AF553711

TOTAL LITERACY CAMPAIGN

WITH SPECIAL REFERENCE TO ADULT DROP-OUTS

TOTAL LITERACY CAMPAIGN

WITH SPECIAL REFERENCE TO ADULT DROP-OUTS

By

Dr. M.C. Obulesu

Dept. of Adult and Continuing Education
S.V. University
Tirupati
(A.P.)

DISCOVERY PUBLISHING HOUSE
NEW DELHI-110002

First Published-2006

ISBN 81-8356-056-3

[Responsibility for the facts stated, opinions expressed, conclusions reached and plagiarism, if any, in this volume is entirely that of the Author. The Publishers bear no responsibility for them, whatsoever.]

Published by

DISCOVERY PUBLISHING HOUSE
4831/24, Ansari Road, Prahlad Street,
Darya Ganj, New Delhi-110002 (India)
Phone: 23279245 • Fax: 91-11-23253475
E-mail:dphtemp@indiatimes.com

Printed at:
Arora Offset Press
Laxmi Nagar, Delhi 110 092.

Dedicated

To

My Beloved Parents

Preface

The success of any development oriented programmes including educational programmes depends on the voluntary participation of the target for whose benefit these programmes are formulated. The success of the adult literacy programmes conceived for promoting literacy also depends on the participation of the illiterates in the programme. The past efforts in this area have revealed that this programmes could not attained their objectives due to heavy dropout rate among the participants. As a result the money materials and human resources invested on this programme has gone as a waste. Keeping of these in view, an attempt was made to investigate into the courses for the adult dropouts from the literacy programmes. The findings of the study helps the programme administrators and field functionaries to understand the anticipated problems of the participants and developing the competencies among the functionaries to overcome the dropout problems.

The present book has five chapters. Chapter-I describes the History and Current Adult Education Programmes implemented for the Promotion of Literacy. The Chapter-II presents a brief review of earlier efforts to identify the causes of dropouts in adult literacy programmes. The Chapter-III focusses on the main theme of the study objectives, hypotheses and methodology adopted. The causes for dropouts and associated factors are presented in Chapter-IV. The last chapter presents the findings and recommendations.

The present book is a boon for the social science researchers, trainers of adult education functionaries of State Resource Centres, Zilla Saksharatha Samithi and the administrators of Adult Education, to carryout their work in improving the quality of adult education programmes.

Author

Acknowledgements

I deem it a rare privilege to work under the supervision of Prof. P. Vasantha Kumari, *Department of Adult and Continuing Education, Sri Venkateswara University, Tirupati. It gives me an immense pleasure to place a record the deepest wholehearted gratitude and indebtedness to her for meticulous care with which she rendered concrete suggestions at every stage of my research work a special mention.*

I wish to place a record to Prof. V.L.N. Reddy *(Retd.), Founder and Former Head, Department of Adult Education,* Prof. M.A.K. Sukumar, *Former Head, Department of English, O.S.D. to Vice-Chancellor, S.V. University, Tirupati,* Prof. G. Prakash Reddy, *(Retd.), Department of Anthropology,* Dr. P. Adinarayana Reddy, Dr. T. Kumaraswamy, *Assistant Directors, Department of Adult Education, S.V. University, Tirupati,* Sri K. Venkoba Rao, *Lecturer in History, Government Degree College, Nagari, for their helpful suggestions in improving the quality of research work.*

I take the opportunity to express my profound honour, love and gratitude to my beloved parents, my brother Mr. M. Barnabas, *and friends, who have given me constant support and encouragement in the completion of my work.*

Dr. M.C. Obulesu

Contents

List of Abbreviations

INC	:	Indian National Congress
NAEP	:	National Adult Education Programme
NBEA	:	National Board of Adult Education
MPFL	:	Mass Programme for Functional Literacy
NLM	:	National Literacy Mission
TLC	:	Total Literacy Campaign
EIC	:	East India Company
MSAEC	:	Mysore State Adult Education Council
RELP	:	Rural Functional Literacy Programme
IEC	:	Indian Education Commission
CABE	:	Central Advisory Board on Education
GSM	:	Gram Shikshan Mohim
NSS	:	National Service Scheme
JSNs	:	Jana Shikshana Nilayams
SRC	:	State Resource Centre
DAEO	:	District Adult Education Centre
DAEB	:	District Adult Education Board
DRU	:	District Resource Unit

SAEP	:	State Adult Education Programme
CECs	:	Continuing Education Centres
SD	:	Standard Deviation
NCEs	:	Nodal Continuing Education Centres
RP	:	Resource Person

1

Total Literacy Campaigns Adult Drop-outs *Problems and Perspectives*

"An educated citizenry are greater to a democratic country than a vague standing army"

—Bruke

IMPORTANCE EDUCATION

Since the beginning of human civilization, education has occupied vital place in the life of an individual. Education has helped man to acquire supremacy over environment. In the present world, one cannot live a complete life without education.

Education is a perennial phenomenon. It continues from the cradle to the grave. The growth of its citizens is the quality of education provided to its citizens. No investment is likely in human resource of which the most important component is education. Education is all the more greater in a society where democracy is a way of life. Democratic institutions cannot be built, nurtured and sustained with a large number of illiterate population. An educated man will develop his personality to the fullest extent possible and contributes to the progress and the prosperity of the community and the country as well.

The role of education in national development is to impart knowledge, understanding, attitudes and skills to human resources and make these resources qualified to utilise the physical resources fully and effectively.

Education provides the individual the ability to reshape his shapeless shape, explore his ideas with logical collaboration. It facilitates steady but proper attitude, sharpness, shrewdness, strategy craftsmanship, creativity, understanding ability and proper vision. Education plays predominant role to transform the social structure as well as to establish modernity. There is urgent need for education to change the socio and economic foundation as the country is witnessing the rapid growth in the field of Science and Technology. There is a greater but wider responsibility from the work side in tackling the perennial problems like illiteracy, exploitation etc., by transforming the illiterate masses virtually literate and economically productive.

Education is a major means for social change and modernization. In the growing scientific and technological knowledge, the pathetic situation of illiterate masses suffering from poverty, disease and ignorance in the social, political and economic changes calls for an urgent need for education. There is greater responsibility on the Government of India in tackling the problem, namely making the vast majority (48%) of illiterate masses functionally literate and economically productive. Education is now recognized as the birth right of every citizen, whatever his/her age may be education is not confined to childhood only but is a continuous and life long process.

CONCEPT AND MEANING OF ADULT EDUCATION

There is a considerable diversity in the use of 'Adult Education' (AE) or an equivalent term in several countries. It is used in a comprehensive manner and also with restricted meaning such as providing basic education for adults. Down through the ages the concept of 'Adult Education' has undergone radical changes. The literal meaning of adult education implies educational facilities to the adults who were not able to undergo a regular course of formal education during their school age. The term non-formal education has recently been adopted by several countries, used and their meanings attached to them are changing in several countries, reflecting the change in actual policy, priorities and programmes. In India, the terms Adult Education and Non-Formal Education are quite familiar. Moreover adult education is understood as a part of the non-formal education.

Phillip H. Coombs and Mazoor Ahmed (1975) defined Non-Formal Education (NFE) as "Organised and semi-organised educational activity operating outside the regular structure and routines of the formal system aimed at serving a great variety of learning needs of different sub-groups in the population, both young and old".

Live Right and Haygood (1966) proposed that "Adult education is the process whereby persons who no longer attend a school on a regular full-time basis undertake sequential and organised activities with a conscious intention of bringing about change in information, knowledge, understanding or skills of appreciation and solving personal or community problems". The first International Conference (1949) on education held in Denmark stated that "Adult education has taken the task of satisfying the needs and aspirations of adults in all their diversity".

According to UNESCO (1972) the term "Adult Education denotes the entire body of organised educational process, whatever content level and method may be, whether formal or otherwise or they prolong or replace initial education in schools, colleges and universities as well as in apprenticeship, whereby persons regarded as adults by the society to which they belong, develop their abilities, enrich their knowledge, improve their technical or professional qualifications and skills and bring about changes in their attitude or behaviour in the two-fold perspective of full personal development and participation in balanced and independent social economic and cultural development". "Adult education embraces all forms of educative experience needed by men and women according to their varied interests and requirements, as their differing levels of comprehension and ability, and in their changing roles and responsibilities throughout the life". The aforesaid definitions give a complete picture of adult education in all respects.

NEED FOR ADULT EDUCATION

Poverty, illiteracy and ignorance are the basic problems of the Third World Countries in general and India in particular. These are the root causes of all the global problems stagnating and degrading the development of individual and the country as well. On one side, illiteracy, ignorance and exploitation make vast masses the poorer and poverty keeps them under constant stress and strain of economic, social and cultural degradation on the other side.

In a broad sense, adult education involves all kinds of learning from the casual and incidental which may occur in the normal environment to that which may take place in formal institutionalised settings. Adult education according to the international encyclopedia (1980) is "an action of external educational agent in purposefully ordering, behaviour into planned systematic exercises that can result in learning those for whom this activity is supplemented to their primary role in society and which involves some continuity in an exchange of relationship between the agent and the learner, so that the educational process is under constant supervision and direction".

The Constitution of India conceived universalisation of elementary education by 1961, but by 1991, the country is still faraway from this target. After Independence, there is a little progress in achieving literacy among the masses, achieving the level of only 52.11% in 1991 from 16.67% in 1951. This situation therefore, is quite alarming and disastrous. It reveals that the constitutional promise of free and compulsory education could not be realized, in practice, because, the educational programmes could not embrace and centre to the needs and aspirations of the poor in the country. Nearly 60% of the population belonging to the weaker sections are deprived of educational facilities owing to poverty and ignorance. It is, in this context of our economic, political and social goals of development, the country has to consider the legitimate roles of adult education.

Adult Education is, therefore, based on the assumptions (a) that illiteracy is a great hurdle to an individual's growth and hence to country's socio-economic progress; (b) that education is not confined to schooling, but takes place in most work and life situation; (c) that learning, working and living are inseparable and each acquires a meaning only when correlated with one another; (d) that the means by which people are involved in the process of formal education systems has failed to realize this. Not only a large number of population is still outside the schools but also the high percentage of drop-outs is making the situation still worse.

ADULT EDUCATION IN INDIA—PRE-BRITISH PERIOD

Adult education is the newest and paradoxically also the oldest discipline in India, which is famous for its ancient cultural heritage studied with the philosophical contribution by saints and sages. It is very difficult to trace the beginning of education in Archaic period. But, it is believed that Indian education extended from 2000 BC to 1200 AD. During this period, various educational systems were developed in terms of social and philosophic relevance. Religion dominated the national life and influenced the educational thought and practices. Learning was pursued not for its own sake but as part of religion.

The country was conceived as a cultural or a spiritual entity rather than a geographical and material entity, not confined within physical bounds. India thus was the first country to rise to the conception of an extra-territorial nationality and obviously became the happy home of different races, each carrying its particular traditions and institutions. Indians have greater reverence and love for education. Since their first appearance in authentic history they have enjoyed the reputation of being a learned people. Learning had exercised a lasting and powerful influence in India and has left an indelible imprint on the literature of the country. In our ancient tradition, education was regarded as the most important tool for self-realisation.

The title of the ancient Indian scriptures, the Vedas, signifies knowledge having been derived from the word "Vid" meaning to know. Thus, knowledge or learning was the cornerstone of the ancient Indian educational system, and was sought as the climax of life. Of all the peoples of the world, the Indians are the most impressed and affected by death as the central fact of life.

During the Vedic period, the society was simple, men and women had equal rights, caste system had not taken root but idol worship was known. During this period, education was imparted through the word of mouth and was confined to upper classes. In the Upanishadic period, the society began to be divided gradually into groups and apart from philosophical education, skills also began to be imparted.

The Dharmashanstrik period saw a good deal of development in art, literature, mathematics and dramatics, Sanskrit had become classical language, but the language, of popular communication was prakrit. The caste system became rigid and before the educational system which was evolved at that time, catered to vocation as well. The Puranic period was the Buddhist period where in the universities of Nalanda and Vikramashilla were erected. Their language was Pali. Institutional education for the first time in this period, when no student who earnestly desired to be educated in a school was ever disappointed. The 'Guru' (Teacher) and pupil lived together. The pupil lived in the teachers house which was known as 'Gurukula', where students shunned all comforts and lived a life of austerity and followed a strict code of conduct and discipline. In some parts, these Gurukulas were also known as 'Ashramas' where pupils from the families of the rich and the poor alike used to dwell together and learn from the Guru.

The education imparted in these 'Gurukulas' and 'Ashramas' was liberal as well as vocational and technical. The art of fighting or martial skills were taught to all those who were attending the Gurukulas. These Ashramas were run by raising funds from the people as well as from the kings. The teachers not only imparted knowledge but instilled moral values among pupils. Education was free and broad-based. The aim was to make a whole man, capable of helping his fellow beings to lead a comfortable life. Individually the objective was emancipation of the soul and collectively the betterment of the society and the country. For a long period in ancient times, the Indian universities of Nalanda, Vikramshila and Takshasila attracted a large number of foreigners, for learning for life. It is said that India had set a high profile in medicine, astronomy and logic.

In the earlier times, education was imparted to the priestly class only. But later it spread to other two classes i.e., Kshtriyas and Vaishyas. This Sudras were denied an opportunity to be educated. However, education was more or less compulsory for every male of the three varnas viz., Brahmins, Kshtriyas and Vaishyas. As stated earlier, education of boys and girls began with the upanayana which was performed at the age of 7. The period of study lasted till the age of 16 and sometime till the age of 24 when the student got married and entered Grihasth Ashram. The student had to learn how to pray, offer sacrifices and perform his social and religious duties.

During the Buddhist and Jain periods, education took a different turn. One difference between Aryan and Buddhist education was that in the latter the teachers were not from the priestly class and education was not based on Vedic study. Education was open to all irrespective of caste, creed and sex. All education was in the hands of monks. Some of monasteries, especially those at Nalanda and Takshasila acquired an international reputation. Scholars from foreign countries visited India to study and take advantage of the Indian culture.

ADULT EDUCATION IN INDIA—BRITISH PERIOD

India had a glorious past of education, to educate man and make him fully conscious of his moral and social obligations.

The political, social and economic changes had their impact on the shape of education of the period. Howell (1765), in his sum up wrote, "Education in India under the British Government was first ignored, then violently and successfully opposed, then conducted on a system now universally admitted to be erroneous". During 1765-1813, the East India Company (EIC) took no interest in the education of the people. It was afraid of educating Indians who were not to be appointed to responsible posts. However, missionaries were encouraged to come and work in this country. In 1813, the EIC felt source and the British Parliament inserted a clause in the character of the company allowing a sum of not less than one lack rupees per year was allocated for the revival and improvement of literature and encouragement of learned Indians, and for the introduction and promotion of knowledge of science among the people.

In 1824, a Sanskrit college was proposed to be opened in Calcutta which was opposed by Raja Rammohan Rai and resulted in a controversy. Lord William Bentick's Government (1835) uprooted the same when the British policy was clearly outlined "We want a class of Indians in blood and coloured, but English in taste, in opinion, in morals and in intellect".

In 1882, the Government of India appointed Hunter Education Commission to enquire into the working of the education departments following the Woods' dispatch. The most important recommendations from the point of view of adult education was that the aim of primary education was instruction of masses and not instruction leading to higher education. Classes were to be organised for backward tribes and aboriginal races through liberal grants. Moreover, the nationalist movement brought the question of mass education to the fore and in 1910, Gokhale moved a resolution in the imperial legislative council to establish the principle of free and compulsory education.

Thus, we find that while during the last years of the 18th century, India was lying prostrate economically, politically and culturally, in the following century new India began to rise from the ashes of the old and by 1885 she had recovered her last soul due to the contribution of individuals who grasped new ideas, learned new techniques and took to new ways of life. In this process of free-education, non-formal and informal agencies of adult education played a notable role. The newspapers, vernacular books, communication media and voluntary association brought about desirable changes in the ideas and attitudes of adult men and women.

By 1878, India has shaken off the hypnotic effect of the British conquest and Indians had begun to demand a greater participation in the Government of their own country. This consciousness among the intelligentsia was brought about by the Indian newspapers, which had provided political education to such an extent that in 1885, the Indian National Congress (INC) was founded. The Congress was able to carry on its struggle for freedom from the British imperialism in various phases, finally being successful in 1947. The newspapers and magazines were the first to take steps towards adult education and became pre-censor to political education and thinking.

Vernacular Literature

Development of Vernacular literature was another informal adult education offshoot of the printing press, which made an impact on the minds and action of the masses. This has been described by Naik and Nurullah (1951) stating that "One of the most important results of the new education was the birth of a new literature and press in the modern Indian languages. The pioneering work in this direction was done by the missionaries. It was they who started the first printing press in India and established the first newspaper. They studied the modern Indian languages, compiled dictionaries, wrote grammar and translated the Bible into them.

Communications

The rapid development of the means of transport constituted another informal agency of adult education bringing people separated by long distance into contact with one another, thus forging unity among them. This coming togetherness helped the people to take new ways of living and thinking. These people ceased to think in sole terms of their own village or town.

Voluntary Agencies

With the closer contact with Europeans, Indians learned to move from new social groups and voluntary associations for joint action for purposes of education and social reform. These organisations became a focal point for the education of the Indian people in the wider sense of term. The people got new ideas and also learnt new methods of group action to achieve their limited objectives. The members of these associations met together to bring about reforms in their social customs and institutions and later for political agitation. Some of these agencies founded schools and libraries. The first few voluntary organisations came into existence in the three metropolitan towns of Madras, Bombay and Calcutta. These made some pioneering efforts towards broad-based education and taking it to the common people. Of these, the students, literacy and scientific society was a model for voluntary organisations. It was established by students and teachers of the Elphinstone Institutions for dissemination of knowledge through vernacular literature, for discussion of scientific and social subjects and for publication of its Marathi version in February, 1850. Later, a Marathi monthly for women was also started. The society also established 16 schools. The Central Province in 1885-86 had 16 printing presses, publishing books and periodicals, 12 public libraries and reading clubs and 14 literacy societies. In the 19th century, thus we find newspapers, vernacular books and voluntary agencies providing informal and non-formal education to the people of India. These had become part of the social and cultural life of the country.

Libraries and Museums

In addition to these non-formal agencies, there were formal agencies which had its impact on adult education. These agencies were the libraries and the museums.

The first modern library in India was established by the Royal Asiatic Society of Bombay. This was however, a research library and not a reformal library which could be an agency of adult education. Bihar instituted many libraries as adjunct to its literacy campaign in the fourth decade of the century. But by the end of 1914, it had only two libraries, both in Patna, the Bihar, Hitaishi Library founded in 1882 and the Oriental Public Library donated by Khunda Baksh in 1891. The Punjab Library was founded in 1885. In the united provinces, the libraries for teachers to improve themselves by private study during out of school hours were established.

Night Schools

In the early years of the 19th century, the Indian Education Commission (IEC) emerged as the dominant power in the country and therefore, the English ways and culture acquired prestige among the upper class Indians. In the three metropolitan cities of Bombay, Calcutta and Madras, there was an increasing tendency on the part of Indians to imitate Englishmen. Many well-to-do Indians spoke and read English language and wear English dresses. At the same time, missionaries were also active among middle class families.

The prestige for English language increased when in 1834 English was established as the state language through the famous minutes of Macaulay. The announcement in 1894 by Lord Hustings Government that English knowing candidates would be preferred for Government service, gave a persistent demand for English all over the country. Thus, the need for adult schools was felt, and these schools would have grown, but for the economic depression.

By 1882, when the Indian Education Commission (IEC) submitted its report, almost every province had made rules to provide night schools for adults. In Bombay, an extra allowance was given to teachers for conducting these schools. A night school attached to a mill or a factory had an average attendance. However, there was no enthusiasm for the schools and as soon as the immediate need for them passed away, the schools slipped back into oblivion. Besides, the separate night schools for adults, there were in some places night classes attached to day schools. There were religious schools also. These were started in Mosques and Gurudwars in Northern India and they enrolled a large number of adults. In Bengal, the education authorities took little interest in adult schools in the beginning, but later on they acted on a proposal to establish night schools in association with village pathashalas with the object of providing elementary instruction to the masses whose occupation was such that they could not attend schools during day time.

In the central province, a tentative scheme of adult education received the approval of the Chief Commissioner in 1868-69, but nothing much came out of it. However, an interesting project was launched in 1860 for the education of policemen. In 1865-66, there were two police schools in each district of the province, one of which was for adults and the other for boys and girls. In every year, a total of 529 constables received education. These schools were under the management of the Superintendent of Police and were reported to be in good order.

In Punjab, adult education had a more democratic beginning. Around 1860, some Government employees in Lahore joined together to engage a teacher, who would teach them in out-of-office hours. Soon, several bankers, traders and other citizens desirous of learning English swelled for membership. During 1863-64, an adult school was opened in Delhi, which was attended by 108 students, but this along with the schools opened in Ambala and Rewari were closed following year. A new adult school at Gurgaon and Jagadhri however made tolerable progress. In Uttar Pradesh State, there were two night schools attached to industrial centres at Lucknow and Gorakhpur. There were many adult schools in other parts of India apart from those mentioned here. But in the absence of a strong movement many of them died down.

In 1912, M. Visveswarayya, then the Dewan of Mysore, opened night schools and established a network of circulating libraries in the state. Nearly six to seven thousand literacy classes flourished at that time. A Magazine 'Vigyan' was also published to popularise scientific knowledge. But as soon as Sir Visveswarayya left the state, all his schemes bleeked out and in 1948, about 75 adult schools were handed over to the Mysore State Adult Education Council (MSAEC).

ADULT EDUCATION IN INDEPENDENT INDIA

Attainment of independence provided a great phillip to the programme of adult education in India. The Government of India tried to reorganised adult education programme and in 1948, Central Advisory Board on Education (CABE) set-up a committee for planning various schemes of adult education. Adult education was renamed as social education by Maulana Azad, the first Education Minister and both literacy as well as general education constituted as essential components of adult education. The programme of social education was implemented by the community development department and the community centres, youth clubs and mahila mandals organised different community programmes basing on domestic crafts, health and nutrition along with literacy classes. The modern mass media like radio, films and television along with traditional media like puppetry, folk theatres, exhibitions and the like were utilised.

Despite painstaking efforts by various agencies and persons, the percentage of literacy has not been raised upto the mark. In India, even after 50 years of independence, the illiterates still remain at 110 million in the 15-35 years age group. Though there is marginal increase in terms of percentage of literacy yet it is far from satisfaction not much consoling. The percentage of literacy went to 16 to 52 during the years 1951-1991, keeping the average annual increase to the tune of 0.66 it has been estimated that by the end of 2000 A.D. India will have more than 50 per cent of the world illiterate population in the age group of 15-35 years.

Adult Schools in Jails (1951)

In 1951, Dr. Walker conducted an interesting experiment in the Agra jail. He organised classes for prisoners to overcome the apathy of the convicts, and attracted them with books, prizes, sweet meats, fruits, picnics, etc. He succeeded in gathering 2000 prisoners. In Bombay, in 1870-71, there were nine schools, of which eight were for prisoners and one for the police. These schools had an enrolment of 160. In 1981-82, there were 30 schools with 1485 learners, two of these schools were for women prisoners. In the Central Province, education was introduced in jails in Dumoh Jail. Several women prisoners were taught how to read and one of them read remarkably well. She was later employed to teach other women prisoners. This was the only jail in the central province when women were taught to read and write.

Gram Shikshan Mohim (1960)

While attempts were made at the national level to eradicate adult illiteracy under social education, a number of smaller projects were also undertaken. Gram Shiksham Mohim (GSM) started in Satara District of Maharashtra in 1960, was one such experiment. Honorable services of primary school teachers, initiation by the local community have been used for these mass programmes. It has achieved remarkable results, but could not be sustained and spread over to the other parts. The reasons for failure can be attributed to (a) the limitation of it to mere literacy to a very inadequate level, (b) failure to create infrastructural needs for post-literacy and follow-up activities and (c) poor financial support.

Indian Education Commission (1964-66)

For the first time, the Indian Education Commission highlighted the role of adult education and felt that it should be possible to eradicate illiteracy by 1985-86. The commission viewed that adult education in a democracy is to provide every adult citizen with an equal opportunity for education of the type he wishes and which he should have for his personal enrichment, professional advancement and effective participation in social and political life. It also realized the importance of adult education for the development of country.

The commission stressed the need for participation of universities in adult education. It has suggested the following for liquidation of illiteracy.

- A massive programme should be launched;
- All academic institutions ranging from universities to primary schools should be involved; and
- All educated men and women should be involved. But, the commission viewed "adult education by its nature is a voluntary activity".

National Board of Adult Education (NBAE) (1970)

A significant feature during Fourth Five Year Plan was establishment of National Board of Adult Education (NBAE) in 1970, which aimed at co-ordinating the programmes of adult education between various State and Central Governments on one hand and among different Ministries of Government of India on the other. Besides this, special efforts were made for production of suitable literature for neo-literates.

During 1975-76, non-formal education programme for the age group of 15-35 years was launched for providing education related to young people's needs, aspirations and local conditions.

National Adult Education Programme (NAEP) (1978)

Several attempts were made for eradication of illiteracy in India, but it was not until 1978 that a systematic attempt was made to this end. The National Adult Education Programme (NAEP) was formally inaugurated on October 2, 1978, with literacy as an indispensable component for approximately 100 million illiterates mainly in the age group of 15-35 years by the end of 1983-84 with a view to provide them with skill for self-directed learning reading to a self-reliant and active role in their own development and in the development of their environment. Unlike the programme which basically oriented to the learning of reading, writing and arithmetic among the illiterates, the major thrust of the NAEP was not only on the spread of reading, writing and arithmetic but on spreading knowledge regarding occupations among the people who are socially and economically disadvantaged. This includes women, Scheduled Castes, Scheduled Tribes, other castes and communities. The NAEP has three basic components viz., literacy, social awareness and functionality.

In order to achieve these tasks, the NAEP was implemented through different agencies such as Government, Nehru Yuvak Kendras, Voluntary Organisations, Universities, Colleges, N.S.S. Units, Industrial and Commercial Organisations and through individual efforts and the Social Voluntary Units.

Adult Education in 20-points Programme (1982)

In 1982, the late Prime Minister Smt. Indira Gandhi introduced the new 20-point programme, the item 16 of the programme envisages the involvement of college and university students and all educated persons, irrespective of their profession in implementing the adult education programme successfully. Voluntary agencies have also played a pivotal role in the eradication of the illiteracy, rooting out dreaded poverty and providing them with facilities for better life.

National Policy on Education (1986) realized the nexus between poverty and illiteracy and the need of education for national development. It has suggested the following three important aspects for adult education.

- Mass literacy programmes
- Large scale involvement of students and teachers
- Centres in rural areas for continuing education

Mass Programme for Functional Literacy (MPFL) (1986)

The programme was started in 1986 with the following objectives:

- to make literacy as peoples mission;
- to harness all agencies for the mission; and
- to post mass literacy programme as a challenge for the youth.

Achievement of these objectives involved the following:

- Stressing functional literacy in National Service Scheme (NSS).
- Increasing coverage of student volunteers;

- Emphasising study service viz., specific project taken up by students as part of work experience for social/national service which should be reflected in their final result; and
- Provision for institutional incentives for eradication of illiteracy.

National Literacy Mission (NLM) (1988)

Ministry of Human Resource Development in collaboration with universities, colleges and other agencies and organisations launched National Literacy Mission (NLM) in 1988 to equip all the citizens themselves of the country with basic skills of literacy. The NLM is intended to focus on rural areas, particularly on women and those belonging to Scheduled Castes and Scheduled Tribes. The main objective of the NLM is to impart functional literacy to 80 million illiterates, 30 millions by 1990 and remaining 50 millions by 1995. The following objectives have been specified by NLM.

- Achieving self-reliance in literacy and numeracy;
- Becoming aware of causes of deprivation;
- Acquiring skills to improve the economic status and general well-being; and
- Imbibing values such as national integration, conservation of the environment, women's equality, observation of small family norm, etc.

Jana Shikshana Nilayam (JSN) (1989)

Given that neo-literates tend to forget what they have learnt. NLM also incorporated Jana Shikshana Nilayams (JSNs) to do the needful. The basic purpose of the JSNs which were established in February, 1989 is to enable the learners to continue their learning beyond elementary literacy. The main objectives of the JSN are:

- Provision of facilities for retention, continuing education and application on functional literacy;
- Broadcasting of information on development programmes, widening and improving participation of traditionally deprived sections of society;

- Creation of awareness, about national concerns such as national integration, conservation and improvement of environment, women's equality and observance of small family norm, and sharing of common problems of the community;
- Improvement of economic condition and general well-being as well as improvement of productivity; and
- Promoting congenial environment for healthy living.

JSN is not limited to neo-literates, but covers school drop-outs, those with primary school education, those who have participated in non-formal education programme as well as other members of the community.

Management of Adult Education Programme

a. National Level

The National Adult Education Programme began with the establishment of National Board of Adult Education in 1977. All important decisions taken by various committees are generally endorsed by the National Board of Adult Education.

The overall responsibility for the administration of the National Adult Education Programme results with the Ministry of Education (presently known as Ministry of Human Resource Development). It provides Secretariat to the National Board of Adult Education. The Ministry also deals with the responsibility of overseeing the implementation of NAEP in various states. The schemes of assistance to voluntary agencies and Shramik Vidyapeeths are directly administered by the Ministry. The rural functional literacy projects, under which a project with central assistance is intended to be established in each district of all the states, as well as the schemes of strengthening of administrative set-up are implemented through the State Governments,.

For effective implementation of the NAEP and to handle the great task ahead, a carefully planned organisational structures introduced right from the Central Government level to the adult education centre level at the grassroots. At the central level, as has already been discussed, the Ministry of Education and the Central

Directorate of Adult Education are the overall incharge of the programme management. The Ministry and the Directorate have a special responsibility for functions of the Directorate including (a) arrangement of training programmes, (b) production of teaching/ learning material and (c) evaluation. The three agencies are also have to involve other developmental Ministries like Agriculture and Rural Development, in the programme. In 1988, the programme has been re-designed as National Literacy Mission (NLM) and target had been extended to 2000.

b. State Level

At state level, the adult education programmes are administered by the Directorate of Adult Education with the Director as the functional head. He is assisted by the Deputy Directors at the Directorate. The main functions of the State Directorate are: (a) to provide policy guidelines; (b) to create a favourable environment and (c) to review the progress of the programme.

The specific tasks of the Directorate of Adult Education are: (1) preparation of plans, (2) encouraging voluntary agencies to participate, (3) direction and overall supervision of government programmes, (4) overseeing and co-ordinating of programmes taken up by various agencies other than the government, (5) selection and placement of personal and (6) monitoring and evaluation of the programme.

The other important agency in the National Adult Education Programme is the State Resource Centre (SRC) which is entrusted with such essential functions as (1) preparation of teaching/ learning material, (2) organisations of seminars, (3) development of methodological guidelines for curriculum preparation and (4) training support to the programme, including post-literacy programmes evaluation, research and publications.

c. District Level

At the district level, the Collector is responsible for steering the programme. He is to function on the advice of the District Adult Education Board (DAEB), the members of which include, district level development officers, educationists, teachers, representatives, and voluntary agencies. The District Adult Education Officer (DAEO) is the member secretary of the District Adult Education Board.

The District Adult Education Officer who is the head of the district administrative unit has three types of functions. He assists the district Collector in arranging co-ordiantion and in the various promotional activities. Secondly, he is expected to generally oversee and monitor the programme implemented by the various agencies. Thirdly, he is the co-ordiantor of the District Resource Unit (DRU). In this capacity, he has to arrange necessary technical support, particularly in regard to training for the various project agencies of the district.

d. Project/Central Level

One of the most important innovations introduced in National Adult Education Programme (NAEP) was the project approach—a more or less autonomous administrative unit responsible for implementation of a programme in a compact and contiguous area.

Each project has a Project Officer and a Supervisor for a number of centres. In the projects administered by the State Governments, a supervisor's responsibility extends to 30 centres.

The critical unit in the whole programme is the adult education centre, and it is under the charge of an instructor or an adult education organiser. Retired personnel, preferably ex-servicemen, unemployed youth and social workers are appointed as instructors.

ADULT EDUCATION IN ANDHRA PRADESH—PRE-INDEPENDENCE

Before independence, the work of adult education was taken up by Christian Missionaries and Private (Voluntary) Organisations. The various social reform movements like Bengali Reform Movement, the spread of the ideas of Bramha Samaj in 19th century and the rise of Indian nationalism helped greatly in increasing the necessity for adult literacy. As early as 1848, the Andhra Evangelical Church, Guntur has started literacy as one of its programmes. In 1907, social reformer like Gadicherla Hari Sarvothama Rao started literacy night school in teacher training college, Rajahmundry and various organisations like the servants of Indian Society (1905), the Seva Sadan (1908), Mahila Samaj (1910) and the Socialist League (1911) were instrumental in educating illiterate adults.

The entry of Mahatma Gandhi in the education movement in 1920 gave a new boost to adult education. In 1929, the social reformers like Sanivarapu Subba Rao, Kalidindi Ganga Raju and Bhamidipathi Satyanarayana have started a school for adult education for teacher at Tadepalligudem and Prof. Ranga in 1933 started a summer schools to inculcate some knowledge of political affairs to the farmers at Nidubrolu. By 1939, adult literacy centres were started at Guntur, Vijayawada, Visakhapatnam followed by such others in Godavari and Nellore Districts.

Adult literacy as a reform movement began with the efforts of Kandukuri Veeresalingam, Raghupathi Venkatarathnam Naidu who started adult literacy classes for the untouchable in the late 19th century. Some of those classes were held on the river banks in the evenings to avoid the wrath of orthodox Hindus who protested against this reformist effort. Young nationalist leaders like Ayyadevara Kaleswara Rao, K. Lakshmana Rao participated in these efforts. Schools for girls and widow homes were started and imparted literacy.

The period marks the beginning of literacy movement in Andhra and the importance of regional languages. The first modern library (1886) in Andhra region came into existence at Visakhapatnam. Libraries were established very soon thereafter at Pulivendula in Cuddapah District, Ongole (1890), Guntur (1900), Rajahmundry (1900), Hyderabad (1901) and other places. It must be started that the library movement in Andhra and Telangana regions of Andhra Pradesh prior to 1947 contributed significantly to the spread of literacy among the people and generated an interest in reading books. In 1919, the Andhra Desa Library Society passed a resolution that adult literacy had to be promoted through speeches, puppetry and such other methods. It advocated the establishment of night schools for illiterate weaker sections of society in all libraries.

The importance of adult literacy as a movement has been underscored regularly by consecutive general body meetings of Andhra Desh Grandhalaya Sangham. In 1935, Saranam Ramaswamy Chowdary called upon the educated youth to impart education to the illiterates during their holidays. It was in 1941 at the 22nd Library Mahasabha Conference, its President, Dr. Rama

Chandra Sastry moved the resolution and stressed the need for the establishment of night schools and summer schools to highlight the importance and significance of adult education. He also appealed to have an enlightenment door-to-door campaign for women's education. At the Andhra Desa Library Mahasabha, Suravaram Prathapa Reddy deeply outlined as well as enlarged the growing importance in upholding the value-based adult education centres, to promote and strengthen the adult literacy in 1942. He also felt that those who are willing to run adult education centres voluntarily should be appointed as officers in the libraries. He considered adult education as the key and main instrumental weapon in creating awareness in the field of health care, sanitation and others.

The Andhra Desa Grandha Bhadagara Society has subsequently known as Andhra Desa Grandhalaya for the promotion of adult education. It was felt that adult education programmes organised by the libraries would undoubtedly help make libraries as popular institution. The association felt that libraries ought to be centres of social and cultural change. The President of the Andhra Desa Grandhalaya Association was, hence associated with the South Indian Adult Education Association (1939) as its Vice-President.

With the political climate notting-up, the Madras Government banned adult education activities with effect from June 11, 1941. The Andhra Desa Library Association organised the First Andhra Desa Vayojana Mahasabha at Tenali on 24th August, 1941, to protest and express its concern at the ban. The conference was presided over by G. Harisarvothama Rao where number of speakers advocated the need of adult literacy. A committee of eleven members was consisting of eight members was formed to propose the government to withdraw the ordinance relating to the ban. On adult education, voluntary efforts for adult education continued as a part of the nationalist movement and slowly decreased in its momentum after independence.

ADULT EDUCATION PROGRAMME IN ANDHRA PRADESH—POST-INDEPENDENCE

National Adult Education Programme (NAEP) was formally launched in Andhra Pradesh on October 2, 1978 and it was actually implemented during December, 1979 by grounding 23 projects [18 under centrally sponsored scheme of Rural Functional Literacy Programme (RELP) and 5 under State Adult Education Programme (SAEP)]. This programme implemented the projects in different batches.

A project is the unit of operation consisting about 300 adult education centres, with each centre having a capacity to control 30 learners. The 300 Adult Education Centres or projects cover normally three to four panchayat blocks or four to ten mandals in Andhra Pradesh.

In 1978, it was estimated that there would be 110 lakh illiterates in the State of Andhra Pradesh to be made literate by 1989-90. The number of adults made literate upto 1987-88 was only 24.20 lakhs. With the present rate of progress there would be 95.96 lakh illiterates in the state by the year 1994-95. In order to cover the entire illiterate population by that year, at least 224 adult education projects are required to be launched at the cost of Rs. 33.60 crores. Against this requirement, the adult education programme which started functioning in Andhra Pradesh in 1980-81 with 23 projects increased to only 52 projects by 1987-88. The investment and efforts are very much insignificant compared to the magnitude of goal to be achieved.

In the year of evaluation, 1988-89, the Directorate of Adult Education, Andhra Pradesh was running the adult education programme through 52 projects, divided equally between RFLPs funded by Central Government and the SAEP funded by the State Government.

Apart from the Directorate of Adult Education, the adult education programme is also run by voluntary agencies with funds from Government channelled through the Directorate of Adult Education under the overall supervision of the Directorate. In 1987-88, there were only three voluntary agencies working in the field of adult education, although their number had increased to fifty five in 1988-89.

PRESENT STATUS OF THE LITERACY PROGRAMMES IN ANDHRA PRADESH

Andhra Pradesh is one of the first state in the country to take up comprehensive programme of Total Literacy Campaign (TLC).

At the beginning of the new approach, TLC projects have been sanctioned in 11 districts of Andhra Pradesh in the year 1990-91. The TLC projects have been gradually extended to 23 districts and covered all the districts of the state. The first phase of implementation of TLC covered the 22 districts. At present the Total Literacy Campaign is under implementation in the remaining one district, viz., Adilabad.

The Adult Education Department in Andhra Pradesh has been implementing the Literacy Programme in three stages i.e., (1) Total Literacy Campaign, (2) Post-literacy Campaign, (3) Continuing Education.

(i) Total Literacy Campaign (TLC)

- The Government of India decided in 1990 to re-organise the centre based programme after finding certain major deficiencies in the old approach to an area specific, time bound, cost-effective and result-oriented programme in the name of Total Literacy Campaign in line with the overall strategy of National Literacy Mission i.e., securing people's participation in achieving the task of eradication of illiteracy in the country through the involvement of government, semi-government, voluntary agencies, people's representatives, particularly the students and youth to make it a mass movement and to provide support by supplying standard teaching and learning material on free of cost. Normally, the time span of Total Literacy Campaign is one year.
- The expenditure of Total Literacy Campaign shall be borne by State Government in the ratio of 2 : 1.
- 23 districts have been covered under the Total Literacy Campaign. At present, Total Literacy Campaign is being implemented in Adilabad District only. The operation restoration programme in Kurnool District is yet to be started.

(ii) Post-Literacy Campaign (PLC)

- Post-Literacy Programme is envisaged for a period of 2 years for the benefit of neo-literates after completion of basic literacy. As per the National Literacy Mission norms, 22 districts which have completed literacy phase have been sanctioned with the Post-Literacy Campaign in a phased manner by the end of January, 1998. At present, 5 districts viz., Guntur, Prakasam, Ananthapur, Nalgonda and Mahabubnagar are implementing the post-literacy programme.

- The funding pattern for post-literacy programme is also at the ratio of 2 : 1 by Government of India and State Government respectively.

(iii) Continuing Education

- The Government of India have formulated a new scheme called "Continuing Education for Neo-literates". Continuing education includes post-literacy for neo-literates and school drop-outs, pass-outs and non-formal education drop-outs and pass-outs for retention of their acquired skills.
- After completion of Post-Literacy phase, continuing education programme will be implemented for the benefit of neo-literates for a period of 5 years initially.
- The continuing education programme in Andhra Pradesh has been implemented with the community participation, the main trust of the programme lies with the community involvement and the Continuing Education Centres (CECs) are managed by village level structures which are elected bodies of the end-users.
- The launching of CECs is not automatic. Unless the community comes forward with reasonable amount of corpus fund (Rs. 10,000) and of other physical contributions. It is an encouraging point to note that so far an amount of Rs. 3.88 crores has been collected as corpus fund in 7,846 CECs launched out of 10,952 CECs sanctioned. Further, in order to ensure the learners attendance, the membership fee of Re. 1 for individual for month has been collected in CECs.

- The Government of India have sanctioned 6,370 Continuing Education Centres/Nodal Continuing Education Centres (CECs/NCECs) to 8 districts in 1st phase viz., Srikakulam, Visakhapatnam, West Godavari, Nellore, Cuddapah, Chittoor, Karimnagar and Nizamabad. Out of the above sanctioned CECs/NCECs, 6,027 centres have been started in those districts so far and are under implementation.
- Continuing Education Projects under the scheme will be provided financial assistance on 100% basis by the Central Government for the 1st 3 years from the date of issue of formal sanction. For the next two years, the extent of central assistance will be limited to 50% and the remaining 50% shall be shared by the State Government after a period of five years, the Central Government after a period of five years, the Central Government will not extend any financial assistance for continued running of established CECs. The State Government shall then take over the responsibility for continued running of CECs through Panchayat Raj Institutions or other local bodies. The Government of India have approved the 1 year cost of Rs. 15.76 crores and released Rs. 7.88 crores so far.
- In 2nd phase, the Government of India have sanctioned 4,582 CECs/NCECs to another 8 districts viz., Vizinagaram, East Godavari, Krishna, Rangareddy, Adilabad, Medak, Warangal and Khammam. Out of the above sanctioned Continuing Education Centres/Nodal Continuing Education Centres, 1,819 centres have been started in those districts so far and are under implementation.

TOTAL LITERACY CAMPAIGN (TLC)

Concept

The National Literacy Mission (NLM) was launched in May, 1988 to bringing out 80 million illiterate persons in the 15-35 age group within the literacy ambit by 1995. The emphasis of NLM is on a campaign approach.

The Total Literacy Campaign (TLC) approach is area specific, time bound and volunteer based. The total literacy campaign at the district level has been accepted as an effective step towards removal of illiteracy from the nation. Literacy, dovetailed with aspects such as consciousness, ability and value orientation, has been the objective of this campaign, that is, education that goes beyond merely imparting the knowledge of the three R's (Reading, Writing and Arithmetic). It is the realization that literacy will be sustained only if it is coupled with knowledge related to consciousness, ability and value-orientation that makes the campaign go beyond literacy. Sustainable literacy also calls for broad-based, post-literacy programmes whereby the initial campaign can graduate into a movement on a long term basis.

First Total Literacy Campaign (TLC) was conducted in Ernakulam District in Kerala in 1989. The success of this TLC creates a new trend in India literacy programmes. As of today in 429 districts out of 520 district of the country campaigns are going on for eradication of illiteracy involving all sections of the people-students, teachers, youth, women's organisations, voluntary organisations, employers, trade unions, paramilitary forces and others. The real value of the literacy campaign will be judged only by the number of persons made literate according to NLM norms.

The success of the NLM authority rests on the mobilisation of the social forces and achieving participation of the vast majority of the people. The magnitude of conceiving total literacy campaign with such national proportions is a mind boggling proposition. The TLC is basically a voluntary action oriented and community based education. Implemented through district administration of the planned districts, total literacy for the statistical purpose is conceived as 70.00 per cent achieved of literacy for the total population in the district where TLC is being implemented.

Objectives

The objectives of functional literacy presented by National Literacy Campaign implies:

- Achieving self-reliance through literacy and numeracy.

- Becoming aware of the causes of one's deprivation and moving towards its amelioration through organisation and participation in the process of development.
- Acquiring skills to improve one's economic status and general well-being.
- Imbibing the value of national integration, conservation of environment, women's equality, observance of the small family norm, etc.

Characteristics

- Literacy as a means of empowerment and development.
- Well-defined goals.
  — Area specific
  — Time bound
  — Total coverage for given age group
- Volunteer based approach
  — Under Zilla Saksharatha Samithis
  — Participation of all sections of the society
  — Included NGO's
- Environment building and mass mobilisation
  — Jathas
  — Folk and Electronic media
  — Person to person contact
  — Conversion and pledges
- Improved pedagogy with emphasis on learning outcomes
- Low cost
  — Rs. 65-100 per learner for literacy phase
  — Rs. 40-50 per learner per year for post-literacy phase
- Stress on post-literacy continuing education

Operationalisation Steps

1. **Pre-Jatha**
   - Consultation and consensus
   - Involving political parties, teachers, students, cultural groups.
   - Identification of core team.
   - Project formulation.
2. **Creation of Organisational Structure**
   - ZSS
   - Block/Gram Panchayat/Village level structures
   - Orientation of personnel
3. **Survey**
   - For enumeration
   - For interactivity
   - For identification MT/VT (Monitor/Volunteer)
4. **Jatha**
   - Cultural groups visits every village
   - Standardised messages
   - Repeat-Jatha as necessary
5. **Teaching/Learning Material Development**
   - Local relevance
   - Conforming to IPCL
   - Incorporates national values
6. **Training**
   - Through RP (Resource Person) and MTS
   - Training of volunteers
   - Primer specific
   - Recurrent training
   - At least 9 days

7. Literacy Instruction

— Instruction duration 200 hours roughly

— Volunteer-learner average 1: 10

— Community pressure for regular participation

— Sustained motivation

8. Monitoring and Evaluation

— Ongoing progress and quality monitoring

— External agency on sample basis

— Learning level related

9. Followed by Post-literacy/Continuing Education

Importance

a. Followed by Post-literacy/Continuing Education

The NLM after through analysis of the previous adult education programmes reflected that there are a variety of reasons that hindered the progress of literacy in the country.

- The learning environment was found to be lacking in basic amenities conducive to learning.
- Functions, particularly instructors, were not properly trained.
- Learners motivation being low, attendance was low and drop-out rate was high.
- It is reported that while learning the 3 R's, functionality and social awareness were not adequately covered.
- There was no effective mechanism for post-literacy efforts to sustain what had been taught.
- Bureaucratic procedures made administrative support difficult particularly for voluntary agencies.

The traditional methods/approaches used for removing illiteracy are not yielding the results expected, though lot of money is spent and hence, the need for campaign approach which is result-oriented, time-specific, area-specific, age-specific and volunteer based with adequate arrangements for post-literacy and continuing education.

TOTAL LITERACY CAMPAIGN IN KURNOOL DISTRICT

The Total Literacy Campaign was launched in this district on 28.06.1990 and the actual teaching phase started from 14.04.1991 to cover the illiterates in the age group of 15-35 years.

At the time of launching total literacy programme in this district, there were 5,88,752 illiterates in the age group of 15-35, of them 5,84,027 were enrolled into the centres.

1.	No. of illiterates identified	5,88,752
2.	No. of illiterates enrolled in the centres	5,84,027
3.	Drop-outs who left the centres without completing even Primer-I and before six months of starting the centres	1,93,292

Source: Zilla Aksharasyatha Samithi (ZAS), Kurnool Action Plan Report, DEO Office, Kurnool, 1990.

PROFILE OF KURNOOL DISTRICT

a. Origin

The District lies between 14°-54N and 16°-11N in the latitude and 75°-50E and 78°-25E in the longitude.

b. Boundaries

The district is bound in the north by Mahaboobnagar and on the south by Ananthapur and Cuddapah Districts and west by Karnataka State and on the east Prakasam District.

c. History

Kurnool has been named after the centre in the district. In ancient days, it was known as Kandenavolu. During those days, people used to oil their bullock carts with the available custard oil abundantly. Hence, it was named Kandenavolu and subsequently Kurnool.

Kurnool was under the control of Revati Cholas between 4th to 8th CBC later on Kurnool has been merged into the Kingdom of Western Chalukyas. In 1162 A.D. Prataparudra I, King of Kakatiya has extended his kingdom upto Srisailam. During the period of Ganapathi Deve, the entire district has become a part and parcel of

Kakatiya empire. Kakatiya constructed Rudravaram and other villages in the district. Later the western part of the district was merged into Vijaya Nagar empire and eastern part into the hands of Reddi Kingdom. Afterwards the Nawabs of Kurnool ruled the district as Jagirs during Mughals and Jahir period, of them Dawood Khan was the first and foremost Pathan.

As soon as the completion of Pathan's period, Ibrahim Khan, Aluf Khan and Himmat Bahadur Khan reigned the district. But some parts of the district have been captured and occupied by the Marathan rulers. In course of time, it was again brought under the control of the Nawabs of Kurnool. But by the wake of subsidiary alliance by Wellessley in 1800 AD Kurnool was captured by the British Raj. Hence, Aloof Khan continued his rule by paying huge tribute to the Britishers. Later, Ghulam and Rasool Khan, the successors of the Nawabs were captured by the Britishers on the ground that he had committed a treachery. From 1839 to 1858, the rule of Jagir was continued with the help of the Commissioner and the Military assistance and thereby a District Collector was appointed.

However, some parts of the district were ruled by the Nawabs of Banaganapalli upto 1686 A.D. The founder of the Nawabs of Banaganapalli was Mahammad Baig Khan.

d. Forests

Forests cover 3,18,250 hectares in the district. Almost 19.2% of forests are in the eastern and western parts of the district. These are in the Nallamala forest range as the outcome of abundant availability of teak, regai trees in the district. There is a Rayalaseema Paper Mill in Kurnool city. The greatest wild sanctuary centre is situated between Srisailam and Nagarjuna Sagar.

e. Population

In this district, there are 15,22,618 male and 14,50,406 female populations, a totalling to 29,73,024. The rural population is 22,04,924 and the urban is 7,68,100. The total number of labour is 13,40,980, of them, Scheduled Castes 5,18,108 (17.43%), Scheduled Tribes 54,455 (1.90%) and other labours are 3,13,315.

f. Other Particulars

At the time of formation of Andhra State on October 1, 1953, Kurnool was the capital and made it as Municipality. There are two T.V. Transition Centres functioning in Adoni and Kurnool.

g. Mandals

The entire Kurnool district comprises 54 mandals, three revenue divisions, viz., Kurnool, Adoni and Nandyal and 894 villages.

h. Literacy Position

Literacy position of Kurnool district during the years 1951-2001 is given below:

Year	*% of Literacy*		
	Males	*Females*	*Total*
1951	19.6	4.3	12
1961	32.9	9.6	21.4
1971	34.5	12.7	23.8
1981	39.9	17.0	28.7
1991	53.2	26.0	39.9
2001	67.36	41.07	54.43

Source: State Resource Centre, Hyderabad, A Report, 2001.

The literacy percentage of the district increased from 12 in 1951 to 54.43 in 2001.

2

Drop-outs of Adult Education
A Review

INTRODUCTION

The success of Total Literacy Campaigns depends to larger extent on effective participation of adult learners in the learning activities of Total Literacy Campaign (TLC) centres. How effectively a learner participates in learning activity depends on various factors. They may be individualistic factors (that refer to individuals personally structure) social and cultural factors, environmental factors and alike. A learner enrolled in TLC centre may either continue his participation in learning activity or discontinue depending upon the nature of influence exerted by various internal and external factors operating on learner's learning activity.

The knowledge of various factors that contribute to discontinuance (drop-out) of learners from TLC is essential for applying corrective measures so as to improve effective participation of learners in learning activities of TLC centres. Such knowledge may be acquired only through empirical studies in the area. In the field of adult education, research studies conducted in India and abroad did not give much importance to investigate and explain precisely the nature and dimension of drop-out.

In this context, review of research studies already done in the area may be helpful in giving direction to further research. If one looks for investigations conducted in the field to identify the factors associated with drop-out phenomena, one will find them to be by and large scattered, unsystematic and inconclusive. The studies in general, may be categorized as evaluation studies and other studies which are specific in nature. In evaluation studies, characteristics and reasons relating to dropping out phenomena covered as part of comprehensive evaluation of the adult education programmes where many other issues relating to the programmes were also examined. Other studies which were specific in nature focused only on drop-outs. However, the review presented include personal problems, psychological problems, environmental problems, programme-related and instructor related problems and reasons for dropping out of adult learners.

PERSONAL PROBLEMS

The studies describing association of variables like age, sex, caste, income, occupation, previous education, type of family, education, background of family members, family size with drop-out phenomena were presented in this section. The studies dealing with the above variables were broadly of two types viz., education studies and specific studies. Further, some evaluation studies have described personal factors relating to learners whereas some other evaluation studies illustrate personal factors of both learners and drop-outs. Similarly, among specific studies, some referred to personal and familial factors relating to drop-outs and some others referred to personal factors of learners. In addition, few other specific studies were also carried out on drop-outs.

The relationship between personal characteristics and continuance of drop-outs in TLC centres as observed by some of the evaluation studies was as follows:

Bhandari (1974) compared personal, economic and social characteristics of learners and drop-outs representing literacy centres and functional literacy centres of Udaipur district, Rajasthan. The sample constituted 96 learners and 96 dropouts. The investigator found no significant differences between the characteristics of learners and drop-outs with regard to age, sex, caste, marital status, occupation, affiliation with economic, social and political organisational groups, exposure to schooling in childhood, size of land-holding and use of improved agricultural practices.

Sarma et al. (1979) made an attempt to analyse adult learners characteristics in Gujarath state. The distribution of learners by age, sex, caste and occupation indicated that majority of the learners were men (57%), belonged to target age group i.e., 15-35 years, had agriculture as the main occupation and belonged to Scheduled Caste, Schedule Tribe and backward classes categories. It was also noted that 16% of the learners had some background of schooling earlier to their enrolment in adult education centres.

The evaluation study conducted in Tamilnadu by Ramakrishnan (1980) revealed that about 50% of the respondents were in the age group of 15-19 years, majority (60%). Skilled workers and agriculturists accounted for 22% and 10% respectively. Regarding earlier exposure to schooling, nearly 50% of the adult learners had attended schools for some time in their childhood but were practically illiterates at the time of enrolment in adult education centres. Scheduled Caste and Scheduled Tribe groups accounted for 62%.

The personal characteristics of adult learners as enumerated by the Centre of Advanced Study in Education (1981), showed that majority of the learners were between 15-35 years, 74% of the learners are STs and agriculturists. 205 out of 260 learners studied represented families with illiterates. The study of Dey and Natarajan (1981) found that majority of the learners continuing in adult education programme were agriculturists and represented younger age group. Most of the learners had no formal childhood education. Further, most of their family members were illiterate.

Hebsur et al. (1981) while examining the socio-economic background of adult learners participating in adult education programme in the State of Maharashtra, found that 62% of the learners were in the age group of 15-25 years. In addition, a moderate percentage of the learners belonged to Scheduled Caste (49%), neo-Buddhists (23%)and Scheduled Tribes (17%) were documented. Backward classes accounted for 9% only. With respect to occupation, agricultural labourers and domestic servants formed 42% of the learners. Farming was the occupation of another 39% of the learners.

The study conducted by Pestonjee et al. (1981) on 768 adult learners in the state of Rajasthan reported that the average age of learners was about 21 years. Most of the women learners belonged to the age group of 15-20 years while men belonged to 15-30 years age group. Most of the learners were from higher dominant castes. The proportion of higher castes was more among women than men. About two-third respondents had farming background. The sample, however, also represented other occupation such as farm-labour, trade, artisans, service, etc. As regards to literacy, about 90% of the respondents were illiterates at the time of joining the centres. The rest of them were either able to sign or had some education.

Ray and Nandi (1981) made a study on a sample of 88 drop-outs in West Bengal and identified certain factors associated with dropouts. They were (a) persons younger in age had a tendency to drop-out from the adult education centres, (b) smaller the family size, more the learners were forced to remain in the adult education centres, (c) a large majority of the drop-outs from the adult education centres belonged to Scheduled Castes and Scheduled Tribes, (d) daily labourers in non-agricultural occupation had the highest tendency to drop-out and (e) persons with very low income had a tendency to drop-out.

Sachidananda et al. (1981) interviewed 339 adult learners in Bihar drawing the sample from such adult education centres which had completed at least six months duration. The study reported that most of the learners were women and were within the age range of 15-35 years. Further, majority of them belonged to the Scheduled Caste and other backward classes. The occupation of two-third of the learners was agriculture. Most of the learners were first time learners.

Sarma et al. (1981) found that more than 70% of dropout of adult education centres organised by voluntary agencies (Gujarath) belonged to Scheduled Castes, Scheduled Tribes and other backward castes. An overwhelming proportion of drop-outs were cultivators, agricultural and casual labours. Interestingly they found higher drop-out rate (34.8%) in the younger age group (15-20 years). Further, they found that drop-out rate tends to decline with higher age group.

Verma et al. (1981) observed that there was no definite relationship between age and drop-out phenomena. Most of the drop-outs were men and belonged to either Scheduled Castes or other backward classes. Further, the drop-outs were either agricultural labourers or labourers on daily wages. In addition, it was noted that drop-outs were either economically deprived people or were facing socio-psychological problems.

Harihar and Rao (1982) found that majority of the learners who attended the centres regularly were married. The learners by and large represented both upper and lower castes equally. As many as 76% of the sample had agriculture as their main occupation. A good majority of them had no educational environment in their families.

Acharji (1983 A) found that majority of the adult learners who dropped out from the TLC centres were men. Most of them were unmarried and in the age group of 15-25 years. Further, majority of them were farmers and agricultural labourers. Only a few learners had early childhood schooling (12%). Majority of them had no educational environment in the family due to literate members in the family.

The study conducted by Acharji (1983 B) revealed that majority of the drop-outs were in the mean age group of 21 years. Most of them were married and belonged to Scheduled Caste and Scheduled Tribes. Almost all of their family members were illiterates.

According to the profile of adult learners developed by Madras Institute of Development Studies (1983-84) majority of the learners were below 25 years of age. Further, the proportion of unmarried learners was higher than married.

Aikara (1984) through his survey in Maharashtra state, found that majority of learners who were participating in the programme were men in the age group of 15-25 years. As many as 51% of the learners were engaged in agriculture and good number of other learners (32%) were agricultural labourers. As many as 40% of the learners had previous schooling. Most of the learners belonged to low income group.

Ganguli et al. (1984) through a study on adult learners in different blocks of Bihar state developed profiles of adult learners. According to the profile most of the learners in one block were unmarried and contrary to this in another area most of the learners belonged to 15-25 years age group and were earning their livelihood through agriculture. However, few learners were artisans and were doing petty business. Only 10% of the learners had previous schooling.

In addition to the above evaluation studies, some specific studies conducted in the field have also identified the relationship between personal factors and drop-out learners from literacy centres. Rao (1988) found that among persons attending adult education centres, young persons, unmarried men and individuals with joint family background had been benefitted much from adult education programme.

Omana (1989) found drop-out rate was higher among women learners and among those above 35 years. Further, she noticed that daily labours had high tendency to drop-out. In addition, the people representing backward communities and low income group were high among drop-outs.

Vanaja (1989) in her study on women drop-outs found that majority of them who dropped out from adult education centres had no formal education and were in the age group of 15-35 years and married and belonged to backward classes.

PSYCHOLOGICAL PROBLEMS

Investigations describing the relationship between learners dropping out and factors like motivation on the part of the learners, attitude of the learners, shyness, impact of conservatism/ traditionalism and such other factors associated with personality structure of the learners were considered under this head.

Bhandari and Mehta (1974) studied the influence of motivation and discouragement on learners and drop-outs phenomena. It was observed that there existed a marked impact of the source of influence on learners and dropping out. They also found positive relationship between learners and the extent to which the teacher can sustain the interest of learners. Significant difference was found for the source of discouragement and continuance or discontinuance of attending literacy classes by the learners. In addition, the influence of relatives on dropping out of learners from adult literacy classes was marginal.

Lowe (1975) indicted fear of ridicule, emotional in security, feeling of social inadequacy, negative attitude towards learning and uncertainty of future rewards as factors leading to non-participation in learning activity.

The study of Khajapeer (1978) showed that persons with high achievement motivation, high aspirations in literacy and favourable attitude towards adult literacy fared well in the acquisition of literacy skills. In other words, these may be considered as qualities of learners. In contrast, he also found that persons with conservative outlook, fatalistic thinking and authoritarian attitude would be very poor in the attainment of literacy skills. These, in other words, may be viewed as qualities of drop-outs.

Reddy (1981) examined the association of 16 personality factors with dropouts and active participants (learners). He opined that active participants were by and large cheerful, active, talkative, careful, matured in their outlook and possessed confidence in their capacities to deal with things. In contrast, the dropouts were found impatient, impractical in outlook and doubtful and had mistrusting nature.

Brist (1983) indicated that lack of flexibility and shyness on the part of learners were the factors leading to drop-out. In addition, he indicated that personal ego of learners with reference to caste and status of instructors, in comparison to learners, may also lead to dropping out.

Sense of belongingness was also observed to have some influence on learners and dropping out phenomena. Seth et al. (1983) observed that learners who felt that they belonged to the group and were liked by others continued their participation in adult education programme.

Mali (1984) noticed that persons who joined literacy classes on their own initiative were deemed to have strong motivation and continued till they acquired literacy skills. Further, he observed that adults who joined the literacy classes because of pressure from others were found to have poor motivation, as such pressure, and persuasion did not lose till the completion of the period required for acquiring skills in reading and writing.

Boss (1985) realized that majority of non-completers of basic education course believed that their destinies were controlled by fate, luck, powerful others. In contrast, the course completers (learners) were found to be internally controlled individuals who believed in their potential to acquire necessary change in their life of overcoming frustrations.

An overview of the above studies showed that no systematic attempt is made to comprehensively explore association of various psychological factors with learners and dropping out. However, studies have identified factors like motivation, interest, shyness, conservation, aspirations in literacy, discouragement, fatalistic thinking which may have bearing on learners and dropping out phenomena.

ENVIRONMENTAL PROBLEMS

Studies indicating the significance of physical facilities like accommodation, lighting, location, etc., and investigations highlighting the role of social support and continuance of learners in TLC centres were reviewed under this head.

Physical facilities provide favourable environment to learners in the form of comfort for learning in an undisturbed way. In addition, encouragement from community, friends and family members and awareness about the benefits of learning provide positive learning environment to the learners. The findings relating to environmental factors by and large were based on the views of learners or views of investigators drop-out views on environmental factors were rarely studied.

Physical Facilities Related Problems

Some studies have revealed that continuance of learners in the centres was found to have not been affected because of their functioning in instructors houses. This fact was emphasized in the evaluation study in Tamilnadu by Ramakrishnan (1980). He found that as many as 90% of the adult education centres evaluated by him were located in instructors house. Rao et al. (1980) reported that provisions of better lighting facilities and running the centre at convenient place were some of the conditions stimulated by the drop-outs for rejoining the centres.

Sachachidananda et al. (1981) also highlighted that a good number of adult education centres were located in the houses of instructors. Further, they concluded that most of the centres surveyed by them had adequate seating arrangement for learners. This indicated additional emphasis on the significance of need for satisfactory accommodation in adult education centres for continuance of learners.

Drop-outs interviewed by Pestonjee et al. (1981) suggested that by providing proper arrangements for lighting, seating, drinking water and facilities for games and recreation etc., attendance rate in the centres can be improved.

The finding of Harihar and Rao (1982) regarding the location of the centre was similar to studies discussed earlier i.e., majority of the centres surveyed by them were located in instructors houses.

Acharji (1983) found that adequate seating and lighting arrangement and convenient location of the centres had facilitated the continuance of learners in the centres if they were satisfied with the arrangements.

The evaluation studies conducted by Ganguli et al. (1983) reported that sufficient lighting and adequate sitting accommodation were available in most of the centres evaluated by them in the state of Bihar. This also means that proper lighting and sitting accommodation are the minimum requirements in any adult education centre for continuance of learners in the centres.

Mathew (1983) tried to list out the views of learners (who continued their participation in adult education programme) about physical facilities.

Aikara (1984) found that in the centres evaluated by him in the state of Maharashtra. Physical facilities like location of the centres, accommodation of the centres and lighting in them moderate. This may mean that the centres should be located at least at a moderate distance and also sitting accommodation to the learners and lighting arrangement at the centres should at least be moderately convenient for continuance of learners.

But in adult education centres evaluated by Ganguli (1984), it was observed that in most of the centres space provided for the learners for the purpose of sitting was inadequate. However, the centres were found to be clean. This may mean inadequate space might not have affected the learners continuance. This might have been compensated by the cleanliness of the centre for the continuance of learners.

According to Pangotra and Sween (1989) over 50% of the adult learners were dissatisfied with the physical environment in the centres.

The studies on physical facilities showed that the findings were inconclusive. Few studies dealt with learners perception of physical facilities. Most of the studies had just presented status reports on physical environment. On the other hand, some studies presented investigators, perception of physical facilities. A few studies covered the views of drop-outs on physical facilities. In the light of these, it would be difficult to know the extent to which the physical facilities influenced learners to drop-out.

Learning Environment Related Problems

In addition to physical facilities, encouragement and support received by learners from family members, friends and community provide favourable learning environment. Added to this knowledge of benefits of literacy may have additional significance in providing favourable environment. Hebsur et al. (1981) observed significant lower rate of drop-out in those adult education centres where support to the instructors was available from local leaders and government officials.

Harihar and Rao (1982) also noted that majority of the learners were encouraged by the instructors. Considerable number of learners were encouraged by both instructors and family members. Neither encouragement nor discouragement from the influential persons in the village of learners attending the centres was found.

Ganguli et al. (1983) found that the instructors were the main source of motivation to join the centres for majority of the learners. Considerable number of learners interviewed by them were also motivated by family members, friends and relatives. The role of village elite and village panchayath officials in motivating the learners to join the centres was limited.

Visaria and Mathew (1983) reported that majority of the learners received encouragement from instructors for joining the centres. Learners who joined the centres with the encouragement of relatives were few in number. Further, a notable feature was that the learners did not receive any opposition from anybody i.e., family members, relatives and village leaders to participate in adult education programme.

A survey conducted by Parik (1985) in the State of Gujarath, indicates that the involvement of village leaders in the promotion of adult education activities was meagre.

An overview of the studies covering factors facilitating learning environment indicate instructor as the main source of inspiration to learners for joining the centres. Others in the list who encouraged the learners considerably to participate in adult education programme were family members, friends and relatives. Interestingly, many studies pointed out different attitude of community representatives for not taking interest in the promotion of adult education programme. This means that they, by and large, had not taken any interest in motivating the illiterate learners to join the TLC centres. Further, all the studies discussed above tried to describe learning environment in terms of learners and none of the studies attempted to investigate the impact of various factors i.e., instructor, relatives, friends, family members and community members on drop-outs. In other words, studies had not attempted to note whether dropping out has any relationship with lack of encouragement from instructors, family members, relatives and the like.

PROGRAMME-RELATED AND INSTRUCTOR-RELATED PROBLEMS

Programme-related Problem

Programme-related problems like course content, teaching methods, duration of the course, timing of the course, class size, etc., may also have a bearing on learners and dropping out phenomena.

Hussain (1980) considered that drop-out rate can be reduced if care was taken of the factors listed by him. The factors include clear statement of course objectives, careful selection and proper training of instructors, motivation of adult learners to learn, supply of adequate teaching and learning materials, convenient class things and location, effective supervision and proper evaluation of learner progress.

Hebsur et al. (1981) reported that provision of adequate teaching and learning materials, functionally and social awareness-oriented curriculum, adequate support from local leaders and government officials exposure to mass media as factors positively influencing retention rate of learners in adult education centres.

Rao (1983) made a comparative study of relative effectiveness of sentence and alphabetic method. He found that alphabetic method was better than sentenced method. Further, within the alphabetic method, teaching, reading for the first two months followed by writing was found more effective than the conventional alphabetic method in which reading and writing were done simultaneously.

In a study conducted by Pangotra and Sween (1989), it was found that course content was not relevant to the every day needs of adult learners. Language and vocabulary used in primers were not suitable to the local conditions. Further, there was no clarity of purpose i.e., basic purpose of adult learning was not clear to adult learners.

On the whole, studies relating to programme-related factors highlighted the need to take proper care about programme related factors to reduce drop-out rate i.e., care about appropriate course content, duration of the course, timing of the classes, and application of appropriate method of teaching enhanced retention of learners in the classes.

Instructor-related Problems

Instructor-related problems like age, sex and caste of the instructor, regularity and punctuality of the instructor, teaching efficiency of the instructor, social and personal relations of the instructor with learners and interest shown by the instructor in learners may also influence learners and dropping out.

Hamadachi (1973) reported that personality of the instructor had significant influence on learners. He observed that more the instructor can create interest in the subject matter, lower was the drop-out rate.

Okara (1975) observed low drop-out rate in literacy centres where instructor treated adult learners with due respect and provided them opportunity to discuss problems relating to their way of life.

Reddy (1986) found that caste, sex and economic status of the instructor should be similar to that of adult learners to ensure better understanding and interaction between learners and instructors.

Rao (1988) found that learner's performance was effective in centres managed by instructors regularly and punctually. Further, he found that learners taught by men instructors gained indore literacy, functionality and awareness than those learners taught by female instructors. In addition, he also found that learners taught by young instructors (below 25 years) performed better than learners taught by instructors of older age group.

Reddy (1989) in his study on factors associated with instructors' effectiveness found the following: women instructors functioned more effectively than men (instructors), instructor with high achievement motivation were more successful and instructions with high positive attitude towards adult education programme were more devoted.

The studies on the whole, though unsystematic and scattered, indicated the significance of an instructor who has interest and concern for the learners, who attempted to teach learners in the best possible way and who was regular and punctual in his teaching and enhanced motivation of learners.

REASONS FOR DROPPING OUT OF ADULT LEARNERS

Illiterate adults join adult education centres with the intention of becoming literates. But, considerable number leave the centres without accomplishing their objectives. A good number of evaluation studies, as specific studies tried to identify the reasons for drop-out from adult education centres. The reasons listed by the studies cover wide spectrum of various issues. Directorate of Adult Education (1973), Laharia and Dixit (1981), Acharji, Ganguli, Pathak Mirza and Shah (1983), Pestonjee (1984) through their evaluation studies listed a number of reasons for dropping out from adult education centres.

The study conducted by Pillai (1974) in Kerala state, revealed several listening reasons for dropping out, besides usual occupational and familial problems. The problem mentioned by the respondents other than occupational and family responsibilities include, lack of interest, uninteresting subjects, fear of ridicule, no English teaching, distance of the centre, teachers too young, difficulty in memorizing, futility in becoming literate, illness, poor eye sight and monotonous class work.

According to Jhansi (1981), the factors promoting participation of learners were: (1) high motivation, (2) family encouragement, (3) family education background, (4) awareness of deprivation of childhood education, (5) ability to take risks, (6) locational factors/physical proximity, (7) favourable perception of the teacher, (8) joint family and availability for leisure time.

As part of evaluation study in the state of Bihar, Ganguli (1983) identified the reasons for early withdrawal from adult education centres. The main reasons were: family problems, poverty, inadequacy of teaching and learning materials, unsuitability of the place of the centre, inconvenient timing, no future benefit in attending the centre and ill-health, etc. Further, the investigators had also examined drop-out reasons as perceived by the instructors. The reasons as perceived by the instructors were migration to far off places in search of livelihood, family problems, sickness and loss of interest.

Shah (1983) made an attempt to explore the reasons for discontinuance of course by the participants enrolled in adult education centres in the state of Gujarath. He found that more than 50% of the respondents left the course due to pressure of work, family problems and migration. About one-fourth of the learners dropped out due to inadequate physical facilities, inconvenient location and timings of the class. In addition, about one-sixth of the subjects interviewed mentioned inadequate and delayed supply of teaching and learning materials, irrelevant course content, irregularity of instructors as reasons for dropping out.

According to Pillai (1986), the major reasons for continuing in adult education centres were: (a) availability of better physical arrangements (seating and lighting), (b) opportunity to mix with a lot of people, (c) exposure to family welfare schemes, (d) interesting learning materials, (e) cordial atmosphere among learners and (f) co-operation from local agencies. Other reasons listed by him were: proximity of adult education centres, availability of healthcare facilities, help in solving their family problems and the like.

Rajyalaxmi (1986) examined motivational problems in functional literacy programmes in Mahaboobnagar district of Andhra Pradesh. On the basis of the study conducted on women, she concluded that the factors accounted for lack of motivation were: lack of leisure, family resistance, absence of any monetary or material incentives, irrational beliefs, geographical distance, perceived negative norms about literacy, negative attitude towards women's literacy in awareness of the programme, time constraints, etc. She observed that the basic factor for non-participation and drop-out was low level of motivation. The women in the study area had no interest for literacy, they did not consider these programmes as useful in the context of their environmental needs either immediately or in the long run.

Smith (1987) investigated the reasons for dropping out from foundation courses. The study revealed that majority of the respondents had abandoned the course because of conflict of interest of one kind or other rather than because of disappointment with the course and its presentation or with their own performance. The term conflict of interest means conflict either with work or with family and social responsibilities. Other reasons were: course too difficult to follow, changed circumstances—new jobs, change of residence, and health problems. The study concluded that perceived inability to cope intellectually with work involved (whatever the actual ability may be) was not the main reasons for abandonment. Rather it was an unwillingness to give the study task the priority that was needed for success.

According to Omana (1989) distance of the centres, family opposition, tiresomeness, to stay at home to look after the family migration from one place to another, lack of motivation, shyness were the reasons for dropping out of learners from adult education centres.

Vanaja (1989) through a study conducted on female drop-outs listed three major reasons for the phenomena of drop-out. The first reasons was the household drudgery which caused tiresomeness and allowed no time to attend the centres. The second reason was social inhibitions and discouraging environment. Most of the young unmarried girls were inhibited to go out of home due to unfavourable custom and traditions prevailing and timings of the centre. Other reasons of equal importance listed by her were shyness, due to their old age and lack of interest in the programme.

An analysis of reasons listed for phenomena of drop-out from adult education centres showed that many major reasons identified by various investigators were similar and complementary. The reasons expressed both for dropping out may be classified into three broad categories namely, learners-related reasons, programme-related reasons and miscellaneous reasons. The learner-related reasons referred to work and family obligations, social and physical factors like interest, motivation, beliefs and so on. The programme related factors referred to organisational factors (class size, time, course duration, distance, accommodation, lighting and the like) and instructional reasons (suitability of curriculum, teaching methodology, efficiency of instructor, availability of teaching/ learning materials). Under miscellaneous reasons, issues like family encouragement, community encouragement, food habits, etc., may be included.

An overview of related literature presented in preceding pages showed: (1) much the attempts made to explore and explain the phenomena of dropping out from adult education centres was through evaluation studies, which were more general in nature covering wide range of issues, relating to entire adult education programme and not dealing in depth with particular aspects; (2) in addition to evaluation studies, specific studies conducted by some investigators to understand the factors associated with learners and dropping out of learners were, by and large, incomplete and unsystematic; (3) when both evaluation studies and specific studies were considered together, most of the investigators focused their attention on highlighting the factors associated with phenomena of dropping out than to suggest remedial measures. (4) Even the limited number of studies done on learners had not attempted to identify systematically the facilitating factors that made an individual stay and learn. (5) Among studies on drop-outs, most of the investigators confined themselves to explore the reasons for dropping out by just putting the question "Why did you dro-pout". But, they had not carefully examined the wide range of factors contributing to drop-out phenomena.

On the whole, the studies indicated personal and familial factors (age, sex, caste, occupation, income, family size, family educational background, childhood education, etc.), psychological factors (motivation attitude, conventional beliefs, shyness, etc.), environmental factors (physical facilities like accommodation support, family encouragement, literacy consciousness, etc.), programme and instructor related factors influenced learners to some degree or other resulting in the promotion of continuance of learners attending the centres or leading them to drop-out. Researches highlighting systematically the effect of the above factors on learners or dropping out of learners from total literacy campaign centres are needed to open new avenues, provide clarity and help an understanding of the conceptual nature of phenomena of learners drop-out from total literacy campaigns.

3

Adult Drop-outs
A Study

The success of any educational programme including adult education programme depends on the participation of target. The extent of participation of the target also depends on various factors including the background of the target, opinion of the target towards the programme and the benefits expected by the target after attending the programmes. In case of adult education, the returns for the targets participation in the programme will not be immediate but it takes some time to yield results. As a result of this, the drop-outs are many and the reasons are also many. In view of this, it is necessary to identify the reasons for drop-outs in adult education and measures to prevent them. Keeping in view of the above, the present study was taken up to identify the problems of the drop-outs. To be specific, the problem to be tackled the operational definitions of certain terms used, objectives, hypothesis, importance and limitations of the study, selection and development of the tool, sample selection, collection of data and statistical techniques used in the study are presented below:

TITLE OF THE PROBLEM

An enquiry into the problems of dropouts in Total Literacy Campaign (TLC) of Kurnool district.

OPERATIONAL DEFINITIONS OF CERTAIN TERMS USED IN THE STUDY

(i) Problem

1. A difficult or puzzling question proposed for solution (Oxford English Dictionary, 1961).
2. Dealing with a problem of human conduct or social relationship (Webster's Dictionary, 1963).
3. Any puzzling or difficult circumstance or person (Standard Desk Dictionary, 1977).
4. Treating subject of social or other problem (The New Oxford Encyclopedic Dictionary, 1981).
5. A question raised for inquiry, consideration or solution.

According to Fernaid C. James (1919), problem is a "perplexing question demanding settlement".

In this study, problem is considered as a set of difficulties growing out of inadequacies of adjustment, demanding settlement or solution on the part of an individual of a society.

(ii) Dropout

Dropout has been defined in many ways: 1) one who leaves a class a few days after enrolling; (2) one who attends the course but does not continue in the class for more than three months; (3) one who leaves the course without completing it and there is no intention of returning to it; (4) one who separates himself from the programme for any other reason than successful completion, temporary illness, or vocation. These definitions are based on the point in time at which the learner becomes a dropout. In some cases, the student who either does not sit or does not pass the final examination is considered a dropout (The International Institute for Adult Literacy Methods, 1980). The duration of Total Literacy Campaign is one year, and the learner has to complete three primers viz., Primer-I, Primer-II and Primer-III. It may take 5 to 6 months for completing Primer-I. One who leaves the campaign without completing even Primer-I and before 6 months is considered as a dropout in the present study.

(iii) Problems of Drop-outs

Problems of drop-outs are the problems or difficulties faced by the drop-outs in attending the Total Literacy Campaign (TLC) and thereby leaving the campaign.

(iv) Total Literacy Campaign

Total Literacy Campaign is an area specific (Mandal/District), time bound (6-12 months), learner age specific (9-35/15-35), cost-effective and result-oriented. It aims at achieving total literacy in specific area in the specific target group in the specified time. The total literacy campaign of Kurnool district covers the entire district, within one year, all the illiterate adults in the age group of 15-35 years as per NLM norms. However, the upper age limit is relaxed in the district upto 45 years.

(v) Kurnool District

Kurnool District is one of the 23 districts of Andhra Pradesh.

OBJECTIVES OF THE STUDY

The following are the objectives of the study.

To study the learners enrolment and drop-outs in TLC of Kurnool district.

To study the problems of dropouts in TLC of Kurnool district as expressed by the drop-outs.

(i) to identify the problems which have different difficulty level/different effects.

(ii) to identify the problems which have same difficulty level/same effect.

(iii) to identify the very significant, significant and less significant problems.

(iv) to identify the very significant, significant and less significant problems of drop-outs in each problem area i.e., economic, social, psychological, familial, instructor-related, community-related, personal and programme-related problems.

To study the different effects (differences in the difficulty level) of each problem of drop-outs between the following groups of drop-outs

(i) Male and Female (Sex)

(ii) With previous schooling and no schooling (education)

(iii) Married and unmarried (Marital Status)

(iv) With different age groups—20 years and below, between 21-35 years, and 36 years and above age groups (Age).

(v) Belonging to different castes—Scheduled Caste, Scheduled Tribe (SC/ST), Backward Castes (BC) and Other Castes (OC) (Caste)

(vi) Belonging to different occupations—agriculture, labour and others (Occupation).

(vii) Different annual income groups—Rs. 20,000 and below, between Rs. 21-30 thousands and Rs. 31 thousands and above (Annual Income)

(viii) With different levels of attendance at the centres—1-2 months, 2-4 months, and 4-6 months (Attendance).

To study the differential effects of each problem area of drop-outs between the following groups of drop-outs.

(i) Male and female (Sex)

(ii) With previous schooling and no schooling (Education)

(iii) Married and unmarried (Marital Status)

(iv) With different age groups—20 years and below, between 21-35 years, and 36 years and above age groups (Age).

(v) Belonging to different castes—Scheduled Caste, Scheduled Tribe (SC/ST), Backward Castes (BC) and Other Castes (OC) (Caste)

(vi) Belonging to different occupations—agriculture, labour and others (Occupation).

(vii) Different annual income groups—Rs. 20,000 and below, between Rs. 21-30 thousands and Rs. 31 thousands and above (Annual Income)

(viii) With different levels of attendance at the centres—1-2 months, 2-4 months, and 4-6 months (Attendance).

To study the relative effect of the problem areas on total drop-outs.

To suggest remedial measures for solving the problems of drop-outs.

Hypotheses of the Study

Hypothesis-1

The drop-out rate in TLC of Kurnool district is higher than 50.

Hypothesis-2

The problem of drop-outs are various and varied.

Hypothesis-3

The problems of drop-outs have varying levels of difficulty/effect.

Hypothesis-4

There are some groups of problems which have same difficulty levels/effect.

Hypothesis-5

There is no difference in the effect/difficulty levels of each problem between the following groups of drop-outs.

(i) Male and Female (Sex)

(ii) With previous schooling and no schooling (Education)

(iii) Married and unmarried (Marital Status)

(iv) With different age groups—20 years and below, between 21-35 years, and 36 years and above age groups (Age).

(v) Belonging to different castes—Scheduled Caste, Scheduled Tribe (SC/ST), Backward Castes (BC) and Other Castes (OC) (Caste)

(vi) Belonging to different occupations—agriculture, labour and others (Occupation).

(vii) Different annual income groups—Rs. 20,000 and below, between Rs. 21-30 thousands and Rs. 31 thousands and above (Annual Income).

(viii) With different levels of attendance at the centres—1-2 months, 2-4 months, and 4-6 months (Attendance).

NEED FOR THE STUDY

The problems of drop-outs have to be identified and solved urgently for various and varied reasons.

- There are studies identifying the problems of drop-outs, but they are not exhaustive. The results are also not conclusive.
- The instruments used earlier for finding out causes/ problems of drop-outs were not standardised. The sample coverage was inadequate. The method used for finding the problems was mainly problem checklist which do not quantify exactly the level of difficulty of the problem. The results arrived at were not trustworthy.
- If the drop-out rate is high, the unit cost of running the programme is high. The expected returns are less and thereby the wastage is more. The society has to bare the cost.
- If once the learners are dropped out/pushed out/thrown out from the programme, they may not be interested to join in any programme in future in view of the demoralizing effect of the earlier programme.
- If the drop-outs are not recognised and checked, the drop-outs may induce other learners also to drop-out by acting as demotivating agents.
- Dropping out may result in not acquiring the skills needed to meet the demands of the technological advances in industry and agriculture and the individuals may not play an effective role as works.

LIMITATIONS OF THE STUDY

- In studying the problems of drop-outs, the sample is limited to 400 drop-outs, drawn only from 6 mandals out of 54 mandals in the district.
- The findings of the study may not be applicable to other districts of Andhra Pradesh. Therefore, these findings cannot be generalized. There may be some problems and problem areas not covered by the present study.

- The problems are limited to only 80 and 8 areas of problems.

SELECTION OF THE TOOL FOR IDENTIFYING PROBLEMS

In order to obtain the problems of the drop-outs, the researcher may use tools like Questionnaire, Checklist, Interview Schedule, Case Study, Observation and Rating Scale.

Keeping in view, the previously employed instruments for studying the problems of drop-outs, the investigator has chosen to employ the technique of rating scale for studying the problems of drop-outs. Rating scale was used since it helps to know the extent of difficulty of each problem.

DESCRIPTION OF RATING SCALE

Rating Scale is a tool which records judgements or opinions and indicates degree of amount. It is a very useful device in assessing quality.

According to A.S. Barr and others (Khanna, D., 1983, pp. 64-67) Rating Scale is "a term applied to expression of opinion or judgement regarding some situation, object or character". Opinions are usually expressed on a scale of values. Rating techniques are "devices by which such judgements may be quantified".

Purposes of Rating Scale

Rating scales have been successfully utilised for purpose of:

(a) Teaching rating—for selection, evaluation and prediction;

(b) Personality rating—for various purposes;

(c) Testing and validity of many objective instruments like paper-pencil inventories of personality;

(d) School appraisals-including appraised of courses, practices and programmes.

Making use of rating scales is a very flexible and simple procedure but it depends on judges instead of independent criteria and is thus not wholly objective.

Characteristics of Rating Scale

The rating scale should possess the following characteristics:

(a) Traits should be judged on the basis of past and present accomplishments;

(b) In self-rating, over and under-estimates should be avoided;

(c) Rating scale should be used only when data cannot be obtained by other more reliable tools;

(d) In describing traits, the use of adjectives should be avoided;

(e) A trait should not be a composite of two or more independent traits;

(f) Only significant traits should be selected.

(g) Several judges should be employed for making judgements.

(h) A trait should refer to a single type of activity or quality.

(i) Traits should be described objectively.

(j) A trait should be described unequivocally.

(k) Only those should be employed who are interested in the ratings they make.

(l) Only those raters should be employed who have adequate educational and professional background.

Useful Hints on the Construction and Use of Rating Scale

(a) Rating scales include three factors :

(i) the subjects or the phenomena to be rated.

(ii) the continuum along which they will be rated; and

(iii) the judges who will do the rating.

All these three factors must be very carefully selected.

(b) The subjects or phenomena to be rated are usually a limited number of aspects of a thing, or of traits of a person.

(c) The degree of the trait should be defined. Each trait is rated on a scale, most frequently of five or seven intervals.

(d) Items may be arranged in ascending or descending order from left to right.

(e) At least three divisions of quality must be kept. Practically, most scales have no more than seven divisions, usually they contain five divisions. By numbering each division in sequence the descriptions can be converted into arithmetic value for averaging.

(f) The rating scale is always composed of two parts:

(i) an instruction which names the subject and defines the continuum; and

(ii) a scale which defines the points to be used in rating.

Merits and Demerits of Rating Scale

Merits

(a) Rating requires much less time than ranking methods.

(b) The procedure becomes interesting when graphic method is employed.

(c) They can be used with persons having minimum of training for making ratings.

(d) The range of their application is very wide. They can be used for teaching ratings, personality ratings, testing validity or paper-pencil inventories, school appraisal, etc.

Demerits

(a) It is difficult to convey to the rater just what quality one wishes to evaluate.

(b) It is difficult for raters to get rid of the hallow effect.

(c) Raters tend to be generally generous.

(d) Subjectivity element influences raters.

Types of Rating Scale

The Rating Scales are classified into six categories. They are :

(a) *Numerical Scale:* In a five-point scale, for example, the "average" person scored 0; the deviants scored +2, +1, -2 or -1, or the scores to eliminate signs, can all be positive 1 being the lowest, 3 the average, 5 the highest. For example: How was the lesson introduced in the class?

No.	*Trait*
1.	Very unsatisfactory
2.	Unsatisfactory
3.	Satisfactory
4.	Good
5.	Outstanding

(b) *Graphic Scale:* A common variant of the scoring method is graphic rating scale. The several levels of degrees of the trait are defined and placed at points along a horizontal line. The judge places a mark any where he chooses on this line between the two extremes. Although a graphic scale theoretically permits scoring at a large number of points, such refinement and spurious accuracy are not warranted. This may be expressed under:

(c) *Descriptive Scale:* The rater puts a check (ü) in the blank before the trait which is described in a word or phrase. Example: Has this pupil initiative?

- Shows marked originality
- Willing to take initiative
- Quite inventive
- On the whole unenterprising
- Very dependent on others

(d) *Cumulative Points Scale:* An individual rates himself. He checks his traits on a list of objectives. He then counts his favourable and unfavourable responses. For each item, there are two responses to be weighed as +1 and 0.

(e) *Standard Scale:* A set of standards are represented to the ratings. Ratings through this scale become easier and more meaningful. For example: Man to man ratings, handwriting comparison.

(f) *Pooled Judgement Scale:* Pooled judgements increase the reliability of any rating scale. Employ several judges, depending on the rating situation, to obtain desirable reliability.

Selection of the Type of Rating Scale

Out of all the six types of Rating Scales, the numerical rating scale was selected for the present study.

Numerical rating scale is a device for making and recording a subjective judgements as to the position of an individual or item in relation to a pre-arranged scale of values typically consists of a trait or characteristic. Three point rating scale was chosen. The subject was asked to choose one of the three alternatives. They may find it difficult to discriminate among five alternatives. Therefore, five point scale was not chosen.

DEVELOPMENT OF RATING SCALE FOR IDENTIFYING THE PROBLEMS OF DRO-OUTS FROM TOTAL LITERACY CAMPAIGN CENTRES

Selection of Areas and Problems

The researcher surveyed the literature available on the subject, consulted the experts in the field, visited some of the Total Literacy Campaign Centres and met the drop-out learners. Basing on the knowledge of the researcher, 113 problems were listed in the rating scale. The problems cover different areas like economic problems, social problems, psychological problems, family problems, instructor-related problems, community-related problems, personal problems and programme related problems.

A panel consisting of 15 experts (5 Adult Education Project Officers, 5 Supervisors and 5 university level teachers) who had experience in the field were constituted as the panel and they were requested to go through the items written by the researcher under different areas. They were also requested to check the repetitions, ambiguous items, unrelated items as well as language errors, if any and change the area of the item, if it falls under different category. Out of 113 problems after incorporating the suggestions and modifications, as many as 96 problems remained. These 96 problems, under different areas, were rewritten and the rating scale was tested on a sample of 50 drop-out learners of Koilkuntla Mandal to test its workability. Based on the experience gained and after incorporation of a few modifications (language) the items of the rating scale consisting of 96 items were tried out.

Try-out of Items

A sample of 370 drop-outs were chosen randomly for pilot study from Velugodu, Atmakur, Banaganapalli Mandals of Nandyal Revenue Division, Kurnool district.

The drop-outs chosen represent different sex, age, occupation, caste, and income groups. The rating scale was administered to the drop-outs. The instructions relating to the method of indicating the responses to the problems were first read out to the subjects. Then the problems were read out one after the other and the subject was requested to indicate his/her answer by agreeing with any one of the three alternatives readout against each item.

The three alternatives given are— Not at all, To some extent, and Much. The alternatives thus obtained from the subjects were scored.

Scoring of the Items

For the purpose of scoring of the items, the following numerical values were assigned to each of the three alternatives against each item.

Alternative	*Numerical Value Assigned*
Not at all	1
To some extent	2
Much	3

Item Analysis

As the pilot study (try-out) was conducted on 370 drop-outs, a group of 100 drop-outs (27%) with highest scores constituted the high group and a group of 100 drop-outs (27%) with the lowest total scores formed the low group. These two groups were selected to be the criterion groups for calculating the critical ratio for each item. The critical ratio was calculated by using the formula suggested by Edwards (1969). The 't' values calculated for each item gave discriminating index of each item and the 't' values are shown in Table 3.1. As suggested by Edwards (1957), the items with 't' value of less than 1.75 were rejected. On the whole, 16 items were rejected from all the problem areas—economic problems 1, from social problems 2, from psychological problems 3, from familial problems 1, from instructor related problems 4, from community related problems 2, and from personal problems 3, psychological problems, 1 from familial problems, 4 from instructor related problems, 2 from community related problems, 3 from personal problems and 0 from programme-related problems. Finally, only 80 items were retained in the Rating Scale.

Table 3.1: Showing 't' values of the Items included in the Pilot Form of the Rating Scale

Item S.No. in the Pilot form	*'t' Value*	*Item S.No. in the final form*	*Item S.No. in the Pilot form*	*'t' Value*	*Item S. No. in the final form*
1	2	3	4	5	6
1.	3.43	1	25.	4.30	21
2.	2.99	2	26.	6.31	22
3.	1.70@		27.	3.76	23
4.	2.46	3	28.	1.99	24
5.	4.82	4	29.	0.97@	
6.	3.33	5	30.	3.08	25
7.	3.91	6	31.	4.79	26
8.	2.84	7	32.	1.61@	
9.	2.53	8	33.	5.23	27
10.	3.10	9	34.	3.36	28
11.	3.42	10	35.	2.49	29
12.	1.67@		36.	3.89	30
13.	2.91	11	37.	5.94	31

(Table Contd...)

1	*2*	*3*	*4*	*5*	*6*
14.	2.70	12	38.	4.93	32
15.	4.57	13	39.	7.66	33
16.	3.03	14	40.	5.62	34
17.	1.02@		41.	0.84@	
18.	4.91	15	42.	3.39	35
19.	3.53	16	43.	4.40	36
20.	4.09	17	44.	2.93	37
21.	2.37	18	45.	7.77	38
22.	3.01	19	46.	1.23@	
23.	1.55@		47.	6.87	39
24.	2.40	20	48.	4.37	40
49.	5.49	41	73.	8.88	61
50.	3.92	42	74.	6.48	62
51.	3.71	43	75.	0.97@	
52.	2.83	44	76.	4.83	63
53.	7.55	45	77.	3.99	64
54.	1.44@		78.	5.52	65
55.	6.97	46	79.	5.87	66
56.	0.99@		80.	4.12	67
57.	5.99	47	81.	0.79@	
58.	4.38	48	82.	6.27	68
59.	1.06@		83.	1.70@	
60.	4.33	49	84.	7.16	69
61.	3.86	50	85.	3.25	70
62.	2.42	51	86.	2.66	71
63.	5.92	52	87.	4.72	72
64.	4.37	53	88.	0.66@	
65.	6.79	54	89.	2.37	73
66.	0.75@		90.	3.17	74
67.	2.37	55	91.	3.96	75
68.	3.89	56	92.	2.42	76
69.	8.02	57	93.	7.10	77
70.	7.39	58	94.	7.73	78
71.	5.73	59	95.	6.94	79
72.	4.24	60	96.	5.93	80

@ Item rejected.

List showing the details of items rejected is given below:

1. Lack of weightage to the certificates issued by Zilla Aksharasyatha Samithi (ZAS) at the time of jobs (Instructor Related Problem)
2. Lack of respect at the village (Instructor Related Problem)
3. Lack of attractive charts, pamphlets and books useful in daily life (Personnel Problem).
4. Lack of adoption of certain measure of compulsion for learners to participate in TLC centres (Personal Problem).
5. Lack of providing identity cards, prizes, certificates, fair price shops to learners (Personal Problem).
6. Absence of demand for frequent/long outstation stay (Familial Problem).
7. Late supply of learning materials (Programme Problem).
8. Lack of quality in learning materials like pencils, erasers (Programme-related problem).
9. Lack of support from village leaders (Community-related problem).
10. Lack of knowledge among leaders about the TLC programme (Community-related problem).
11. Lack of awareness among learners that education facilitates in reducing the economic disparities in the society (Social Problem).
12. Lack of vocational training in the centres (Economic Problem).
13. Lack of equality in the society (Social Problem).
14. Accompanying family members in the centres (Psychological Problem).
15. Lack of feeling in learning alphabets (Psychological Problem).
16. Girls does not require education (Psychological Problem).

The final form of the Rating Scale consists of 80 problems covering eight areas as shown in Table-3.2.

Table 3.2: Areas and Problems

Sl. No.	*Area*	*No. of Items*	*Sl. No. of the items in the rating scale*
1.	Economic problems	6	1-6
2.	Social problems	10	7-16
3.	Psychological problems	14	17-30
4.	Familial problems	6	31-36
5.	Instructor related problems	21	37-57
6.	Community related problems	8	58-65
7.	Personal problems	12	66-77
8.	Programme related problems	3	78-80

It is observed that the number of items/problems in 8 problems areas is not equal and then number varies from 3 to 121. The inclusion of items in each area depends upon:

1. Problems identified in previous research studies;
2. Opinion of panel consisting 15 experts;
3. Item analysis (Statistical Treatment) of the items; and
4. Relative weightage of each problem area.

These considerations forced the researcher to choose unequal number of items in different problem areas.

Validity of the Rating Scale

The rating scale does possess face validity, content validity, item validity and intrinsic validity as it has been established. The details of each of these are given below:

(a) Face Validity

When the rating scale was readout to few lay persons (adult learners and drop-outs), who had no knowledge of rating scale, they felt that it measured the problems of dropouts. Lindquist (1966) says, "a test is face valid particularly if it looks valid to layman" and therefore the test has face validity.

(b) Content Validity

Content validity indicates how adequate is the content of a test sampling the domain of which inferences are to be made. To restore this type of validity to the test, an attempt was made to see that all the areas of drop-outs were included in the test constructed. Under each are an adequate number of sample items were included. The preparation of scale items was proceeded by a thorough and systematic examination of all the areas of drop-outs found in books and journals. Experts were also conducted. The test items were reviewed in the light of the suggestions of the experts for content adequacy and accuracy. In view of these, it may be said that the test possess content validity.

(c) Item Validity

The items of the rating scale were selected on the basis of item analysis. Each item selected and included in the final test had satisfactory level of item discrimination. Hence, the items included in the rating scale possess item validity.

(d) Intrinsic Validity

The degree to which a test measures what it measures may be called its intrinsic validity. The definition can also be stated in terms of how well the obtained scores measure the test true-score components. The validity is indicated by the square root of the preparation of true variance, in other words, the square root of its reliability. Another name for this statistic is the index of reliability (Guilfore, 1954). The intrinsic value of the rating scale was $\sqrt{0.88}$ = 0.9327 which indicates that the scale possesses high intrinsic validity.

Reliability of the Rating Scale

The reliability can be measured by different methods such as Test-retest, Parallel forms, Split-half and Rational-equivalence method. In the present study, test-retest method is used. The rating scale is administered twice on a small sample 30 drop-out learners with a gap of 15 days. The correlation co-efficient is found between the results of two administrations. The test-retest correlation co-efficient is 0.87 and it indicates rather high reliability.

METHOD OF COLLECTION OF DATA

Locale of the Study

The locale of the study is Kurnool district. Kurnool district is one of the 23 districts of Andhra Pradesh.

The reasons for choosing Kurnool district for the study include the following:

(a) Familiarity of the researcher with the region.

(b) Backwardness of the region

(c) The researcher belongs to the district

Sample Selection

In the present study, Stratified Random Sampling Technique is employed. According to S.R. Bajpai, (1960) Stratified Sampling is a combination of both random sampling and purposive selection. Under this system, the universe is first divided into a number of strata or groups. Then from each group certain number of items are taken on random basis. Thus, in the selection of strata we use purposive selection method, but in selecting actual units from each stratum random method is used.

1. Process of Stratifying

- The success of stratified sampling depends upon formation of strata or groups. If a correct stratification has been made even a smaller number of units will form a representative sample, following points may be kept in mind while constructing strata.
- First of all we should note the different variables involved in the study of the problem. The common variables used for stratification are generally region, income, sex, etc. The universe is first divided into these groups and then the required units are selected at random from each group. In selecting the variables, care should be taken to see that they are related to study.
- The size of each stratum in the universe should be large enough to provide selection of items on random basis. If the strata are too small, difficulty may be created in making a random selection.

- Stratification should be so conducted that there should be perfect homogeneity in the different units of strata. The items in the stratum should be similar to each other but they should differ significantly from the units of other strata.
- It is desirable that number of items to be selected from each stratum should be in the same ratio as the total number of units in the stratum bear to the units in whole universe. Thus, for example, if the percentage of education in a certain social groups is 75, the sample percentage of units will be selected from amongst the educated.
- The strata should be clear cut and free from overlapping, so that every unit must find a place in some stratum or the other and no units should be placed in more than one stratum. The total number of units in different strata should be equal to total number of units in universe.

2. Kinds of Stratified Sampling

Stratified sampling itself is of the following types:

- *Proportional Stratified Sample:* In the method, the number of units to be drawn from each stratum is in the same proportion as they stand in the universe. It has already been explained above.
- *Disproportional Stratified Sample:* According to this method, an equal number of cases are taken from each stratum regardless of the size of strata in proportion to universe. It is also known as controlled sampling because it permits inter-strata comparison.
- *Stratified Weighted Sampling:* The method aims at removing the defects of disproportionate sample and combine the advantages of the two stratified samples stated earlier. The disproportionate sample has one defect, that it create bias by over weighing same of the strata. In this system, equal number of units are selected from each stratum. Averages are taken from each stratum but they are given weights in proportion to the size of stratum in the whole universe.

3. Advantages of Stratified Sampling

According to Frederick Stephen (1960), the advantages of stratified sampling are:

- The sample gets a greater control over the sample. In random sample, although every unit has an equal chance of being selected, sometimes important groups are left out by chance. Under stratified sampling, no significant group is left unrepresented.
- If proper stratification has been made a representative character can be achieved with fewer items. If a stratum is perfectly homogeneous selection of even a few items from it is enough.
- Replacement of case can be resorted too easily, if the original case is not accessible to study. If a person refuse to co-operate with the survey, he may be replaced by another man from the same stratum. Stephen rightly point out—"By providing that fixed proportion of the same shall come from each geographic area or income class, stratification automatically brings about the replacement of persons lost to the sample by persons of the same stratum thus partly correcting the bias that would result if there were no replacement of losses".
- By stratification, the sample can be so selected that most of the units are geographically localized. In a purely random sample, there is not such control and the cases actually selected may be very widely dispersed. Concentration of units saves time and cost of surveys.

4. Disadvantages of Stratified Sampling

- Bias may be caused in the sample through improper stratification. If the strata are overlapping, unsuitable or the problem under study are disproportionate the selection of the sample may not be representative.
- A sample in order to be representative must be proportionate. Proportion is attained in random sampling automatically. In stratified sampling, a deliberate attempt has to be made in this respect.

Attainment of proportionate is very difficult through deliberate means specially when the size of different strata is extremely unequal.

- Disproportionate stratification requires weighting which again introduces selective factor in the sample. An undue weighting makes the sample unrepresentative.
- Difficulty may be experienced in a stratum. If the strata is not very clear-cut it may be difficult to decide in which stratum any particular unit is to be placed. Proportional stratified sample method is used stratification being region—Revenue Division and Mandal. Kurnool district has 3 Revenue Divisions (Kurnool, Nandyala and Adoni) and 54 mandals. From each Revenue Division, two mandals are selected. From each mandal 15-25 centres are selected. A total of 400 drop-out learners were selected from 100 literacy centres spread across Kurnool, Nandyala and Adoni Divisions of Kurnool District at the rate of 4 drop-outs from each centre. The drop-outs were selected using random sampling technique for the present study.

Table 3.3: Sample Frame (Universe)

Sl. No.	*Name of the Revenue Division*	*No. of Mandals*	*Total No. of TLC centres*	*Total No. of Dropouts*	
				Before completion of 6 months and not completing Primer-I	*After completion of 6 months*
1	2	3	4	5	6
I.	**Kurnool**				
1.		C. Bengal	1068	3536	2378
2.		Gudur	934	3093	2065
3.		Kurnool	1654	5475	3749
4.		Nandikotkur	891	2950	1964
5.		Pagidyala	857	2837	1884
6.		Kothapalle	687	2277	1488
7.		Atmakur	750	2483	1633

(Table Contd...)

1	*2*	*3*	*4*	*5*	*6*
8.		Srisailam	809	2679	1772
9.		Velgodu	1039	3439	2308
10.		Pamulapadu	1000	3310	2219
11.		Japadu Bungalow	830	2747	1821
12.		Midthur	962	3184	2130
13.		Orvakal	1176	3895	2632
14.		Kallur	1216	4026	2722
15.		Kodumur	1486	4919	3056
16.		Krishnagiri	883	2922	1944
17.		Veldurthi	1320	4370	2967
18.		Bethamcherla	815	2699	1786
19.		Peapalle	1635	5414	3715
20.		Dhone	1240	4104	2779
II.	**Nandyala**				
1.		Panyam	979	3243	2171
2.		Gadivemula	927	3071	9249
3.		Bandi Atmakur	1031	3412	2291
4.		Nandyal	1301	4307	2923
5.		Mahanandi	782	2590	1710
6.		Sirvel	1264	4185	2837
7.		Rudravaram	1040	3444	2311
8.		Allagadda	1647	5453	3732
9.		Chagalamarri	1039	3442	2309
10.		Uyyalawada	673	2230	1455
11.		Dornipadu	600	1988	1284
12.		Gospadu	888	2942	1958
13.		Koilkuntla	985	3261	2183
14.		Banaganapalle	1417	4691	3194
15.		Sanjamala	862	2853	1895
16.		Kolimigundla	1062	3515	2362
17.		Owk	1109	3672	2475
III.	**Adoni**				
1.		Kowthalam	1494	4947	3375
2.		Kosigi	1244	4117	2789
3.		Mantralayam	1080	3576	2406

(Table Contd...)

1	2	3	4	5	6
III.	Adoni				
4.		Nandavaram	1124	3722	2509
5.		Gonegandla	1374	4549	3094
6.		Yemmiganur	1374	4550	3093
7.		Pedda Kadalur	983	3256	2180
8.		Adoni	1129	3737	2520
9.		Holagunda	972	3217	2154
10.		Alur	1187	3930	2656
11.		Apsari	1251	4142	2807
12.		Devanakonda	1295	4289	2910
13.		Tuggali	1214	3218	2720
14.		Pattikonda	1309	4333	2941
15.		Maddikera (East)	850	2813	1867
16.		Chippagiri	774	2564	1690
17.		Halaharvi	868	2875	1090

Table 3.4: Size of the Sample

Sl. No.	Name of selected Mandal	Revenue division	Total No. of centres	Total No. of Drop-outs (A) Before completion of 6 months	(A) After completion of 6 months	No. of centres selected	No. of sample selected
1.	Peapalle	Kurnool	1635	5414	3715	25	100
2.	Kodumur		1486	4919	3056	15	60
1.	Dornipadu	Nandyal	600	1988	1284	15	60
2.	Nandyal		1301	4307	2923	15	60
1.	Chippagiri	Adoni	774	2564	1690	15	60
2.	Gonegandla		1374	4549	3094	15	60

Profile of the Sample

The profile of 400 drop-outs divided according to the variables—Sex, Education, Marital Status, Age, Caste, Occupation, Income, Attendance in centres is given below:

List showing the details of items rejected is given below:

1. Lack of weightage to the certificates issued by Zilla Aksharasyata Samithi (ZAS) at the time of jobs (INS).

2. Lack of respect at the village (INS).
3. Lack of attractive charts, pamphlets and books useful in daily life (PER).
4. Lack of adoption of certain measures of compulsion for learners to participate in TLC centres (PER)
5. Lack of providing identity cards, prizes, certificates, fair price shops to learners (PER).
6. Absence of demand for frequent/long outstation stay (FAM).
7. Late supply of learning materials (PRO).
8. Lack of quality in learning materials like pencils, erasers (PRO).
9. Lack of support from village leaders (COM).
10. Lack of knowledge among leaders about the TLC programme (COM).
11. Lack of awareness among learners that education facilitates in reducing the economic disparities in the society (SOC).
12. Lack of vocational training in the centres (ECO).
13. Lack of equality in the society (SOC).
14. Accompanying family members in the centres (PSY).
15. Lack of feeling in learning alphabets (PSY).
16. Girls does not require education (PSY).

INS	:	Instructor related Problems	*COM*	:	Community related Problems
PER	:	Personal Problems	*SOC*	:	Social Problems
FAM	:	Familial Problems	*ECO*	:	Economic Problems
PRO	:	Programme related Problems	*PSY*	:	Psychological Problems

It is observed that the number of items/problems in 8 problem areas is not equal and the number varies from 3 to 21. The inclusion of items in each area depends upon:

1. Problems identified in previous research studies;
2. Opinion of panel consisting 15 experts;
3. Item analysis (statistical treatment) of the items; and
4. Relative weightage of each problem area. These considerations forced the researcher to choose unequal number of items in different problem areas.

Profile of the Sample

The profile of 400 drop-outs, divided according to the variables Sex, Education, Marital Status, Age, Caste, Occupation, Income, Attendance in centres is given below:

Sl. No.	*Variable*	*Sample*	*Total*
1	2	3	4
1.	**Sex**		
	Male	228	
			400
	Female	172	
2.	**Education**		
	Previous Schooling	229	
			400
	No Schooling	171	
3.	**Marital Status**		
	Married	238	
			400
	Un-married	162	
4.	**Age**		
	20 years and below	134	
	21-35 years	191	400
	36 years and above	075	
5.	**Caste**		
	SC/ST	169	
	BC	117	400
	OC	114	

(Contd...)

1	2	3	4
6.	**Occupation**		
	Agriculture	181	
	Labour	135	400
	Others	084	
7.	**Income**		
	Rs. 20,000 and below	188	
	Rs. 21-30 thousands	146	400
	Rs. 31 thousands and above	066	
8.	**Attendance**		
	1-2 months	185	
	2-4 months	127	400
	4-6 months	088	

The drop-outs covered in the study include different categories of drop-outs classified on the basis of variables namely, Sex, Education, Marital Status, Age, Occupation, Income and Attendance in centres. Though, Total Literacy Campaign was confined to 15-35 years age group, learners above the age of 35 years expressed their willingness to join the centres and they were also enrolled to avoid displeasure from them. Along with others, some of them dropped out from them. Along with others, some of them dropped out from the centres later on. Therefore, drop-outs belonging to 36 years and above age group were also covered in the study since they were there in the campaign.

Method of Administering the Rating Scale and Scoring

With the permission of the nodal officers at the mandal level, researcher approached the centre organiser to identify the dropouts of the centre. With his/her help, the drop-outs were contacted at the time convenient to them. The Rating Scale containing 80 problems usually faced by drop-outs was read to them. If they were the problems for them to drop-out from the centres, they were requested to indicate the difficulty of each problem by choosing one of the three alternatives given below and they were assigned the marks shown against them.

Alternative	*Numerical Value Assigned*
Not at all	1
To some extent	2
Much	3

The alternatives given by the drop-outs were noted by the researcher. It took nearly one hour for collecting data from each drop-out.

The information regarding the learners enrolled and drop-outs was collected from Deputy Director, Adult Education of Kurnool district.

The following variables of the dropouts were covered in the study

Sl. No.	*Variable*	*Sample*	*Total*
1	2	3	4
1.	**Sex**		
	Male		
	Female		
2.	**Education**		
	Previous Schooling		
	No Schooling		
3.	**Marital Status**		
	Married		
	Un-married		
4.	**Age**		
	20 years and below		
	21-35 years		
	36 years and above		
5.	**Caste**		
	SC/ST		
	BC		
	OC		
6.	**Occupation**		
	Agriculture		
	Labour		
	Others		

(Contd...)

1	2	3	4
7.	**Income**		
	Rs. 20,000 and below		
	Rs. 21-30 thousands		
	Rs. 31 thousands and above		
8.	**Attendance**		
	1-2 months		
	2-4 months		
	4-6 months		

An attempt is made to study the problems of the drop-outs classified under the said variables (Sex, Education, Marital Status, Age, Occupation, Income and Attendance in centres) and also the differential effect of each problem and of area-wise problems on the drop-outs belonging to the said variables.

It is expected that the Sex, Education, Marital Status, Age, Caste, Occupation, Income and Attendance in the centres of the drop-outs would lead to differences in the problems faced by them and also have differential effect of each problem/area-wise problems on the Sex, Education, Marital Status, Age, Caste, Occupation, Income and Attendance in the centres of the drop-outs.

STATISTICAL TECHNIQUES USED IN THE STUDY

Drop-out Rate

Drop-out Rate was calculated by taking into account the number of adult learners, enrolled in the centre and the number who left the centres without completing even Primer-I and before 6 months from the date of starting the centres.

$$\text{Drop-out Rate} = \frac{\text{No. of Learners left the centre}}{\text{No. of Adults enrolled in the centres}} \times 100$$

Difficulty or Effect of Problems

The study, the difficulty or effect of each problem of drop-outs, the average difficulty of each problem was found out, by calculating the mean.

Preparation of Rank Order List

After calculating the mean difficulty of each problem, the problems are arranged in rank order, starting from maximum difficulty to minimum difficulty, and thus rank order list was prepared. This list helps to know whether the difficulty or effect of each problems is same or not and also the relative difficulty.

Interpretation of Difficulty Level or Effect of each Problem

The difficulty levels of problems can be interpreted by using one of the following methods, basing on the average difficulty of each problem.

1. The number of problems for which difficulty values are found is 80. When the problems are arranged from minimum to maximum difficulty level we may interpret as follows:

   First 27 problems (1-27) – Less Significant

   Next 27 problems (28-54) – Significant

   Last 26 problems (55-80) – Very Significant

2. The rating of difficulty of each problem varies from 1 to 3. Basing on the average difficulty of each problem, the difficulty of each problem can be interpreted as "not at all, to some extent, much" if the average difficulty level is "1, 2, 3" respectively. But, the "average difficulty" values may not be exactly 1, 2, 3 and interpretation may be difficult.

3. On the basis of the rank order list, first 27 per cent of the problems can be considered "less significant" next 27 per cent of the problems can be considered "significant" and the last 26 per cent of the problems can be considered "very significant", when the problems are arranged from minimum to maximum difficulty level.

4. From the scores of "average difficulty" of each problem for any sample, the mean and S.D. of the scores can be calculated. From this, cut off points on the basis of Mean $\pm \sigma$ can be calculated. Taking into account, the values of Mean $\pm \sigma$, difficulty level of the problems can be interpreted.

5. The values of ratings vary from 1 to 3. The range of 2 can be divided into three intervals of 0.66 each and it may be interpreted as follows:

Value	*Interpretation*
The average value ranging from 1.00 to 1.66	Less Significant
The average value ranging from 1.66 to 2.32.	Significant
The average value ranging from 2.32 to 3.00	Very Significant

6. In the present study, besides, total sample, drop-outs are divided into 21 groups on the basis of variables like Sex, Education, Marital Status, Age, Caste, Occupation, Annual Income and Attendance in the centres. The minimum and maximum difficulty value/effect of the items in each group for 21 groups, beside total sample were noted. Then the lowest of the minimum and the highest of the maximum value were identified. The highest value was 2.43 and the lowest was 1.53. The range between highest and lowest was 0.90. This range was divided into 3 intervals of 0.30 each and 3 categories were made and interpreted as shown below:

Item Value	*Interpretation*
1.53-1.83 (1.53 + 0.30)	Less Significant
1.84-2.13 (1.83 + 0.30)	Significant
2.14-2.43 (2.13 + 0.30)	Very Significant

In any group, the item will never be above 2.43 and never be below 1.53. The item values of each group were arranged from maximum to minimum. The items were classified as very significant, significant and less significant according to the criterion set above.

For the present study, the method 6 was followed. It takes into account the exact limits of range difficulty of items experienced by the group and the uniform criterion was followed in classifying the items as very significant, significant and less significant problems.

Differential Effects of Problems or Areas of Problems on the Sex, Education, Marital Status, Age, Caste, Occupation, Income and Attendance of the Drop-outs

The differential effects of different problems and problem areas namely economic, social, psychological, familial, instructor related, community-related, personal, programme related problems of the drop-out on their sex, education, marital status, age, caste, occupation, income and attendance was found out by finding mean and S.D. of the groups. The 't' test was used for checking the significant differences between means of the two groups.

Analysis of variance was employed when groups to be compared are more than two. When 'F' test was significant indicating the difference among the groups, the exact group was further analysed by calculating 't' test. For analyzing data computer facility is used.

The sample covered in the study is 400 drop-outs. The groups compared vary from 2-3 and the degrees of freedom (df) will be 398 or 397. For testing whether 'F' or 't' is significant. df is taken as 400 and the tables 'D' and 'E' found in Garrett, H.E. (1981) and used. The 'F' value should be 6.70 and above to be significant at 01 level and 3.86 and above but below 6.70 to be significant at 0.05 level. The 't' value has to be 2.59 and above to be significant at 0.01 level and 1.97 and above but below 2.59 to be significant at 0.05 level.

Summary of the Chapter

In order to identify the problems of drop-outs rating scale techniques was used. Rating scale helps to measure to the extent of difficulty of each problem. A 3-point rating scale was specifically developed for the purpose of the study and the instruments covered different problems like economic, social, psychological, familial, instructor related, community related, personal and programme related. A pilot study was conducted in Nandyal Revenue Division to improve the efficiency of the instruments. Reliability and validity were also established. A sample of 400 drop-outs were selected in Kurnool district by using stratified random sampling techniques. The sample was drawn from 100 Total Literacy Campaign Centres. Various statistical techniques like 't' test analyse of variance were employed to analyse the data.

Sum-up

The chapter described the problems to be tackled objectives and hypothesis of the study, operational definitions of the terms used in the study, limitations of the study, selection and description of the study, research instrument, selection and size of the sample methods adopted for data collection, statistical techniques applied, etc.

The next chapter provides the details relating to the enrolment of adult learners, extent of problems of drop-outs.

Education plays a vital role in the life of an individual. Similarly adult education is an important input for social economic development of the society. Recognising the need for adult education, individual and institutional efforts were made since a long time towards the eradication of illiteracy. Efforts for the eradication of illiteracy were made during pre-British period, British period and post-independence period. Similarly, attempts were also put in the state of Andhra Pradesh in general and Kurnool district in particular. Recent Government have accorded much importance for the promotion of adult education. A number of illiterates were enrolled in adult education centres to impart functional literacy but there is much gap between enrolment and achievement. The present study is an attempt to probe the several reasons as to why the enlisting could not produce the coveted achievement.

The literature on drop-outs of adult education and total literacy campaign was reviewed to get a better inside into the problems of drop-outs. The studies reviewed were categorized into different sections viz., personal problems, psychological problems, environmental problems relating to physical facilities and learning environment, programme related problems, instructor related problems are but few reasons among several dropping out from total literacy campaign centres. The studies conducted by different workers, institutions across India and overseas were reviewed. The studies revealed that some attempts have been made to examine the factors associated with drop-outs of adult education centres. These centres were designed on the basis of centre based approach, the current programme of total literacy was based on campaign approach i.e., volunteer based approach. No depth studies were conducted on the drop-outs of total literacy campaign.

This chapter covers the problems for research study, operational definitions of certain terms are described. The Objectives and Hypotheses of the study were presented. The research study was undertaken with the major objectives of examining learners enrolment and achievement. Problems of dropouts, differential effects of each problem relative effects of the problem area and dropouts and to suggest remedial measures for solving the problem of drop-outs. In total, there were six (6) main objectives and 13 hypotheses of the study. The need for the study and the limitations were also summarised.

4

Problems of the Drop-outs

The participants of the Total Literacy Campaigns are enrolled with a motive of learning literacy coupled with life skills, however all could not survive the entire duration of the campaign but due to various interventions they were forced to discontinue and become drop-outs of the campaign. The extent of dropouts are found to be alarming and the campaign could not able to attain its objectives. The knowledge of the problems of the adults who have dropped out of the campaign will be useful for the administrators and programme planners to equip the functionaries with the skills required by the field functionaries to prevent such drop-outs. Keeping in view of the above, an attempt was made in the following pages to present the enrolment and drop-out rate in the Total Literacy Campaign of Kurnool district. For the problems of the drop-outs area-wise, intensity-wise and character-wise of the drop-outs.

PART-I

Enrolment and Drop-out Rate

The TLC of Kurnool district covered the illiterates in the age group of 15-35 years. The number of illiterates enrolled into the centres, drop-outs who left the centres without completing even Primer-I and before 6 months are given:

No. of illiterates identified	:	5,88,752
No. of illiterates enrolled in the centres	:	6,84,027
Adults who drop-out without completing even Primer-I or before 6 months after starting the centre	:	1,93,292

Drop-out Rate

The drop-out rate was calculated on the basis of the formula presented in Chapter-3.

$$\text{Drop-out Rate} = \frac{\text{No. of Learners left the centre}}{\text{No. of Adults enrolled in the centres}} \times 100$$

$$= \frac{1{,}93{,}292}{5{,}84{,}027} \times 100 = 33.1$$

The drop-out rate is 33.1. The hypothesis that the drop-out rate in TLC of Kurnool district is higher than 50 is not supported.

PART-II

Problems of Dropouts

The problems of total drop-outs and problems of 21 groups of drop-outs divided on the basis of Sex (1) Males, (2) Females; Education (3) Previous Schooling, (4) No Schooling, Merital Status, (5) Married, (6) Unmarried, Age, (7) 20 years and below, (8) 21-31 years, (9) 36 years and above caste, (10) SC/ST, (11) BC, (12) Other Caste, Occupation, (13) Agriculture, (14) Labour, (15) Others, Annual Income, (16) Rs. 20,000 and below (17) Rs. 21-30,000, (18) Rs. 31,000 and above, (19) Attendance 1-2 months, (20) 2-4 months, (21) 4-6 months are presented and discussed in the succeeding pages.

The effect or the difficulty level of the problems felt by different groups of drop-outs (mean difficulty) is found out and the problems are classified as very significant, significant and less significant problems on the basis of difficulty level of the problems.

Problems of Total Drop-outs

The problems of dropouts are arranged in rank order of difficulty i.e., from maximum average difficulty to minimum average difficulty of each problem and rank order list is prepared. The list of rank order for 80 problems of total drop-out has been detailed in the Tables 5.03, 5.04 and 5.05. The data revealed that (1) out of 80 problems, the difficulty levels of 17 problems appear to be different from each other. (2) With regard to their remaining 63 problems, they fall under 20 groups of problems which have same difficulty levels, so far as the group is concerned, but each group differs from the other.

Problems with different difficulty levels

The 17 problems with different difficulty levels are shown in following Table 4.01.

Table 4.1: Showing the problems with differential difficulty levels

Sl. No.	*Problem Area and S.No. in Rank Order List*	*Problems*	*Mean Difficulty*
1.	PSY 1	Easily getting tired	2.36
2.	INS 2	The instructor lacks good voice and fluency	2.29
3.	PRO 3	The centre is at a distance	2.26
4.	ECO 7	There are no specific working hours in different professions	2.23
5.	COM 13	I am not permitted to go with my friends	2.20
6.	PRO 20	Minimum amenities are not found at the centre (Air/Ventilation)	2.15
7.	PER 21	The instructor is male	2.14
8.	SOC 30	Personal position is at stake in the society	2.11
9.	PRO 35	The centre is started at inconvenient place/environment with sounds and smell	2.07
10.	PER 58	The other learners also are average in learning	1.99
11.	COM 66	The time of the programme is short	1.94
12.	PSY 71	Feeling that education is only for wealthy people	1.90
13.	FAM 72	Looking after the children	1.88
14.	SOC 75	The instructor utilises the learners for his personal work	1.84
15.	PER 78	Getting newly married	1.77
16.	SOC 79	There are some fights in the village	1.70
17.	ECO 80	Owners and landlords do not permit	1.69

ECO: Economic Problems area
SOC: Social Problems area
PSY: Psychological Problems area
FAM: Familial Problems area
COM: Community Related Problems area
PER: Personal Problems area
PRO: Programme Related Problems
INS: Instructor Related Problems area

The groups of problems which have same difficulty levels

Table 4.2: The 20 groups of problems which have same difficulty levels

Group	*Problem Area and S. No. in Rank Order List*	*Problems*	*Mean Difficulty*
1	2	3	*4*
I.	PSY 4	The learner is not able to answer to the instructor	2.25
	FAM 5	There is none else at home	2.25
	INS 6	The books are difficult to learn	2.25
II.	PSY 8	Unwilling to get educated	2.21
	PSY 9	Feeling that the age to study has passed	2.21
	PSY 10	Feeling that others would mock	2.21
	FAM 11	Other family members refuse permission to attend during nights	2.21
	INS 12	The instructor fails to enthuse the learner to participate	2.21
III.	PSY 14	Feeling that studying at the centre is a waste	2.16
	INS 15	Instruction is limited only to literacy	2.16
	INS 16	The instructor does not personally reveal and development	2.16
	INS 17	Teaching aids are not available at the right time	2.16
	COM 18	Friends do not go to the centre	2.16
	COM 19	The time of the centre is inconvenient	2.16
IV	FAM 22	Unable to go to the centre because of heavy work	2.13
	INS 23	The lessons are not according to the requirements and tastes	2.13
	PER 24	Due to ill-health	2.13
	PER 25	Lack of knowledge about this programme	2.13
V	SOC 26	The instructor does not belong to his caste	2.12
	SCO 27	Attending functions and going to movies	2.12
	FAM 28	The time of the centre is the supper time	2.12
	PER 29	The other learners are mocking because of backwardness in learning	2.12

(Table Contd...)

1	2	3	4
VI	PSY 31	The fellow learners do not listen to the thoughts and ideas	2.12
	PER 32	The relevant lessons are not taught at the centre	2.10
VII	COM 33	There is no encouragement from the village elders	2.10
	COM 34	The centre is co-educated	2.08
VIII	PSY 36	There is no understanding between the learner and the instructor	2.08
	COM 37	No one else visits the centre except the instructor	2.06
	PER 38	Getting the marriage age	2.06
IX	PSY 39	Feeling shy to go to centre	2.06
	INS 40	The instructor does not treat all the learners equally	2.05
	INS 41	The instruction is not relevant to the learners.	2.05
	INS 42	The instructor uses difficult languages, pictures and symbols	2.05
	COM 43	Good friends are not available at the centre	2.05
X	ECO 44	Busy with farm work	2.05
	INS 45	Providing too much information within a short time	2.04
	PER 46	Becoming a slave to bad habits	2.04
XI	ECO 47	There is no immediate use by getting educated	2.03
	SOC 48	The instructor and the learner are not friends	2.03
	PSY 49	Feeling why one should get educated when the age is so much	2.03
	PSY 50	Feeling shy during conversation with others	2.03
XII	INS 51	The instructor is negligent	2.01
	INS 52	The absence of audio-visual aids useful for instruction	2.01
	INS 53	Related primary teaching books are not in order	2.01
	PER 54	The other learners are much older	2.01

(Table Contd...)

1	2	3	4
XIII	ECO 55	No immediate financial benefit by education	2.00
	PSY 56	Learners calling by nicknames	2.00
	INS 57	The instructional methods specified by the government are not liked	2.00
XIV	PSY 59	Feeling that learning at home instead of at the centre is better	1.98
	INS 60	The instructor is unable to explain clearly	1.98
	SOC 61	The instructor does not belong to his place	1.96
XV	INS 62	The instructor is not well-versed with his learning	1.96
	SOC 63	Some learners have enmity in the centre	1.95
XVI	SOC 64	Many of the learners belong to upper caste	1.95
	INS 65	The instructor does not accept criticism with open heart	1.95
	INS 67	The instructor is not punctual to the centre	1.91
XVII	INS 68	There is no teaching experience to the instructor	1.92
	ECO 69	My family economically backward	1.91
XVIII	FAM 70	Other family members do not co-operate in matters of education	1.91
	SOC 73	There are some learners with bad behaviour in the centre	1.85
XIX	INS 74	The centre is not well maintained	1.85
	PER 76	Quarrelling with other learners	1.79
XX	PER 77	Getting discouraged after working hard to get educated and feeling that this attempt is useless	1.79

ECO: Economic Problems area
SOC: Social Problems area
PSY: Psychological Problems area
FAM: Familial Problems area
COM: Community related Problems area
PER: Personal Problems area
INS: Instructor related Problems area

Very Significant, Significant and Less Significant Problem

As explained in Chapter 3 (under point 3.05.4) the problems are divided into three categories—very significant, significant and less significant on the basis of difficulty levels of the problems.

The problems with difficulty level from 1.53 to 1.83, 1.84 to 2.13 and from 2.14 to 2.43 were classified as less significant, significant and very significant problems respectively. The problems are presented in Tables 4.03, 4.04 and 4.05 respectively.

Table 4.3: Showing Very Significant Problems

S.No. in the Rank Order List	*Problem Area and S.No. in Rating Scale*	*Problem*	*Mean Difficulty*
1	*2*	*3*	*4*
1.	PSY 23	Easily getting tired	2.36
2.	INS 46	The instructor lacks good voice and fluency	2.29
3.	PRO 80	The centre is at a distance	2.26
4.	PSY 18	The learner is not able to answer to the instructor	2.25
5.	FAM 35	There are none else at home	2.25
6.	INS 56	The books are difficult to learn	2.25
7.	ECO 6	There are no specific working hours in different professions	2.23
8.	PSY 19	Unwilling to get educated	2.21
9.	PSY 20	Feeling that the age to study has passed	2.21
10.	PSY 22	Feeling that others would mock	2.21
11.	FAM 31	Other family members refuse permission to attend during nights	2.21
12.	INS 47	The instructor fails to enthuse the learner to participate	2.21
13.	COM 60	I am not permitted to go with my friends	2.20
14.	PSY 29	Feeling that studying at the centre is waste	2.16
15.	INS 48	Instruction is limited only to literacy	2.16
16.	INS 50	The instructor does not reveal in learner's progress	2.16
17.	INS 52	Teaching aids are not available at the right time	2.16

(Table Contd...)

1	2	3	4
18.	COM 59	Friends do not go to the centre	2.16
19.	COM 62	The time of the centre is inconvenient	2.16
20.	PRO 78	Minimum amenities are not found at the centre (air/ventilation)	2.15
21.	PER 75	The instructor is male	2.14

ECO: Economic Problems area
COM: Community related Problems area
PSY: Psychological Problems area
FAM: Familial Problems Area
INS: Instructor related Problems area
PER: Personal Problems area
PRO: Programme related Problems area

Table 4.4: Showing Significant Problems

S. No. in the Rank Order List	*Problem Area and S. No. in Rating Scale*	*Problem*	*Mean Difficulty*
1	2	3	4
22.	FAM 36	Unable to go to the centre because of heavy work	2.13
23.	INS 55	The lessons are not according to the requirements and tastes	2.13
24.	PER 68	Due to ill-health	2.13
25.	PER 76	Lack of knowledge about this programme	2.13
26.	SOC 8	The instructor does not belong to this caste	2.12
27.	SOC 16	Attending functions and going to movies	2.12
28.	FAM 34	The time of the centre is supper time	2.12
29.	PER 72	The other learners are mocking because of backwardness in learning	2.12
30.	SOC 10	Personal position is at stake in the society	2.11
31.	PSY 28	The fellow learners do not listen to the thoughts and ideas	2.10
32.	PER 77	The relevant lessons are not taught at the centre	2.10
33.	COM 58	There is no encouragement from the village elders	2.08

(Table Contd...)

1	2	3	4
34.	COM 63	The centre is co-educated	2.08
35.	PRO 79	The centre is started at inconvenient place/environment with sounds and bad smell	2.07
36.	PSY 17	There is no understanding between the learner and the instructor	2.06
37.	COM 64	No one else visits the centre except the instructor	2.06
38.	PER 70	Getting the marriage age	2.06
39.	PSY 21	Feeling shy to go to the centre	2.05
40.	INS 42	The instructor does not treat all the learners equally	2.05
41.	INS 45	The instruction is not relevant to the learners	2.05
42.	INS 51	The instructor uses difficult language, pictures and symbols	2.05
43.	COM 61	Good friends are not available at the centre	2.05
44.	ECO 2	Busy with farm work	2.04
45.	INS 49	Providing too much information within a short time	2.04
46.	PER 66	Becoming a slave to bad habits	2.04
47.	ECO 4	There is no immediate use by getting educated	2.03
48.	SOC 12	The instructor and the learners are not friends	2.03
49.	PSY 24	Feeling why one should get educated when the age is so much	2.03
50.	PSY 26	Feeling shy during conversation with others	2.03
51.	INS 43	The instructor is negligent	2.01
52.	INS 53	The absence of audio-visual aids useful for instruction	2.01
53.	INS 54	Related primary teaching books are not in order	2.01
54.	PER 71	The other learners are much older	2.01
55.	ECO 1	No immediate financial benefit by education	2.00

(Table Contd...)

1	2	3	4
56.	PSY 27	Learners calling by nicknames	2.00
57.	INS 57	The instructional methods specified by the government are not liked	2.00
58.	PER 74	The other learners also are average in learning	1.99
59.	PSY 30	Feeling that learning at home instead of at the centre is better	1.98
60.	INS 41	The instructor is unable to explain clearly	1.98
61.	SOC 7	The instructor does not belong to his place	1.96
62.	INS 39	The instructor is not well-versed with his teaching	1.96
63.	SOC 11	Some learners have enmity in the centre	1.95
64.	SOC 14	Many of the learners belong to the upper caste	1.95
65.	INS 44	The instructor does not accept criticism with open heart	1.95
66.	COM 65	The time of the programme is short	1.94
67.	INS 38	The instructor is not punctual to the centre	1.92
68.	INS 40	There is no teaching experience to the instructor	1.92
69.	ECO 5	My family economically backward	1.91
70.	FAM 33	Other family members do not co-operate in matters of education	1.91
71.	PER 25	Feeling that education is only for wealthy people	1.90
72.	FAM 32	Looking after the children	1.88
73.	SOC 15	There are some learners with bad behaviour in the centre	1.85
74.	INS 37	The centre is not well maintained	1.85
75.	SOC 9	The instructor utilise the learners for his personal work	1.84

FAM: Familial Problems Area
INS: Instructor related Problems area
PER: Personal Problems area
SOC: Social Problems
PSY: Psychological Problems area
COM: Community related Problems area
ECO: Economic Problems area
PRO: Programme related Problems area

Table 4.5: Showing Less Significant Problem

S. No. in the Rank Order List	*Problem Area and S. No. in Rating Scale*	*Problem*	*Mean Difficulty*
76.	PER 69	Quarrelling with other learners	1.79
77.	PER 73	Getting discouraged after working hard to get educated and feeling that this attempt is useless	1.79
78.	PER 67	Getting newly married	1.77
79.	SOC 13	There are some fights in the village	1.70
80.	ECO 3	Owners and landlords do not permit	1.69

PER: Personal Problems area *SOC:* Social Problems

ECO: Economic Problems area

Very Significant, Significant and Less Significant Problems in each Problem Area

The difficulty levels of problems in each problem area i.e., economic problems, social problems, psychological problems, familial problems, instructor related problems, community related problems, personal problems and programme related problems are presented. Following the previous criteria, the problems in each area are presented under three categories namely very significant, significant and less significant problems.

I. Economic Problems

The very significant, significant and less significant problems in 'Economic problems area' are presented in the Table 4.06.

Table 4.6: Showing the Very Significant, Significant and Less Significant Problems in the area of 'Economic Problems'

S. No.	*S. No. in the Rating Scale*	*Economic problems*	*Mean Difficulty*
1	2	3	4
		Very Significant	
1.	ECO 6	There are no specific working hours in different professions	2.23

(Table Contd...)

1	2	3	4
		Significant	
2.	ECO 2	Busy with farm work	2.04
3.	ECO 4	There is no immediate use by getting educated	2.03
4.	ECO 1	No immediate financial benefits by education	2.00
5.	ECO 5	My family economically backward	1.91
		Less Significant	
6.	ECO 3	Owners and landlords do not permit	1.69

ECO: Economic Problems Area.

II. Social Problems

The very significant, significant and less significant problems in 'social problems area' are presented in the Table 4.07.

Table 4.7: Showing the Very Significant, Significant and Less Significant Problems in the area of 'Social Problems'

S. No.	*S. No. in the Rating Scale*	*Social problems*	*Mean Difficulty*
		Significant	
7.	SOC 8	The instructor does not belong to his caste	2.12
8.	SOC 16	Attending functions and going to movies	2.12
9.	SOC 10	Personal position is at stake in the society	2.11
10.	SOC 12	The instructor and the learners are not friends	2.03
11.	SOC 7	The instructor does not belong to his place	1.96
12.	SOC 11	Some co-learners have enmity in the centre	1.95
13.	SOC 14	Many of the learners belong to the upper caste	1.95
14.	SOC 15	There are some learners with bad behaviour in the centre	1.85
15.	SOC 9	The instructor utilises the learners for his personal work	1.84
		Less Significant	
16.	SOC 16	There are some fights in the village	1.70

SOC: Social Problems Area

There are '*no very significant problems*' in this problem area.

III. Psychological Problems

The very significant, significant and less significant problems in 'psychological problems area' are presented in the Table 4.08.

Table 4.8: Showing the Very Significant, Significant and Less Significant Problems in the area of 'Psychological Problems'

S. No.	*S. No. in the Rating Scale*	*Psychological Problems*	*Mean Difficulty*
		Very Significant	
17.	PSY 23	Easily getting tired	2.36
18.	PSY 18	The learner is not able to answer to the instructor	2.25
19.	PSY 19	Un-willing to get educated	2.21
20.	PSY 20	Feeling that the age to study has passed	2.21
21.	PSY 22	Feeling that other would mock	2.21
22.	PSY 29	Feeling that studying at the centre is a waste	2.16
		Significant	
23.	PSY 28	The fellow learners do not listen to the thoughts and ideas	2.10
24.	PSY 17	There is no understanding between the learner and the instructor	2.06
25.	PSY 21	Feeling shy to go the centre	2.05
26.	PSY 24	Feeling why one should get educated when the age is so much	2.03
27.	PSY 26	Feeling shy during conversation with others	2.03
28.	PSY 27	Learners calling by nicknames	2.00
29.	PSY 30	Feeling that learning at home instead of at the centre is better	1.98
30.	PSY 25	Feeling that education is only for wealthy people	1.90

PSY: Psychological Problems Area

There are *'no less significant problems'* in this area.

IV. Familial Problems

The very significant, significant and less significant problems in 'Familial problems area' are presented in the Table 4.09.

Table 4.9: Showing the Very Significant, Significant and Less Significant Problems in the area of 'Familial Problems'

S. No.	S. No. in the Rating Scale	Familial Problems	Mean Difficulty
		Very Significant	
31	FAM 35	There is none else at home	2.25
32	FAM 31	Other family members refuse permission to attend during nights	2.21
		Significant	
33	FAM 36	Unable to go to the centre because of heavy work	2.13
34	FAM 34	The time of the centre is the supper time	2.12
35	FAM 33	Other family members do not co-operate in matters of education	1.91
36	FAM 32	Looking after the children	1.88

FAM: Familial Problems Area

There are *'no less significant problems'* in this area.

V. Instructor related Problems

The very significant, significant and less significant problems in 'instructor related problems area' are presented in the Table 4.10.

Table 4.10: Showing the Very Significant, Significant and Less Significant Problems in the area of 'Instructor related Problems'

S. No.	S. No. in the Rating Scale	Instructor related Problems	Mean Difficulty
1	2	3	4
		Very Significant	
37.	INS 46	The instructor lacks good voice and fluency	2.29
38.	INS 56	The books are difficult to learn	2.25
39.	INS 47	The instructor fails to enthuse the learner to participate	2.21
40.	INS 48	Instructor is limited only to literacy	

(Table Contd...)

1	2	3	4
41.	INS 50	The instruction does not reveal learners progress	2.16
42.	INS 52	Teaching aids are not available at the right time	2.16
		Significant	
42.	INS 55	The lessons are not according to requirements and tastes	2.13
43.	INS 42	The instructor does not treat all the learners equally	2.05
44.	INS 45	The instruction is not relevant to the learners	2.05
45.	INS 51	The instructor uses difficult language, pictures and symbols	2.05
46.	INS 49	Providing too much information within a short time	2.04
47.	INS 43	The instructor is negligent	2.01
48.	INS 53	The absence of audio-visual aids useful for instruction	2.01
49.	INS 54	Related primary teaching books are not in order	2.01
50.	INS 57	The instructional methods specified by the Government are not liked	2.00
51.	INS 41	The instructor is unable to explain clearly	1.98
52.	INS 39	The instructor is not well-versed with his teaching	1.96
53.	INS 44	The instructor does not accept criticism with open heart	1.95
54.	INS 38	The instructor is not punctual to the centre	1.92
55.	INS 40	There is no teaching experience to the instructor	1.92
56.	INS 37	The centre is not well maintained	1.85

INS: Instructor Related Problems Area

There are *'no less significant problems'* in this area.

VI. Community related Problems

The very significant, significant and less significant problems in 'community related problems area' are presented in the Table 4.11.

Table 4.11: Showing the Very Significant, Significant and Less Significant Problems in the area of 'Community related Problems'

S. No.	*S. No. in the Rating Scale*	*Community related Problems*	*Mean Difficulty*
		Very Significant	
58.	COM 60	I am not permitted to go with my friends	2.20
59.	COM 59	Friends do not go to the centre	2.16
60.	COM 62	The time at the centre is inconvenient	2.16
		Significant	
61.	COM 58	There is no encouragement from the village elders	2.08
62.	COM 63	The centre is co-educated	2.08
63.	COM 64	No one else visits the centre except the instructor	2.06
64.	COM 61	Good friends are not available at the centre	2.0
65.	COM 65	The time of the programme is short	1.94

COM: Community related Problems Area

There are *'no less significant problems'* in this area.

VII. Personal Problems

The very significant, significant and less significant problems in 'personal problems area' are presented in the Table 4.12.

Table 4.12: Showing the Very Significant, Significant and Less Significant Problems in the area of 'Personal Problems'

S. No.	*S. No. in the Rating Scale*	*Personal Problems*	*Mean Difficulty*
1	2	3	4
		Very Significant	
66.	PER 75	The instructor is male	2.14
		Significant	
67.	PER 68	Due to ill-health	2.13
68.	PER 76	Lack of knowledge about this programme	2.13

(Table Contd...)

1	2	3	4
69.	PER 72	The other learners are mocking because of backwardness in learning	2.12
70.	PER 77	The relevant lessons are not taught at the centre	2.10
71.	PER 70	Getting the marriage age	2.06
72.	PER 66	Becoming a slave to bad habits	2.04
73.	PER 71	The other learners are much older	2.01
74.	PER 74	The other learners also are average in learning	1.99
		Less Significant	
75.	PER 69	Quarrelling with other learners	1.79
76.	PER 73	Getting discouraged after working hard to get educated and feeling that this attempt is useless	1.79
77.	PER 67	Getting newly married	1.77

PER: Personal Problems Area

VIII. Programme related Problems

The very significant, significant and less significant problems in 'Programme related problems area' are presented in Table 4.13.

Table 4.13: Showing the Very Significant, Significant and Less Significant Problems in the area of 'Programme related Problems'

S. No.	*S. No. in the Rating Scale*	*Programme related Problems*	*Mean Difficulty*
		Very Significant	
78.	PER 80	The centre is at a distance	2.26
89.	PER 78	Minimum amenities are not found at the centre (air/ventilation)	2.15
		Significant	
80.	PRO	The centre is started at inconvenient place/ environment with sounds and bad smell	2.07

PRO: Programme related Problems Area

There are *'no less significant'* problems in this area.

There are 21 very significant problems, (Rank order 1-21, Table No. 4.03), 54 significant problems (Rank order 22-75, Table No. 4.04) and 5 less significant problems (Rank order 76-80, Table No. 4.05).

The problems area-wise distribution of very significant, significant and less significant problems found in Tables 4.06 to 4.13 is summarised below:

Table 4.14: Distribution of Very Significant, Significant and Less Significant Problems area wise as indicated by Tables 4.06 to 4.13

Problem Area	*Very Significant Problems*	*Significant Problems*	*Less Significant Problems*	*Total*
Economic Problems (ECO)	1	4	1	6
Social Problems (SOC)	-	9	1	10
Psychological Problems (PSY)	6	8	-	14
Familial Problems (FAM)	2	4	-	6
Instructor related Problems (INS)	6	15	-	21
Community Related Problems (COM)	3	5	-	8
Personnel Problems (PER)	1	8	3	12
Programme Related Problems (PRO)	2	1	-	3
Total	**21**	**54**	**5**	**80**

Action has to be taken to solve all the problems of drop-outs. Instead of suggesting remedial measure to solve the problems for each group of drop-out separately, suggestions are made at the end, taking into account the very significant problems of all the groups together.

Problems of Male Drop-outs

The very significant, significant and less significant problems of male drop-outs are presented in the Table 4.15.

Table 4.15: Showing the Very Significant, Significant and Less Significant Problems in the Case of Male Drop-outs

Rank Order	*Mean Difficulty*	*Problem Area and Sl. No. in the Rating Scale*	*Problem*
1	2	3	4
1.	2.43	INS 47	The instructor fails to enthuse the learners to participate
2.	2.39	PSY 23	Easily getting tired
3.	2.37	INS 50	The instructor does not reveal in learner's progress
4.	2.30	INS 56	The books are difficult to learn
5.	2.29	FAM 35	There are none else at home
6.	2.28	PSY 19	Unwilling to get educated
7.	2.26	PSO 78	Minimum amenities are not found to the centre (air/ventilation)
8.	2.26	PER 68	Due to ill-health
9.	2.26	INS 52	Teaching aids are not available at the right time
10.	2.25	PSY 18	The learners is not able to answer to the instructor
11.	2.25	SOC 10	Personal position is at stake in the society
12.	2.24	PRO 79	The centre is started at inconvenient place/having much sounds and bad smell
13.	2.24	PSY 22	Feeling that others would mock
14.	2.23	INS 46	The instructor lacks good voice and fluency
15.	2.20	PER 74	The other learners also are average in learning
16.	2.20	SOC 8	The instructor does not belong to my caste
17.	2.19	ECO 6	There are no specific working hours in different professions
18.	2.18	PER 72	The other learners are mocking because of my backwardness in learning
19.	2.18	INS 49	Providing too much information within a short time

(Table Contd...)

1	2	3	4
20.	2.18	INS 48	Instruction is limited only to literacy
21.	2.18	PSY 20	Feeling that the age to study has passed
22.	2.18	SOC 16	Attending functions and going to movies
23.	2.17	PER 77	The relevant lessons are not taught at the centre
24.	2.17	PSY 28	The fellow learners do not listen to the thoughts and ideas
25.	2.16	PER 76	Lack of knowledge about this programme
26.	2.16	COM 49	Providing too much information within a short time
27.	2.16	INS 54	Primer and follow-up books are not in order
28.	2.14	COM 60	I am not permitted to go with my friends
			Significant
29.	2.13	INS 55	There is no encouragement from the village elders
30.	2.11	INS 42	The instructor does not treat all the learners equally
31.	2.11	INS 41	The instructor is unable to explain clearly
32.	2.11	PSY 29	Feeling that studying at the centre is a waste
33.	2.11	PSY 17	There is no understanding between the learner and the instructor
34.	2.11	ECO 2	Busy with farm work
35.	2.10	PER 75	The instructor is male
36.	2.10	PER 70	Getting the marriage age
37.	2.10	FAM 31	Other family members refuse permission to attend during nights
38.	2.09	INS 44	The instructor does not accept criticism with open heart
39.	2.08	SOC 11	Some co-learners have enmity in the centre
40.	2.08	ECO 4	There is no immediate use by getting educated
41.	2.07	PER 71	The other learners are much older
42.	2.07	COM 62	The time of the centre is inconvenient
43.	2.07	FAM 34	The time of the centre is the supper time
44.	2.05	PRO 80	The centre is at a distance

(Table Contd...)

1	2	3	4
45.	2.05	INS 51	The instructor uses difficult language, pictures and symbols
46.	2.05	FAM 36	Unable to go to the centre because of heavy work
47.	2.05	PSY 41	The instructor is unable to explain clearly
48.	2.04	INS 57	The instructional methods used by the instructor are not liked
49.	2.04	INS 39	The instructor is not well versed with this teaching
50.	2.03	COM 64	No one else visits the centre except the instructor
51.	2.03	INS 43	The instructor is negligent
52.	2.03	INS 38	The instructor is not punctual to the centre
53.	2.02	PER 66	Becoming a slave to bad habits
54.	2.02	INS 53	The absence of audio-visual aids useful for instruction
55.	2.02	INS 40	There is no teaching experience to the instructor
56.	2.02	PSY 46	The instructor lacks good voice and fluency
57.	2.01	SOC 14	Many learners belong to the upper caste
58.	2.00	PER 73	Getting discouraged after working hard for sometime to get educated and feeling that this attempt is useless
59.	2.00	COM 61	Good friends are not available at the centre
60.	2.00	INS 45	The instruction is not relevant to the learners
61.	2.00	INS 37	The centre is not well maintained
62.	2.00	PSY 30	Feeling that learning at home instead of at the centre is better
63.	2.00	PSY 27	Learners calling by nicknames
64.	1.99	ECO 5	My family is economically backward
65.	1.98	SOC 7	The instructor does not belong to my place
66.	1.97	COM 63	Co-educational centre
67.	1.97	COM 58	There is no encouragement from the village elders
68.	1.97	PSY 25	Feeling that education is only for wealthy people

(Table Contd...)

1	2	3	4
69.	1.97	SOC 12	The instructor and the learners are not friendly
70.	1.96	ECO 1	No immediate financial benefit by education
71.	1.92	COM 65	The time of the programme is short
72.	1.90	SOC 15	There are some learners with bad behaviour in the centre
73.	1.88	FAM 32	Looking after the children
74.	1.87	PSY 64	No one else visits the centre except the instructor
75.	1.85	SOC 9	The instructor utilises the learners for his personal work
			Less Significant
76.	1.83	FAM 33	Other family members do not co-operate in matters of education
77.	1.81	SOC 13	There are some fights in the village
78.	1.80	PER 67	Getting newly married
79.	1.77	PER 69	Quarrelling with other learners
80.	1.65	ECO 3	Owners and landlords do not permit for attending centres

ECO: Economic Problems area — *INS:* Instructor related Problems area
SOC: Social Problems area — *COM:* Community related Problems area
PSY: Psychological Problems area — *PER:* Personal Problems area
FAM: Familial Problems area — *PRO:* Programme related Problems

There are 28 very significant problems (Rank Order 1-28), 47 significant problems (Rank Order 29-75) and 5 less significant problems (Rank Order 76-80).

The problem area-wise distribution of very significant, significant and less significant problems is summarized and presented in Table No. 4.16. By looking at the problems area in the Table 4.15, the exact problem may be located.

Table 4.16:

Problem Areas	*Very Significant*	*Significant*	*Less Significant*	*Total*
Economic Problems (ECO)	1	4	1	6
Social Problems (SOC)	3	6	1	10
Psychological Problems (PSY)	6	8	-	14
Familial Problems (FAM)	1	4	1	6
Instructor related Problems (INS)	8	13	-	21
Community related Problems (COM)	2	6	-	8
Personal Problems (PER)	5	5	2	12
Programme related Problems (PRO)	2	1	-	3
Total	**28**	**47**	**5**	**80**

Problems of Female Dropouts

The very significant, significant and less significant problems of drop-outs are presented in the Table 4.17.

Table 4.17: Showing the Very Significant, Significant and Less Significant Problems in the case of Female Drop-outs

Rank Order	*Mean Difficulty*	*Problem Area and Sl. No. in the Rating Scale*	*Problem*
1	2	3	4
		Very Significant	
1.	2.39	PRO 80	The centre is at a distance
2.	2.36	INS 4	The instructor lacks good voice and fluency
3.	2.33	FAM 31	Other family members refuse permission to attend during nights
4.	2.31	PSY 23	Easily getting tired
5.	2.29	COM 63	Co-educational centre
6.	2.27	COM 62	The time of the centre is inconvenient
7.	2.27	ECO 6	There are no specific working hours in different professions

(Table Contd...)

1	2	3	4
8.	2.26	COM 60	I am not permitted to go with my friends
9.	2.25	PSY 18	The learner is not able to answer to the instructor
10.	2.24	PSY 24	Feeling shy one should get educated when the age is so much
11.	2.24	PSY 20	Feeling that the age to study has passed
12.	2.22	PSY 29	Feeling that studying at the centre is a waste
13.	2.21	COM 58	There is no encouragement from the village elders
14.	2.21	FAM 36	Unable to go to the centre because of heavy work
15.	2.19	PER 75	The instructor is male
16.	2.18	INS 56	The books are difficult to learn
17.	2.18	FAM 35	There are none else at home
18.	2.18	FAM 34	The time of the centre is the supper time
19.	2.16	COM 59	The friends do not go to the centre
20.	2.15	PSY 22	Feeling that others would mock
			Significant
21.	2.13	INS 48	Instructor is limited only to literacy
22.	2.12	INS 45	The instruction is not relevant to the learners
23.	2.11	COM 61	I am not permitted to go with my friends
24.	2.11	INS 55	The lessons are not according to the requirements or tastes
25.	2.10	SOC 12	The instructor and the learners are not friendly
26.	2.09	COM 64	No one else visits the centre except the instructor
27.	2.09	PSY 19	Unwilling to get educated
28.	2.07	PER 76	Lack of knowledge about this programme
29.	2.05	PER 66	Becoming a slave to bad habits

(Table Contd...)

1	2	3	4
30.	2.05	ECO 1	No immediate financial benefit by education
31.	2.03	INS 51	The instructor uses difficult language, pictures and symbols
32.	2.03	PSY 21	Feeling shy to go to the centre
33.	2.03	SOC 16	Attending functions and going to movies
34.	2.02	PSY 26	Feeling shy during conversation with others
35.	2.02	FAM 33	Other family members do not co-operate in matters of education
36.	2.01	SOC 8	The instructor does not belong to my caste
37.	2.00	PRO 78	Minimum amenities are not found at the centre (air/ventilation)
38.	2.00	PER 77	The relevant lessons are not taught at the centre
39.	2.00	INS 52	Teaching aids are not available at the right time
40.	1.99	PSY 27	Learners calling by nicknames
41.	1.99	PSY 17	There is no understanding between the learner and the instructor
42.	1.98	PRO 70	Getting the marriage age
43.	1.97	INS 53	The absence of audio-visual aids useful for instruction
44.	1.97	PSY 28	The fellow learners do not listen to the thoughts and ideas
45.	1.96	INS 43	The instructor is negligent
46.	1.96	ECO 4	There is no immediate use by getting educated
47.	1.95	PSY 30	Feeling that learning at home instead of at the centre, is better
48.	1.94	PER 68	Due to ill-health
49.	1.94	COM 65	The time of the programme is short
50.	1.94	INS 42	The instructor does not treat all the learners equally
51.	1.94	ECO 2	Busy with farm work
52.	1.93	PER 71	The other learners are much older

(Table Contd...)

1	2	3	4
53.	1.93	INS 57	The instructional methods used by the instructor are not liked
54.	1.93	SOC 7	The instructor does not belong to my place
55.	1.91	INS 50	The instructor does not reveal in learner's progress
56.	1.90	INS 47	The instructor fails to enthuse the learners to participate
57.	1.90	SOC 10	Personal position is at stake in the society
58.	1.86	FAM 32	Looking after the children
59.	1.86	SOC 14	Many learners belong to the upper caste
60.	1.84	PRO 79	The centre is started at inconvenient place/having much sounds and bad smell
61.	1.84	INS 49	Providing too much information within a short time
			Less Significant
62.	1.83	INS 39	The instructor is not well-versed with his teaching
63.	1.83	SOC 9	The instructor utilises the learners for his personal work
64.	1.81	PER 69	Quarrelling with other learners
65.	1.81	INS 54	Primer and follow-up books are not in order
66.	1.79	PSY 25	Feeling that education is only for wealthy people
67.	1.78	INS 41	The instructor is unable to explain clearly
68.	1.78	INS 40	There is no teaching experience to the instructor
69.	1.78	ECO 5	My family is economically backward
70.	1.77	SOC 15	There are some learners with bad behaviour in the centre
71.	1.76	INS 44	The instructor does not accept criticism with open heart
72.	1.76	INS 38	The instructor is not punctual to the centre

(Table Contd...)

1	2	3	4
73.	1.75	SOC 11	Some co-learners have enmity in the centre
74.	1.74	ECO 3	Owners and landlords do not permit for attending centres
75.	1.70	PER 74	The other learners also are average in learning
76.	1.70	PER 67	Getting newly married
77.	1.63	INS 37	The centre is not well maintained
78.	1.54	SOC 13	There are some fights in the village
79.	1.53	PER 72	The other learners are mocking because of my backwardness in learning
80.	1.53	PER 73	Getting discouraged after working hard for some time to get educated and feeling that this attempt is useless.

ECO: Economic Problems area
SOC: Social Problems area
PSY: Psychological Problems area
FAM: Familial Problems area
INS: Instructor related Problems area
COM: Community related Problems area
PER: Personal Problems area
PRO: Programme related Problems

There are 20 very significant problems (Rank Order 1-20), 41 significant problems (Rank Order 21-61) and 19 less significant problems (Rank Order 62-80).

The problems area-wise distribution of very significant, significant and less significant problems is summarized and presented in the Table 4.18. By looking at the problem area in the Table 4.17, the exact problem may be located.

Table 4.18: Distribution of Very Significant, Significant and Less Significant Problems as Problems area-wise indicated by Female Drop-outs

Problem Areas	*Very Significant*	*Significant*	*Less Significant*	*Total*
1	2	3	4	5
Economic Problems (ECO)	1	3	2	6
Social Problems (SOC)	-	6	4	10
Psychological Problems (PSY)	6	7	1	14

(Table Contd...)

1	2	3	4	5
Familial Problems (FAM)	4	2	-	6
Instructor related Problems (INS)	2	12	7	21
Community related Problems (COM)	5	3	-	8
Personal Problems (PER)	1	6	5	12
Programme related Problems (PRO)	1	2	-	3
Total	**20**	**41**	**19**	**80**

Problems of Previous Schooling Drop-outs

The very significant, significant and less significant problems of previous schooling drop-outs are presented in the Table 5.19.

Table 4.19: Showing the Very Significant, Significant and Less Significant Problems in the case of Previous Schooling Drop-outs

Rank Order	*Mean Difficulty*	*Problem Area and Sl. No. in the Rating Scale*	*Problem*
1	2	3	4
			Very Significant
1.	2.35	PSY 23	Easily getting tired
2.	2.34	INS 56	The books are difficult to learn
3.	2.31	PSY 20	Feeling that the age to study has passed
4.	2.31	INS 46	The instructor lacks good voice and fluency
5.	2.27	PSY 18	The learner is not able to answer to the instructor
6.	2.27	FAM 36	Unable to go to the centre because of heavy work
7.	2.27	PRO 80	The centre is at a distance
8.	2.26	ECO 6	There are no specific working hours in different professions
9.	2.26	PSY 29	Feeling that studying at the centre is a waste

(Table Contd...)

1	*2*	*3*	*4*
10.	2.26	FAM 35	There are none else at home
11.	2.24	PSY 22	Feeling that others would mock
12.	2.24	INS 52	Teaching aids are not available at the right time
13.	2.24	PRO 78	Minimum amenities are not found at the centre (air/ventilation)
14.	2.23	INS 47	The instructor fails to enthuse the learners to participate
15.	2.22	FAM 28	Other family members refuse permission to attend during night
16.	2.22	INS 55	The lessons are not according to the requirements and tastes
17.	2.21	PER 34	The time of the centre is the supper time
18.	2.20	SOC 16	Attending functions and going to movies
19.	2.20	INS 57	The instructional methods used by the instructor are not liked
20.	2.19	COM 62	The time of the centre is inconvenient
21.	2.19	PER 72	The other learners are mocking because of my backwardness in learning
22.	2.19	COM 60	I am not permitted to go with my friends
23.	2.18	SOC 10	Personal position is at stake in the society
24.	2.18	INS 42	The instructor does not treat all the learners equally
25.	2.18	PER 77	The relevant lessons are not taught at the centre
26.	2.17	SOC 8	The instructor does not belong to my caste
27.	2.17	INS 51	Teaching aids are not available at the right time
28.	2.17	PSY 68	Due to ill-health
29.	2.16	PSY 17	There is no understanding between the learners and the instructor
30.	2.15	PSY 19	Unwilling to get educated
			Significant
31.	2.13	PSY 21	Feeling shy to go to the centre
32.	2.13	COM 63	Co-educational centre
33.	2.13	COM 65	The time of the programme is short

(Table Contd...)

1	2	3	4
34.	2.13	PRO 79	The centre is started at inconvenient place/having much sounds and bad smell
35.	2.12	INS 45	The instruction is not relevant to the learners
36.	2.12	INS 50	The instructor does not reveal in learner's progress
37.	2.12	INS 54	Primer and follow up books are not in order
38.	2.12	COM 64	No one else visits the centre except the instructor
39.	2.11	INS 48	Instruction is limited only to literacy
40.	2.10	ECO 4	There is no immediate use by getting educated
41.	2.09	FAM 31	Other family members refuse permission to attend during nights
42.	2.08	PER 75	The instructor is male
43.	2.08	PER 76	Lack of knowledge about this programme
44.	2.07	EOC 1	No immediate financial benefit by education
45.	2.07	PER 70	Getting the marriage age
46.	2.06	COM 59	Friends do not go to the centre
47.	2.05	PSY 26	Feeling shy during conversation with others
48.	2.05	COM 58	There is no encouragement from the village elders
49.	2.05	PER 71	The other learners are much older
50.	2.04	ECO 2	Busy with farm work
51.	2.04	PER 66	Becoming a slave to bad habits
52.	2.03	PSY 30	Feeling that learning at home instead of at the centre is better
53.	2.03	INS 38	The instructor is not punctual to the centre
54.	2.03	COM 61	Good friends are not available at the centre
55.	2.03	PER 74	The other learners also are average in learning

(Table Contd...)

1	2	3	4
56.	2.02	INS 53	The absence of audio-visual aids useful for instruction
57.	2.00	INS 41	The instructor is unable to explain clearly
58.	2.00	INS 43	The instructor is negligent
59.	1.98	PSY 24	Feeling why one should get educated when the age is so much
60.	1.98	FAM 33	Other family members do not co-operate in matters of education
61.	1.97	SOC 11	Some co-learners have enmity in the centre
62.	1.97	INS 49	Providing too much information within a short time
63.	1.95	INS 39	The instructor is not well versed with this teaching
64.	1.95	INS 40	There is no teaching experience to the instructor
65.	1.95	INS 44	The instructor does not accept criticism with open heart
66.	1.93	SOC 9	The instructor utilises the learners for his personal work
67.	1.93	SOC 12	The instructor and the learner are not friendly
68.	1.93	PSY 27	Learners calling by nicknames
69.	1.92	FAM 32	Looking after the children
70.	1.89	ECO 5	My family is economically backward
71.	1.89	SOC 14	Many learners belong to the upper caste
72.	1.89	PSY 25	Feeling that education is only for wealthy people
73.	1.87	SOC 7	The instructor does not belong to my place
74.	1.76	PER 69	Quarrelling with other learners
75.	1.84	PER 73	Getting discouraged after working hard for sometime to get educated and feeling that this attempt is useless
			Less Significant
76.	1.79	SOC 15	There are some learners with bad behaviour in the centre
77.	1.79	INS 37	The centre is not well maintained

(Table Contd...)

1	2	3	4
78.	1.73	SOC 13	There are some fights in the village
79.	1.70	PER 67	Getting newly married
80.	1.59	ECO 3	Owners and landlords do not permit for attending centres

ECO: Economic Problems area *INS:* Instructor related Problems area
SOC: Social Problems area *COM:* Community related Problems area
PSY: Psychological Problems area *PER:* Personal Problems area
FAM: Familial Problems area *PRO:* Programme related Problems

There are 30 very significant problems (Rank Order 1-30), 45 significant problems (Rank Order 31-75) and 5 less significant problems (Rank Order 76-80).

The problems area-wise distribution of very significant, significant and less significant problems is summarized and presented in the Table 4.20. By looking at the problem area in the Table 4.19, the exact problem may be located.

Table 4.20: Showing the Very Significant, Significant and Less Significant Problems as Problems area-wise indicated by Previous Schooling Dropouts

Problem Areas	*Very Significant*	*Significant*	*Less Significant*	*Total*
Economic Problems (ECO)	1	4	1	6
Social Problems (SOC)	3	5	2	10
Psychological Problems (PSY)	8	6	-	14
Familial Problems (FAM)	3	3	-	6
Instructor related Problems (INS)	8	12	1	21
Community related Problems (COM)	2	6	-	8
Personal Problems (PER)	3	8	1	12
Programme related Problems (PRO)	2	1	-	3
Total	**30**	**45**	**5**	**80**

Problems of No Schooling Drop-outs

The very significant, significant and less significant problems of previous schooling drop-outs are presented in the Table 4.21.

Table 4.21: Showing the Very Significant, Significant and Less Significant Problems in the case of 'No Schooling' Drop-outs

Rank Order	*Mean Difficulty*	*Problem Area and Sl. No. in the Rating Scale*	*Problem*
1	2	3	4
			Very Significant
1.	2.36	PSY 23	Easily getting tired
2.	2.35	FAM 31	Other family members refuse permission to attend during nights
3.	2.29	COM 59	Friends do not go to the centre
4.	2.27	PSY 19	Unwilling to get educated
5.	2.24	PRO 80	The centre is at a distance
6.	2.24	INS 46	The instructor lacks good voice and fluency
7.	2.22	INS 48	Instruction is limited only to literacy
8.	2.21	PER 75	The instructor is male
9.	2.21	INS 50	The instructor does not reveal learner's progress
10.	2.21	PSY 18	The learner is not able to answer to the instructor
11.	2.20	SOC 14	Many learners belong to the upper caste
12.	2.20	ECO 2	Busy with farm work
13.	2.19	COM 60	I am not permitted to go with my friends
14.	2.18	PER 76	Lack of knowledge about this programme
15.	2.18	ECO 6	There are no specific working hours in different professions
16.	2.17	INS 47	The instructor fails to enthuse the learners to participate
17.	2.15	PSY 22	Feeling that others would mock
18.	2.15	SOC 12	The instructor and the learner are not friendly
			Significant
19.	2.13	INS 56	The books are difficult to learn
20.	2.12	COM 62	The time of the centre is inconvenient

(Table Contd...)

1	2	3	4
21.	2.12	FAM 35	There are none else at home
22.	2.11	COM 58	There is no encouragement from the village elders
23.	2.11	INS 49	Providing too much information within a short time
24.	2.09	PSY 27	Learners calling by nicknames
25.	2.09	PSY 24	Feeling why one should get educated when the age is so much
26.	2.08	PSY 20	Feeling that the age to study has passed
27.	2.08	SOC 7	The instructor does not belong to my place
28.	2.07	PER 68	Due to ill-health
29.	2.06	COM 61	Good friends are not available at the centre
30.	2.05	SOC 8	The instructor does not belong to my caste
31.	2.02	PRO 78	Minimum amenities are not found at the centre (air/ventilation)
32.	2.02	PER 70	Getting the marriage age
33.	2.02	PER 66	Becoming a slave to bad habits
34.	2.02	INS 52	Teaching aids are not available at the right time
35.	2.02	PSY 29	Feeling that studying at the centre is a waste
36.	2.01	PER 72	The other learners are mocking because of my backwardness in learning
37.	2.01	SOC 16	Attending functions and going to movies
38.	2.00	INS 43	The instructor is negligent
39.	2.00	FAM 34	The time of the centre is the supper time
40.	2.00	SOC 10	Personal position is at stake in the society
41.	1.99	COM 63	Co-educational centre
42.	1.99	PSY 26	Feeling shy during conversation with other
43.	1.98	PRO 79	The centre is started at inconvenient place/having much sounds and bad smell
44.	1.98	PER 77	The relevant lessons are not taught at the centre

(Table Contd...)

1	2	3	4
45.	1.98	INS 53	The absence of audio-visual aids useful for instruction
46.	1.97	COM 64	No one else visits the centre except the instructor
47.	1.96	INS 39	The instructor is not well versed with his teaching
48.	1.95	PER 71	The other learners are much older
49.	1.95	INS 55	The lessons are not according to the requirements and tastes
50.	1.95	INS 45	The instruction is not relevant to the learners
51.	1.94	INS 44	The instructor does not accept criticism with open heart
52.	1.93	PER 74	The other learners are also average in learning
53.	1.93	INS 41	The instructor is unable to explain clearly
54.	1.93	PSY 21	Feeling shy to go to the centre
55.	1.92	PSY 17	There is no understanding between the learner and the instructor
56.	1.92	ECO 4	There is no immediate use by getting educated
57.	1.91	INS 37	The centre is not well maintained
58.	1.91	FAM 36	Unable to go to the centre because of heavy work
59.	1.91	PSY 30	Feeling that learning at home instead of the centre is better
60.	1.91	PSY 28	The fellow learners do not listen to the thoughts and ideas
61.	1.91	SOC 15	There are some learners with bad behaviour in the centre
62.	1.91	ECO 5	My family is economically backward
63.	1.90	PSY 11	Some co-learners have enmity in the centre
64.	1.90	ECO 1	No immediate financial benefit by education
65.	1.89	PSY 25	Feeling that education is only for wealthy people
66.	1.87	INS 40	There is no teaching experience to the instructor

(Table Contd...)

1	2	3	4
67.	1.86	INS 51	The instructor uses difficult language, pictures and symbols
68.	1.85	INS 54	Primer and follow-up books are not in order
69.	1.85	INS 42	The instructor does not treat all the learners equally
70.	1.84	PER 67	Getting newly married
			Less Significant
71.	1.82	ECO 3	Owners and landlords do not permit for attending centres
72.	1.81	FAM 33	Other family members do not co-operate in the matters of education
73.	1.81	FAM 32	Looking after the children
74.	1.74	INS 38	The instructor is not punctual to the centre
75.	1.72	INS 57	The instructional methods specified by the Government are not liked
76.	1.71	SOC 9	The instructor utilises the learners for his personal work
77.	1.70	PER 73	Getting discouraged after working hard for sometime to get educated and feeling that this attempt is useless
78.	1.68	PER 69	Quarrelling with other learners
79.	1.67	COM 65	The time of the programme is short
80.	1.64	SOC 13	There are some fights in the village

ECO: Economic Problems area *INS:* Instructor related Problems area

SOC: Social Problems area *COM:* Community related Problems area

PSY: Psychological Problems area *PER:* Personal Problems area

FAM: Familial Problems area *PRO:* Programme related Problems

There are 18 very significant problems (Rank Order 1-18), 52 significant problems (Rank Order 19-70) and 10 less significant problems (Rank Order 71-80).

The problem area-wise distribution of very significant, significant and less significant problems is summarized and presented in the Table 4.22. By looking at the problems area in the Table 4.21, the exact problem may be located.

Table 4.22: Showing the Very Significant, Significant and Less Significant Problems as Problems area-wise indicated by No Schooling Drop-outs

Problem Areas	*Very Significant*	*Significant*	*Less Significant*	*Total*
Economic Problems (ECO)	2	3	1	6
Social Problems (SOC)	2	6	2	10
Psychological Problems (PSY)	4	10	-	14
Familial Problems (FAM)	1	3	2	6
Instructor related Problems (INS)	4	15	2	21
Community related Problems (COM)	2	5	1	8
Personal Problems (PER)	2	8	2	12
Programme related Problems (PRO)	1	2	-	3
Total	**18**	**52**	**10**	**80**

Problems of Married Drop-outs

The very significant, significant and less significant problems of married drop-outs are presented in the Table 4.23.

Table 4.23: Showing the Very Significant, Significant and Less Significant Problems in the case of 'Married' Drop-outs

Rank Order	*Mean Difficulty*	*Problem Area and Sl. No. in the Rating Scale*	*Problem*
1	2	3	4
			Very Significant
1.	2.42	PSY 23	Easily getting tired
2.	2.27	PSY 22	Feeling that others would mock
3.	2.27	INS 56	The books are difficult to learn
4.	2.26	ECO 6	There are no specific working hours in different professions
5.	2.26	PSY 18	The learner is not able to answer to the instructor

(Table Contd...)

1	2	3	4
6.	2.25	PSY 19	Unwilling to get educated
7.	2.25	FAM 31	Other family members refuse permission to attend during nights
8.	2.25	PSY 20	Feeling that the age to study has passed
9.	2.24	PRO 80	The centre is at a distance
10.	2.23	PSY 29	Feeling that studying at the centre is a waste
11.	2.23	INS 46	The instructor lacks good voice and fluency
12.	2.18	SOC 10	Personal position is at stake in the society
13.	2.18	INS 48	Instruction is limited only to literacy
14.	2.18	COM 62	The time of the centre is inconvenient
15.	2.16	INS 50	The instructor does not reveal in learner's progress
16.	2.16	INS 55	The lessons are not according to the requirements and tastes
17.	2.16	COM 64	No one else visits the centre except the instructor
18.	2.15	PSY 21	Feeling shy to go to the centre
19.	2.15	PSY 28	The fellow learners do not listen to the thoughts and ideas
20.	2.15	FAM 35	There are none else at home
21.	2.15	ECO 2	Busy with farm work
22.	2.15	INS 57	The instructional methods used by the instructor are not liked
			Significant
23.	2.13	PER 68	Due to ill-health
24.	2.12	FAM 34	The time of the centre is the supper time
25.	2.11	FAM 36	Unable to go to the centre because of heavy work
26.	2.11	PER 74	The other learners are also average in learning
27.	2.10	INS 51	The instructor uses difficult language, pictures and symbols
28.	2.09	INS 45	The instruction is not relevant to the learners

(Table Contd...)

1	2	3	4
29.	2.09	INS 49	Providing too much information within a short time
30.	2.09	PER 77	The relevant lessons are not taught at the centre
31.	2.08	INS 52	Teaching aids are not available at the right time
32.	2.08	COM 59	Friends do not go to the centre
33.	2.08	PRO 78	Minimum amenities are not found at the centre (air/ventilation)
34.	2.08	INS 47	The instructor fails to enthuse the learners to participate
35.	2.06	PRO 79	The centre is started at inconvenient place/having much sounds and bad smell
36.	2.06	PSY 25	Feeling that education is only for wealthy people
37.	2.05	PSY 26	Feeling shy during conversation with others
38.	2.05	PSY 30	Feeling that learning at home instead of at the centre is better
39.	2.05	COM 58	There is no encouragement from the village elders
40.	2.05	PER 75	The instructor is male
41.	2.05	COM 60	I am not permitted to go with my friends
42.	2.04	INS 41	The instructor is unable to explain clearly
43.	2.04	PER 66	Becoming a slave to bad habits
44.	2.04	INS 38	The instructor is not punctual to the centre
45.	2.03	ECO 4	There is no immediate use by getting educated
46.	2.03	SOC 12	The instructor and the learner are not friendly
47.	2.02	ECO 1	No immediate financial benefit by education
48.	2.02	SOC 8	The instructor does not belong to my caste
49.	2.02	PER 72	The other learners are mocking because of my backwardness in learning

(Table Contd...)

1	2	3	4
50.	2.02	PER 76	Lack of knowledge about this programme
51.	2.01	PER 71	The other learners are much older
52.	2.00	PSY 17	There is no understanding between the learner and the instructor
53.	2.00	INS 42	The instructor does not treat all the learners equally
54.	2.00	INS 54	Primer and follow-up books are not in order
55.	2.00	FAM 32	Looking after the children
56.	2.00	SOC 16	Attending functions and going to movies
57.	1.98	COM 65	The time of the programme is short
58.	1.97	SOC 11	Some co-learners have enmity in the centre
59.	1.97	SOC 14	Many learners belong to the upper caste
60.	1.96	SOC 7	The instructor does not belong to my place
61.	1.95	INS 53	The absence of audio-visual aids useful for instruction
62.	1.94	ECO 5	My family is economically backward
63.	1.94	INS 39	The instructor is not well versed with his teaching
64.	1.93	INS 43	The instructor is negligent
65.	1.91	SOC 9	The instructor utilises the learners for his personal work
66.	1.91	PSY 27	Learners calling by nicknames
67.	1.90	INS 40	There is no teaching experience to the instructor
68.	1.89	COM 63	Co-educational centre
69.	1.87	COM 61	Good friends are not available at the centre
70.	1.87	INS 37	The centre is not well maintained
71.	1.86	SOC 15	There are some learners with bad behaviour in the centre
72.	1.86	PSY 26	Feeling shy during conversation with others
73.	1.85	PER 69	Quarrelling with other learners
74.	1.84	PER 70	Getting the marriage age

(Table Contd...)

1	2	3	4
			Less Significant
75.	1.80	FAM 33	Other family members do not co-operate in matters of education
76.	1.80	PER 73	Getting discouraged after working hard for sometime to get educated and feeling that this attempt is useless
77.	1.80	INS 44	The instructor does not accept criticism with open heart
78.	1.77	PER 67	Getting newly married
79.	1.75	ECO 3	Owners and landlords do not permit for attending the centres
80.	1.61	SOC 13	There are some fights in the village

ECO: Economic Problems area
SOC: Social Problems area
PSY: Psychological Problems area
FAM: Familial Problems area
INS: Instructor related Problems area
COM: Community related Problems area
PER: Personal Problems area
PRO: Programme related Problems

There are 22 very significant problems (Rank Order 1-22), 52 significant problems (Rank Order 23-74) and 6 less significant problems (Rank Order 75-80).

The problem area-wise distribution of very significant, significant and less significant problem is summarized and presented in the Table 4.24. By looking at the problems area in the Table 4.23, the exact problem may be located.

Table 4.24: Showing the Very Significant, Significant and Less Significant Problems as Problems area-wise indicated by Married Drop-outs

Problem Areas	*Very Significant*	*Significant*	*Less Significant*	*Total*
1	2	3	4	5
Economic Problems (ECO)	2	3	1	6
Social Problems (SOC)	1	8	1	10
Psychological Problems (PSY)	8	6	-	14
Familial Problems (FAM)	2	3	1	6

(Table Contd...)

1	2	3	4	5
Instructor related Problems (INS)	6	14	1	21
Community related Problems (COM)	2	6	-	8
Personal Problems (PER)	-	10	2	12
Programme related Problems (PRO)	1	2	-	3
Total	**22**	**52**	**6**	**80**

Problems of Unmarried Dropouts

The very significant, significant and less significant problems of unmarried drop-outs are presented in the Table 4.25.

Table 4.25: Showing the Very Significant, Significant and Less Significant Problems in the case of 'Unmarried' Dropouts

Rank Order	*Mean Difficulty*	*Problem Area and Sl. No. in the Rating Scale*	*Problem*
1	*2*	*3*	*4*
			Very Significant
1.	2.41	COM 60	I am not permitted to go with my friends
2.	2.38	FAM 35	There are none else at home
3.	2.38	INS 47	The instructor fails to enthuse the learners to participate
4.	2.36	INS 46	The instructor lacks good voice and fluency
5.	2.35	PER 70	Getting the marriage age
6.	2.34	COM 63	Co-educational centre
7.	2.30	SOC 16	Attending functions and going to movies
8.	2.30	COM 61	Good friends are not available at the centre
9.	2.28	PRO 80	The centre is at a distance
10.	2.27	PSY 23	Easily getting tired
11.	2.27	COM 59	Friends do not go to the centre
12.	2.27	PER 76	Lack of knowledge about this programme
13.	2.27	PSY 26	Feeling shy during conversation with others

(Table Contd...)

1	2	3	4
14.	2.26	PER 72	The other learners are mocking because of my backwardness in learning
15.	2.25	SOC 8	The instructor does not belong to my caste
16.	2.25	INS 52	Teaching aids are not available at the right time
17.	2.24	PRO 78	Minimum amenities are not found at the centre (air/ventilation)
18.	2.23	PSY 18	The learner is not able to answer to the instructor
19.	2.22	INS 56	The books are difficult to learn
20.	2.20	PER 75	The instructor is male
21.	2.17	ECO 6	There are no specific working hours in different professions
22.	2.16	INS 44	The instructor does not accept criticism with open heart
23.	2.15	PSY 20	Feeling that the age to study has passed
24.	2.14	PSY 17	There is no understanding between the learner and the instructor
25.	2.14	INS 50	The instructor does not reveal in learner's progress
			Significant
26.	2.13	PSY 19	Unwilling to get educated
27.	2.13	FAM 36	Unable to go to the centre because of heavy work
28.	2.13	COM 62	The time of the centre is inconvenient
29.	2.12	PSY 27	Learners calling by nicknames
30.	2.12	FAM 31	Other family members refuse permission to attend during nights
31.	2.12	INS 48	Instruction is limited only to literacy
32.	2.11	FAM 34	The time of the centre is the supper time
33.	2.11	INS 43	The instructor is negligent
34.	2.11	COM 58	There is no encouragement from the village elders
35.	2.11	PER 68	Due to ill-health
36.	2.11	PER 77	The relevant lessons are not taught at the centre
37.	2.10	PSY 22	Feeling that others would mock

(Table Contd...)

1	2	3	4
38.	2.10	INS 42	The instructor does not treat all the learners equally
39.	2.08	PRO 79	The centre is started at inconvenient place/having much sounds and bad smell
40.	2.07	INS 53	The absence of audio-visual aids useful for instruction
41.	2.06	FAM 33	Other family members do not co-operate in matters of education
42.	2.06	INS 55	The lessons are not according to the requirements and tastes
43.	2.04	PSY 29	Feeling that studying at the centre is a waste
44.	2.03	PER 66	Becoming a slave to bad habits
45.	2.02	ECO 4	There is no immediate use by getting educated
46.	2.02	INS 54	Primer and follow up books are not in order
47.	2.01	SOC 12	The instructor and the learner are not friendly
48.	2.00	PSY 24	Feeling why one should get educated when the age is so much
49.	2.00	PSY 28	The fellow learners do not listen to the thoughts and ideas
50.	2.00	PER 71	The other learners are much older
51.	1.99	SOC 10	Personal position is at stake in the society
52.	1.98	INS 45	The instruction is not relevant to the learners
53.	1.97	INS 39	The instructor is not well versed with his teaching
54.	1.96	ECO 1	No immediate financial benefit by education
55.	1.96	SOC 7	The instructor does not belong to my place
56.	1.95	INS 49	Providing too much information within a short time
57.	1.95	INS 51	The instructor uses difficult language, pictures and symbols
58.	1.91	INS 40	There is no teaching experience to the instructor

(Table Contd...)

1	*2*	*3*	*4*
59.	1.91	SOC 14	Many learners belong to the upper caste
60.	1.89	SOC 11	Some co-learners have enmity in the centre
61.	1.89	COM 64	No one else visits the centre except the instructor
62.	1.88	PSY 21	Feeling shy to go to the centre
63.	1.87	PSY 30	Feeling that learning at home instead of at the centre is better
64.	1.87	INS 41	The instructor is unable to explain clearly
65.	1.87	COM 65	The time of the programme is short
66.	1.86	ECO 2	Busy with farm work
			Less Significant
67.	1.83	ECO 5	My family is economically backward
68.	1.83	SOC 15	There are some learners with bad behaviour in the centre
69.	1.81	SOC 13	There are some fights in the village
70.	1.80	INS 37	The centre is not well maintained
71.	1.80	PER 74	The other learners also are average in learning
72.	1.77	INS 57	The instructional methods used by the instructor are not liked
73.	1.75	PER 73	Getting discouraged after working hard for sometime to get educated and feeling that this attempt is useless
74.	1.74	SOC 9	The instructor utilises the learners for his personal work
75.	1.74	PER 67	Getting newly married
76.	1.72	INS 38	The instructor is not punctual to the centre
77.	1.69	PER 69	Quarreling with other learners
78.	1.69	FAM 32	Looking after the children
79.	1.64	PSY 25	Feeling that education is only for wealthy people
80.	1.69	ECO 3	Owners and landlords do not permit for attending the centres

ECO: Economic Problems area
INS: Instructor related Problems area
SOC: Social Problems area
COM: Community related Problems area
PSY: Psychological Problems area
PER: Personal Problems area
FAM: Familial Problems area
PRO: Programme related Problems

There are 25 very significant problems (Rank Order 1-25), 41 significant problems (Rank Order 26-66) and 14 less significant problems (Rank Order 67-80).

The problem area-wise distribution of very significant, significant and less significant problems is summarized and presented in the Table 4.26. By looking at the problems area in the Table 4.25, the exact problem may be located.

Table 4.26: Distribution of Very Significant, Significant and Less Significant Problems as Problems area-wise indicated by Unmarried Drop-outs

Problem Areas	*Very Significant*	*Significant*	*Less Significant*	*Total*
Economic Problems (ECO)	1	3	2	6
Social Problems (SOC)	2	5	3	10
Psychological Problems (PSY)	5	8	1	14
Familial Problems (FAM)	1	4	1	6
Instructor related Problems (INS)	6	12	3	21
Community related Problems (COM)	4	4	-	8
Personal Problems (PER)	4	4	4	12
Programme related Problems (PRO)	2	1	-	3
Total	**25**	**41**	**14**	**80**

Problems of 20 years and below Age Group Drop-outs

The very significant, significant and less significant problems of 20 years and below age group drop-outs are presented in Table 4.27.

Table 4.27: Showing the Very Significant, Significant and Less Significant Problems in the case of 'Unmarried' Drop-outs

Rank Order	*Mean Difficulty*	*Problem Area and Sl. No. in the Rating Scale*	*Problem*
1	2	3	4
			Very Significant
1.	2.41	COM 60	I am not permitted to go with my friends
2.	2.38	FAM 35	There are none else at home
3.	2.38	INS 47	The instructor fails to enthuse the learners to participate
4.	2.36	INS 46	The instructor lacks good voice and fluency
5.	2.35	PER 70	Getting the marriage age
6.	2.34	COM 63	Co-educational centre
7.	2.30	SOC 16	Attending functions and going to movies
8.	2.30	COM 61	Good friends are not available at the centre
9.	2.28	PRO 80	The centre is at a distance
10.	2.27	PSY 23	Easily getting tired
11.	2.27	COM 59	Friends do not go to the centre
12.	2.27	PER 76	Lack of knowledge about this programme
13.	2.27	PSY 26	Feeling shy during conversation with others
14.	2.26	PER 72	The other learners are mocking because of my backwardness in learning
15.	2.25	SOC 8	The instructor does not belong to my caste
16.	2.25	INS 52	Teaching aids are not available at the right time
17.	2.24	PRO 78	Minimum amenities are not found at the centre (air/ventilation)
18.	2.23	PSY 18	The learner is not able to answer to the instructor

(Table Contd...)

1	2	3	4
19.	2.22	INS 56	The books are difficult to learn
20.	2.20	PER 75	The instructor is male
21.	2.17	ECO 6	There are no specific working hours in different professions
22.	2.16	INS 44	The instructor does not accept criticism with open heart
23.	2.15	PSY 20	Feeling that the age to study has passed
24.	2.14	PSY 17	There is no understanding between the learner and the instructor
25.	2.14	INS 50	The instructor does not reveal in learner's progress
			Significant
26.	2.13	PSY 19	Unwilling to get educated
27.	2.13	FAM 36	Unable to go to the centre because of heavy work
28.	2.13	COM 62	The time of the centre is inconvenient
29.	2.12	PSY 27	Learners calling by nicknames
30.	2.12	FAM 31	Other family members refuse permission to attend during nights
31.	2.12	INS 48	Instruction is limited only to literacy
32.	2.11	FAM 34	The time of the centre is the supper time
33.	2.11	INS 43	The instructor is negligent
34.	2.11	COM 58	There is no encouragement from the village elders
35.	2.11	PER 68	Due to ill-health
36.	2.11	PER 77	The relevant lessons are not taught at the centre
37.	2.10	PSY 22	Feeling that others would mock
38.	2.10	INS 42	The instructor does not treat all the learners equally
39.	2.08	PRO 79	The centre is started at inconvenient place/having much sounds and bad smell
40.	2.07	INS 53	The absence of audio-visual aids useful for instruction
41.	2.06	FAM 33	Other family members do not co-operate in matters of education
42.	2.06	INS 55	The lessons are not according to the requirements and tastes

(Table Contd...)

1	2	3	4
43.	2.04	PSY 29	Feeling that studying at the centre is a waste
44.	2.03	PER 66	Becoming a slave to bad habits
45.	2.02	ECO 4	There is no immediate use by getting educated
46.	2.02	INS 54	Primer and follow-up books are not in order
47.	2.01	SOC 12	The instructor and the learner are not friendly
48.	2.00	PSY 24	Feeling why one should get educated when the age is so much
49.	2.00	PSY 28	The fellow learners do not listen to the thoughts and ideas
50.	2.00	PER 71	The other learners are much older
51.	1.99	SOC 10	Personal position is at stake in the society
52.	1.98	INS 45	The instruction is not relevant to the learners
53.	1.97	INS 39	The instructor is not well versed with this teaching
54.	1.96	ECO 1	No immediate financial benefit by education
55.	1.96	SOC 7	The instructor does not belong to my place
56.	1.95	INS 49	Providing too much information within a short time
57.	1.95	INS 51	The instructor uses difficult language, pictures and symbols
58.	1.91	INS 40	There is no teaching experience to the instructor
59.	1.91	SOC 14	Many of the learners belong to the upper caste
60.	1.89	SOC 11	Some co-learners have enmity in the centre
61.	1.89	COM 64	No one else visits the centre except the instructor
62.	1.88	PSY 21	Feeling shy to go to the centre
63.	1.87	PSY 30	Feeling that learning at home instead at the centre is better

(Table Contd...)

1	2	3	4
64.	1.87	INS 41	The instructor is unable to explain clearly
65.	1.87	COM 65	The time of the programme is short
66.	1.86	ECO 2	Busy with farm work
			Less Significant
67.	1.83	ECO 5	My family is economically backward
68.	1.83	SOC 15	There are some learners with bad behaviour in the centre
69.	1.81	SOC 13	There are some fights in the village
70.	1.80	INS 37	The centre is not well maintained
71.	1.80	PER 74	The other learners also are average in learning
72.	1.77	INS 57	The instructional methods used by the instructor are not liked
73.	1.75	PER 73	Getting discouraged after working hard for sometime to get educated and feeling that this attempt is useless
74.	1.74	SOC 9	The instructor utilises the learners for his personal work
75.	1.74	PER 67	Getting newly married
76.	1.72	INS 38	The instructor is not punctual to the centre
77.	1.69	PER 69	Quarreling with other learners
78.	1.69	FAM 32	Looking after the children
79.	1.64	PSY 25	Feeling that education is only for wealthy people
80.	1.69	ECO 3	Owners and landlords do not permit for attending the centres

ECO: Economic Problems area
INS: Instructor related Problems area
SOC: Social Problems area
COM: Community related Problems area
PSY: Psychological Problems area
PER: Personal Problems area
FAM: Familial Problems area
PRO: Programme related Problems

There are 26 very significant problems (Rank Order 1-26), 39 significant problems (Rank Order 27-65) and 15 less significant problems (Rank Order 66-80).

The problem area-wise distribution of very significant, significant and less significant problems is summarized and presented in Table 4.28. By looking at the problems area in the Table 4.27, the exact problem may be located.

Table 4.28: Distribution of Very Significant, Significant and Less Significant Problems as Problems area-wise indicated by 20 years and below age group drop-outs

Problem Areas	*Very Significant*	*Significant*	*Less Significant*	*Total*
Economic Problems (ECO)	1	3	2	6
Social Problems (SOC)	2	5	3	10
Psychological Problems (PSY)	5	7	2	14
Familial Problems (FAM)	1	4	1	6
Instructor related Problems (INS)	6	12	3	21
Community related Problems (COM)	5	2	1	8
Personal Problems (PER)	4	5	3	12
Programme related Problems (PRO)	2	1	-	3
Total	**26**	**39**	**15**	**80**

Problems of 21-35 years Age Group Drop-outs

The very significant, significant and less significant problems of 21-35 years age group drop-outs are presented in Table 4.29.

Table 4.29: Showing the Very Significant, Significant and Less Significant Problems in the case of 21-35 years Age Group Drop-outs

Rank Order	*Mean Difficulty*	*Problem Area and Sl. No. in the Rating Scale*	*Problem*
1	2	3	4
			Very Significant
1.	2.43	PER 66	Becoming a slave to bad habits
2.	2.41	PER 69	Quarrelling with other learners
3.	2.40	INS 56	The books are difficult to learn
4.	2.33	PSY 23	Easily getting tired
5.	2.30	INS 46	The instructor lacks good voice and fluency
6.	2.28	PSY 22	Feeling that others would mock

(Table Contd...)

1	2	3	4
7.	2.25	COM 65	The time of the programme is short
8.	2.24	FAM 31	Other family members refuse permission to attend during nights
9.	2.23	INS 55	The lessons are not according to the requirements and tastes
10.	2.21	INS 57	The instructional methods used by the instructor are not liked
11.	2.21	PSY 21	Feeling shy to go to the centre
12.	2.20	INS 50	The instructor does not reveal in learner's progress
13.	2.20	SOC 11	Some co-learners have enmity in the centre
14.	2.20	PSY 29	Feeling that studying at the centre is a waste
15.	2.18	COM 59	Friends do not go to the centre
16.	2.16	PER 77	The relevant lessons are not taught at the centre
17.	2.16	PSY 19	Unwilling to get educated
18.	2.15	PRO 78	Minimum amenities are not found at the centre (air/ventilation)
19.	2.15	FAM 35	There are none else at home
20.	2.15	COM 58	There is no encouragement from the village elders
21.	2.10	PRO 80	The centre is at a distance
			Significant
22.	2.10	PSY 18	The learner is not able to answer to the instructor
23.	2.09	PSY 20	Feeling that the age to study has passed
24.	2.08	INS 49	Providing too much information within a short time
25.	2.C3	PSY 24	Feeling why one should get educated when the age is so much
26.	2.08	INS 45	The instruction is not relevant to the learners
27.	2.08	INS 47	The instructor fails to enthuse the learners to participate
28.	2.08	COM 64	No one else visits the centre except the instructor

(Table Contd...)

1	2	3	4
29.	2.08	PER 75	The instructor is male
30.	2.07	INS 54	Primer and follow-up books are not in order
31.	2.07	COM 62	The time of the centre is inconvenient
32.	2.05	COM 60	I am not permitted to go with my friends
33.	2.04	PER 74	The other learners are also average in learning
34.	2.04	PER 68	Due to ill-health
35.	2.03	INS 48	Instruction is limited only to literacy
36.	2.03	PSY 26	Feeling shy during conversation with other
37.	2.02	SOC 10	Personal position is at stake in the society
38.	2.01	FAM 34	The time of the centre is the supper time
39.	2.00	ECO 2	Busy with farm work
40.	2.00	SOC 12	The instructor and the learner are not friendly
41.	2.00	FAM 36	Unable to go to the centre because of heavy work
42.	2.00	INS 38	The instructor is not punctual to the centre
43.	2.00	INS 51	The instructor uses difficult language, pictures and symbols
44.	2.00	INS 52	Teaching aids are not available at the right time
45.	2.00	PER 72	The other learners are mocking because of my backwardness in learning
46.	1.99	ECO 5	My family is economically backward
47.	1.98	SOC 8	The instructor does not belong to my caste
48.	1.98	INS 41	The instructor is unable to explain clearly
49.	1.95	ECO 1	No immediate financial benefit by education
50.	1.95	PSY 30	Feeling that learning at home instead of at the centre is better
51.	1.95	INS 43	The instructor is negligent

(Table Contd...)

1	2	3	4
52.	1.94	PSY 27	Learners calling by nicknames
53.	1.94	PRO 79	The centre is started at inconvenient place/having much sounds and bad smell
54.	1.92	SCO 16	Attending functions and going to movies
55.	1.92	ECO 4	There is no immediate use by getting educated
56.	1.90	PSY 428	The fellow learners do not listen to the thoughts and ideas
57.	1.90	INS 40	There is no teaching experience to the instructor
58.	1.89	FAM 32	Looking after the children
59.	1.89	SOC 15	There are some learners with bad behaviour in the centre
60.	1.89	PSY 25	Feeling that education is only for wealthy people
61.	1.89	INS 39	The instructor is not well versed with his teaching
62.	1.89	PER 71	The other learners are much older
63.	1.87	PER 70	Getting the marriage age
64.	1.87	SOC 14	Many learners belong to the upper caste
65.	1.86	PER 76	Lack of knowledge about this programme
66.	1.89	SOC 9	The instructor utilises the learners for his personal work
67.	1.86	INS 42	The instructor does not treat all the learners equally
			Less Significant
68.	1.83	COM 61	Good friends are not available at the centre
69.	1.82	COM 63	Co-educational centre
70.	1.82	SOC 7	The instructor does not belong to my place
71.	1.81	INS 37	The centre is not well maintained
72.	1.80	PSY 17	There is no understanding between the learner and the instructor
73.	1.77	INS 44	The instructor does not accept criticism with open heart

(Table Contd...)

1	2	3	4
74.	1.75	INS 53	The absence of audio-visual aids useful for instruction
75.	1.75	FAM 33	Other family members do not co-operate in matters of education
76.	1.73	PER 73	Getting discouraged after working hard for sometime to get educated and feeling that this attempt is useless
77.	1.70	ECO 3	Owners and landlords do not permit for attending centres
78.	1.69	SOC 13	There are some fights in the village
79.	1.60	PER 67	Getting newly married
80.	1.54	ECO 6	There are no specific working hours in different professions

ECO: Economic Problems area *INS:* Instructor related Problems area
SOC: Social Problems area *COM:* Community related Problems area
PSY: Psychological Problems area *PER:* Personal Problems area
FAM: Familial Problems area *PRO:* Programme related Problems

There are 21 very significant problems (Rank Order 1-21), 46 significant problems (Rank Order 22-67) and 13 less significant problems (Rank Order 68-80).

The problem area-wise distribution of very significant, significant and less significant problems is summarized and presented in the Table 4.30. By looking at the problems area in the Table 4.29, the exact problem may be located.

Table 4.30: Distribution of Very Significant, Significant and Less Significant Problems as Problems area-wise indicated by 21-35 years age group drop-outs

Problem Areas	*Very Significant*	*Significant*	*Less Significant*	*Total*
1	2	3	4	5
Economic Problems (ECO)	-	4	2	6
Social Problems (SOC)	1	7	2	10
Psychological Problems (PSY)	5	8	1	14
Familial Problems (FAM)	2	3	1	6

(Table Contd...)

1	2	3	4	5
Instructor related Problems (INS)	5	13	3	21
Community related Problems (COM)	3	3	2	8
Personal Problems (PER)	3	7	2	12
Programme related Problems (PRO)	2	1	-	3
Total	**21**	**48**	**13**	**80**

Problems of 36 years Age Group Drop-outs

The very significant, significant and less significant problems of 36 years and above age group drop-outs are presented in the Table 4.31.

Table 4.31: Showing the Very Significant, Significant and Less Significant Problems in the case of 36 and above Age Group Drop-outs

Rank Order	*Mean Difficulty*	*Problem Area and Sl. No. in the Rating Scale*	*Problem*
1	2	3	4
			Very Significant
1.	2.62	PSY 18	The learner is not able to answer to the instructor
2.	2.57	INS 84	Instruction is limited only to literacy
3.	2.53	PSY 28	The fellow learners do not listen to the thoughts and ideas
4.	2.53	PSY 23	Easily getting tired
5.	2.52	PSY 20	Feeling that the age to study has passed
6.	2.52	PSY 17	There is no understanding between the learner and the instructor
7.	2.42	FAM 34	The time of the centre is the supper time.
8.	2.41	SOC 16	Attending functions and going to movies
9.	2.41	FAM 36	Unable to go to the centre because of heavy work

(Table Contd...)

1	2	3	4
10.	2.40	ECO 2	Busy with farm work
11.	2.40	ECO 6	There are no specific working hours in different professions
12.	2.38	SOC 10	Personal position is at stake in the society
13.	2.37	PRO 79	The centre is started at inconvenient place/having much sounds and bad smell
14.	2.34	PSY 9	The instructor utilises the learners for his personal work
15.	2.34	PER 68	Quarrelling with other learners
16.	2.33	INS 53	The absence of audio-visual aids useful for instruction
17.	2.33	FAM 31	Other family members refuse permission to attend during nights
18.	2.33	PER 71	The other learners are much older
19.	2.32	PER 76	Lack of knowledge about this programme
20.	2.32	INS 42	The instructor does not treat all the learners equally
21.	2.32	COM 64	No one else visits the centre except the instructor
22.	2.29	PER 74	The other learners also are average in learning
23.	2.29	FAM 35	There are none else at home
24.	2.29	PRO 80	The centre is at a distance
25.	2.28	COM 63	Co-educational centre
26.	2.28	SOC 14	Many learners belong to upper caste
27.	2.28	COM 62	The time of the centre is inconvenient
28.	2.25	SOC 12	The instructor and the learner are not friendly
29.	2.25	PSY 22	Feeling that others would mock
30.	2.25	PSY 29	Feeling that studying at the centre is a waste
31.	2.24	INS 52	Teaching aids are not available at the right time
32.	2.22	FAM 32	Looking after the children
33.	2.22	PSY 30	Feeling that learning at home instead of at the centre is better

(Table Contd...)

1	2	3	4
34.	2.22	INS 51	The instructor uses difficult language, pictures and symbols
35.	2.18	PSY 25	Feeling that education is only for wealthy people
36.	2.18	INS 47	The instructor fails to enthuse the learners to participate
37.	2.17	SOC 8	The instructor does not belong to my caste
38.	2.16	INS 56	The books are difficult to learn
39.	2.14	ECO 4	There is no immediate use by getting educated
			Significant
40.	2.13	PER 67	Getting newly married
41.	2.13	INS 38	The instructor is not punctual to the centre
42.	2.13	INS 41	The instructor is unable to explain clearly
43.	2.13	PER 66	Becoming a slave to bad habits
44.	2.12	ECO 1	No immediate financial benefit by education
45.	2.12	PRO 78	Minimum amenities are not found at the centre (air/ventilation)
46.	2.10	INS 44	The instructor does not accept criticism with open heart
47.	2.10	INS 46	The instructor lacks good voice and fluency
48.	2.10	INS 50	The instructor does not reveal in learner's progress
49.	2.10	INS 55	The lessons are not according to the requirements and tastes
50.	2.09	SOC 7	The instructor does not belong to my place
51.	2.09	PER 75	The instructor is male
52.	2.08	COM 60	I am not permitted to go with my friends
53.	2.08	INS 43	The instructor is negligent
54.	2.06	SOC 9	The instructor utilises the learners for his personal work

(Table Contd...)

1	2	3	4
55.	2.06	INS 39	The instructor is not well versed with his teaching
56.	2.06	INS 40	There is no teaching experience to the instructor
57.	2.06	INS 49	Providing too much information within a short time
58.	2.05	PSY 27	Learners calling by nicknames
59.	2.04	FAM 33	Other family members do not co-operate in matters of education
60.	2.02	INS 57	The instructional methods used by the instructor are not liked
61.	2.02	PER 70	Getting the marriage age
62.	2.02	PSY 21	Feeling shy to go to the centre
63.	2.02	COM 65	The time of the programme is short
64.	2.01	PER 72	The other learners are mocking because of my backwardness in learning
65.	2.00	ECO 5	My family is economically backward
66.	2.00	INS 45	The instruction is not relevant to the learners
67.	1.97	COM 61	Good friends are not available at the centre
68.	1.97	INS 37	The centre is not well maintained
69.	1.94	COM 58	There is no encouragement from the village elders
70.	1.93	PER 77	The relevant lessons are not taught at the centre
71.	1.92	INS 54	Primer and follow-up books are not in order
72.	1.92	COM 59	Friends do not go to the centre
73.	1.90	SOC 11	Some co-learners have enmity in the centre
74.	1.88	PSY 24	Feeling why one should get educated when the age is so much
75.	1.86	ECO 3	Owners and landlords do not permit for attending centres
76.	1.86	PSY 26	Feeling shy during conversation with others
77.	1.86	PER 69	Quarrelling with other learners

(Table Contd...)

1	2	3	4
			Less Significant
78.	1.82	SOC 15	There are some learners with bad behaviour in the centre
79.	1.81	PER 73	Getting discouraged after working hard for sometime to get educated and feeling that this attempt is useless
80.	1.71	SOC 13	There are some fights in the village

ECO: Economic Problems area
SOC: Social Problems area
PSY: Psychological Problems area
FAM: Familial Problems area
INS: Instructor related Problems area
COM: Community related Problems area
PER: Personal Problems area
PRO: Programme related Problems

There are 39 very significant problems (Rank Order 1-39), 38 significant problems (Rank Order 40-77) and 3 less significant problems (Rank Order 78-80).

The problem area wise distribution of very significant, significant and less significant problems is summarized and presented in Table 4.32. By looking at the problems area in the Table 4.31, the exact problem may be located.

Table 4.32: Showing the Very Significant, Significant and Less Significant Problems as Problems area-wise indicated by 36 years and above age group dropouts

Problem Areas	*Very Significant*	*Significant*	*Less Significant*	*Total*
Economic Problems (ECO)	3	3	-	6
Social Problems (SOC)	5	3	2	10
Psychological Problems (PSY)	10	4	-	14
Familial Problems (FAM)	5	1	-	6
Instructor related Problems (INS)	7	14	-	21
Community related Problems (COM)	3	5	-	8
Personal Problems (PER)	4	7	1	12
Programme related Problems (PRO)	2	1	-	3
Total	**39**	**38**	**3**	**80**

Problems of SC/ST Caste Group Drop-outs

The very significant, significant and less significant problems SC/ST caste group drop-outs are presented in the Table 4.33.

Table 4.33: Showing the Very Significant, Significant and Less Significant Problems in the case of SC/ST Caste Group Drop-outs

Rank Order	*Mean Difficulty*	*Problem Area and Sl. No. in the Rating Scale*	*Problem*
1	*2*	*3*	*4*
			Very Significant
1.	2.40	PSY 23	Easily getting tired
2.	2.36	PRO 80	The centre is at a distance
3.	2.30	ECO 6	There are no specific working hours in different professions
4.	2.28	PSY 20	Feeling that the age to study has passed
5.	2.26	PSY 22	Feeling that others would mock
6.	2.25	INS 42	The instructor does not treat all the learners equally
7.	2.24	COM 60	I am not permitted to go with my friends
8.	2.22	COM 63	Co-educational centre
9.	2.22	PER 72	The other learners are mocking because of my backwardness in learning
10.	2.20	INS 48	Instruction is limited only to literacy
11.	2.20	PER 75	The instructor is male
12.	2.19	COM 62	The time of the centre is inconvenient
13.	2.18	SOC 10	Personal position is at stake in the society
14.	2.18	FAM 31	Other family members refuse permission to attend during nights
15.	2.18	INS 51	The instructor uses difficult language, pictures and symbols
16.	2.17	PSY 17	There is no understanding between the learner and the instructor
17.	2.16	FAM 35	There are none else at home
18.	2.16	INS 56	The books are difficult to learn

(Table Contd...)

1	2	3	4
19.	2.15	PER 77	The relevant lessons are not taught at the centre
20.	2.14	PER 70	Getting the marriage age
21.	2.14	SOC 8	The instructor does not belong to my caste
22.	2.14	PSY 29	Feeling that studying at the centre is a waste
23.	2.14	INS 47	The instructor fails to enthuse the learners to participate
			Significant
24.	2.12	PSY 18	Unwilling to get educated
25.	2.12	INS 46	The instructor lacks good voice and fluency
26.	2.12	COM 59	Friends do not go to the centre
27.	2.11	PSY 18	The learner is not able to answer to the instructor
28.	2.11	INS 55	The lessons are not according to the requirements and tastes
29.	2.10	INS 50	The instructor does not reveal in learner's progress
30.	2.10	INS 52	Teaching aids are not available at the right time
31.	2.07	ECO 4	There is no immediate use by getting educated
32.	2.07	FAM 36	Unable to go to the centre because of heavy work
33.	2.05	INS 54	Primer and follow-up books are not in order
34.	2.05	COM 58	There is no encouragement from the village elders
35.	2.04	PSY 27	Learners calling by nicknames
36.	2.03	ECO 2	Busy with farm work
37.	2.03	SOC 16	Attending functions and going to movies
38.	2.03	INS 49	Providing too much information within a short time
39.	2.02	FAM 34	The time of the centre is the supper time
40.	2.02	PER 76	Lack of knowledge about this programme
41.	2.01	SOC 7	The instructor does not belong to my place

(Table Contd...)

1	*2*	*3*	*4*
42.	2.00	ECO 1	No immediate financial benefit by education
43.	2.00	SOC 12	The instructor and the learners are not friendly
44.	2.00	SOC 14	Many learners belong to the upper caste
45.	1.98	PSY 21	Feeling shy to go to the centre
46.	1.98	PSY 24	Feeling why one should get educated when the age is so much
47.	1.98	PSY 25	Feeling that education is only for wealthy people
48.	1.98	PSY 28	The fellow learners do not listen to the thoughts and ideas
49.	1.98	COM 61	Good friends are not available at the centre
50.	1.97	INS 45	The instruction is not relevant to the learners
51.	1.95	ECO 5	My family is economically backward
52.	1.94	PSY 26	Feeling shy during conversation with others
53.	1.94	INS 43	The instructor is negligent
54.	1.94	PRO 79	The centre is started at inconvenient place/having much sounds and bad smell
55.	1.92	PRO 78	Minimum amenities are not found at the centre (air/ventilation)
56.	1.91	FAM 33	Other family members do not co-operate in matters of education
57.	1.91	PER 71	The other learners are much older
58.	1.91	COM 64	No one else visits the centre except the instructor
59.	1.90	INS 41	The instructor is unable to explain clearly
60.	1.89	INS 44	The instructor does not accept criticism with open heart
61.	1.89	COM 65	The time of the programme is short
62.	1.89	PER 74	The other learners also are average in learning
63.	1.86	PER 68	Due to ill-health
64.	1.86	INS 53	The absence of audio-visual aids useful for instruction

(Table Contd...)

1	2	3	4
65.	1.85	PER 69	Quarrelling with other learners
66.	1.82	PER 66	Becoming a slave to bad habits
67.	1.81	SOC 9	The instructor utilises the learners for his personal work
68.	1.80	INS 39	The instructor is not well versed with his teaching
69.	1.79	PSY 30	Feeling that learning at home instead of at the centre is better
70.	1.78	INS 38	The instructor is not punctual to the centre
71.	1.78	PER 73	Getting discouraged after working hard for sometime to get educated and feeling that this attempt is useless
72.	1.76	ECO 3	Owners and landlords do not permit for attending centres
73.	1.75	INS 40	There is no teaching experience to the instructor
74.	1.72	SOC 15	There are some learners with bad behaviour in the centre
75.	1.71	INS 57	The instructional methods used by the instructor are not liked
76.	1.70	INS 37	The centre is not well maintained
77.	1.66	FAM 32	Looking after the children
78.	1.65	PER 67	Getting newly married
79.	1.63	SOC 11	Some co-learners have enmity in the centre
80.	1.59	SOC 13	There are some fights in the village

ECO: Economic Problems area *INS:* Instructor related Problems area
SOC: Social Problems area *COM:* Community related Problems area
PSY: Psychological Problems area *PER:* Personal Problems area
FAM: Familial Problems area *PRO:* Programme related Problems

There are 23 very significant problems (Rank Order 1-23), 42 significant problems (Rank Order 24-65) and 15 less significant problems (Rank Order 66-80).

The problem area-wise distribution of very significant, significant and less significant problems is summarized and presented in Table 4.34. By looking at the problems area in the Table 4.33, the exact problem may be located.

Table 4.34: Showing the Very Significant, Significant and Less Significant Problems as Problems area-wise indicated by SC/ST Caste Group Drop-outs

Problem Areas	*Very Significant*	*Significant*	*Less Significant*	*Total*
Economic Problems (ECO)	1	4	1	6
Social Problems (SOC)	2	4	4	10
Psychological Problems (PSY)	5	8	1	14
Familial Problems (FAM)	2	3	1	6
Instructor related Problems (INS)	5	11	5	21
Community related Problems (COM)	3	5	-	8
Personal Problems (PER)	4	5	3	12
Programme related Problems (PRO)	1	2	-	3
Total	**23**	**42**	**15**	**80**

Problems of BC Caste Group Dropouts

The very significant, significant and less significant problems of BC caste group dro-outs are presented in Table 4.35.

Table 4.35: Showing the Very Significant, Significant and Less Significant Problems in the case of BC Caste Group Drop-outs

Rank Order	*Mean Difficulty*	*Problem Area and Sl. No. in the Rating Scale*	*Problem*
1	*2*	*3*	*4*
			Very Significant
1.	2.43	PER 69	Due to ill-health
2.	2.43	INS 56	The books are difficult to learn
3.	2.43	INS 39	The instructor is not well versed with his teaching
4.	2.43	PSY 18	The learner is not able to answer to the instructor
5.	2.41	PSY 28	The fellow learners do not listen to the thoughts and ideas

(Table Contd...)

1	2	3	4
6.	2.40	INS 46	The instructor lacks good voice and fluency
7.	2.37	PRO 78	Minimum amenities are not found at the centre (air/ventilation)
8.	2.35	SOC 8	The instructor does not belong to my caste
9.	2.34	PSY 19	Unwilling to get educated
10.	2.33	INS 52	Teaching aids are not available at the right time
11.	2.32	PER 71	The other learners are much older
12.	2.32	PSY 23	Easily getting tired
13.	2.32	COM 60	I am not permitted to go with my friends
14.	2.29	FAM 32	Looking after the children
15.	2.29	FAM 34	The time of the centre is the supper time
16.	2.29	PER 66	Becoming a slave to bad habits
17.	2.28	FAM 31	Other family members refuse permission to attend during nights
18.	2.26	COM 59	Friends do not go to the centre
19.	2.25	PER 76	Lack of knowledge about this programme
20.	2.23	SOC 15	There are some learners with bad behaviour in the centre
21.	2.23	PER 75	The instructor is male
22.	2.22	SOC 12	The instructor and the learners are not friends
23.	2.22	INS 45	The instruction is not relevant to the learners
24.	2.20	COM 58	There is no encouragement from the village elders
25.	2.19	SOC 11	Some co-learners have enmity in the centre
26.	2.19	COM 62	The time of the centre is inconvenient
27.	2.17	ECO 6	There are no specific working hours in different professions
28.	2.14	SOC 10	Personal position is at stake in the society
29.	2.14	PSY 26	Feeling shy during conversation with others
30.	2.14	COM 61	Good friends are not available at the centre

(Table Contd...)

1	2	3	4
			Significant
31.	2.12	PSY 29	Feeling that the age to study has passed
32.	2.12	PRO 79	The centre is started at inconvenient place/having much sounds and bad smell
33.	2.12	PRO 80	The centre is at a distance
34.	2.11	FAM 33	Other family members do not co-operate in matters of education
35.	2.11	INS 53	The absence of audio-visual aids useful for instruction
36.	2.10	INS 57	The instructional methods used by the instructor are not liked
37.	2.10	COM 64	No one else visits the centre except the instructor
38.	2.09	SOC 7	The instructor does not belong to my place
39.	2.07	SOC 16	Attending functions and going to movies
40.	2.07	FAM 36	Unable to go to the centre because of heavy work
41.	2.07	INS 37	The center is not well maintained
42.	2.07	INS 43	The instructor is negligent
43.	2.07	INS 47	The instructor fails to enthuse the learners to participate
44.	2.06	PSY 21	Feeling shy to go to the centre
45.	2.06	INS 40	There is no teaching experience to the instructor
46.	2.05	PSY 24	Feeling why one should get educated when the age is so much
47.	2.05	INS 50	The instructor does not reveal in learner's progress
48.	2.05	INS 55	The lessons are not according to the requirements and tastes
49.	2.05	PER 70	Getting the marriage age
50.	2.05	PER 72	The other learners are mocking because of my backwardness in learning
51.	2.03	ECO 2	Busy with farm work
52.	2.02	FAM 35	There are none else at home
53.	2.02	COM 65	The time of the programme is short
54.	2.01	INS 51	The instructor uses difficult language, pictures and symbols

(Table Contd...)

1	2	3	4
55.	2.00	INS 49	Providing too much information within a short time
56.	2.00	PER 77	The relevant lessons are not taught at the centre
57.	1.99	INS 41	The instructor is unable to explain clearly
58.	1.98	PSY 25	Feeling that education is only for wealthy people
59.	1.98	PSY 27	Learners calling by nicknames
60.	1.98	PSY 29	Feeling that studying at the centre is a waste
61.	1.98	PER 67	Getting newly married
62.	1.97	SOC 14	Many learners belong to the upper caste
63.	1.97	PER 74	The other learners also are average in learning
64.	1.96	ECO 1	No immediate financial benefit by education
65.	1.95	PSY 22	Feeling that others would mock
66.	1.94	INS 38	The instructor is not punctual to the centre
67.	1.94	INS 48	Instruction is limited only to literacy
68.	1.92	COM 63	Co-educational centre
69.	1.91	ECO 4	There is no immediate use by getting educated
70.	1.91	INS 42	The instructor does not treat all the learners equally
71.	1.90	SOC 9	The instructor utilises the learners for his personal work
72.	1.90	PSY 30	Feeling that learning at home instead of at the centre is better
73.	1.88	INS 44	The instructor does not accept criticism with open heart
			Less Significant
74.	1.82	ECO 5	My family is economically backward
75.	1.82	PER 73	Getting discouraged after working hard for sometime to get educated and feeling that this attempt is useless
76.	1.81	ECO 3	Owners and landlords do not permit for attending centre

(Table Contd...)

1	2	3	4
77.	1.80	INS 54	Primer and follow-up books are not in order
78.	1.76	PSY 17	There is no understanding between the learner and the instructor
79.	1.56	SOC 13	There are some fights in the village
80.	1.55	PER 69	Quarrelling with other learners

ECO: Economic Problems area
SOC: Social Problems area
PSY: Psychological Problems area
FAM: Familial Problems area
INS: Instructor related Problems area
COM: Community related Problems area
PER: Personal Problems area
PRO: Programme related Problems

There are 30 very significant problems (Rank Order 1-30), 43 significant problems (Rank Order 31-73) and 7 less significant problems (Rank Order 74-80).

The problem area-wise distribution of very significant, significant and less significant problems is summarized and presented in Table 4.36. By looking at the problems, area in Table 4.35, the exact problem may be located.

Table 4.36: Showing the Very Significant, Significant and Less Significant Problems as Problems area-wise indicated by BC Caste Group Drop-outs

Problem Areas	*Very Significant*	*Significant*	*Less Significant*	*Total*
Economic Problems (ECO)	1	3	2	6
Social Problems (SOC)	5	4	1	10
Psychological Problems (PSY)	5	8	1	14
Familial Problems (FAM)	5	3	-	6
Instructor related Problems (INS)	5	15	1	21
Community related Problems (COM)	5	3	-	8
Personal Problems (PER)	5	5	2	12
Programme related Problems (PRO)	1	2	-	3
Total	**30**	**43**	**7**	**80**

Problems of Other Caste Group Drop-outs

The very significant, significant and less significant problems of other caste group drop-outs are presented in Table 4.37.

Table 4.37: Showing the Very Significant, Significant and Less Significant Problems in the case of Other Caste Group Drop-outs

Rank Order	*Mean Difficulty*	*Problem Area and Sl. No. in the Rating Scale*	*Problem*
1	2	3	4
			Very Significant
1.	2.43	FAM 35	There are none else at home
2.	2.43	INS 47	The instructor fails to enthuse the learners to participate
3.	2.41	INS 46	The instructor lacks good voice and fluency
4.	2.37	PSY 22	Feeling that others would mock
5.	2.35	PSY 29	Feeling that studying at the centre is a waste
6.	2.35	INS 50	The instructor does not reveal in learner's progress
7.	2.34	PSY 30	Feeling that learning at home instead of at the centre is better
8.	2.32	PSY 23	Easily getting tired
9.	2.32	INS 48	Instruction is limited only to literacy
10.	2.29	SOC 16	Attending functions and going to movies
11.	2.25	PRO 78	Minimum amenities are not found at the centre (air/ventilation)
12.	2.25	PSY 18	The learner is not able to answer to the instructor
13.	2.25	PRO 80	The centre is at a distance
14.	2.24	FAM 36	Unable to go to the centre because of heavy work
15.	2.21	INS 55	The lessons are not according to the requirements or tastes

(Table Contd...)

1	2	3	4
16.	2.21	COM 64	No one else visits the centre except the instructor
17.	2.21	PRO 79	The centre is started at inconvenient place/having much sounds and bad smell
18.	2.20	PSY 17	There is no understanding between the learners and the instructor
19.	2.19	PSY 20	Feeling that the age to study has passed
20.	2.19	INS 57	The instructional methods used by the instructor are not liked
21.	2.18	PSY 19	Unwilling to get educated
22.	2.18	FAM 31	Other family members refuse permission to attend during nights
23.	2.17	ECO 6	There are no specific working hours in different professions
24.	2.15	INS 54	Primer and follow-up books are not in order
25.	2.15	PER 74	The other learners also are average in learning
26.	2.14	SOC 11	Some co-learners have enmity in the centre
27.	2.14	PER 76	Lack of knowledge about this programme
			Significant
28.	2.11	PSY 21	Feeling shy to go to the centre
29.	2.11	INS 56	The books are difficult to learn
30.	2.11	COM 59	Friends do not go to the centre
31.	2.10	INS 44	The instructor does not accept criticism with open heart
32.	2.10	PER 66	Becoming a slave to bad habits
33.	2.08	PER 77	The relevant lessons are not taught at the centre
34.	2.08	ECO 4	There is no immediate use by getting educated
35.	2.08	FAM 34	The time of the centre is the supper time
36.	2.08	INS 38	The instructor is not punctual to the centre
37.	2.07	PER 68	Due to ill-health
38.	2.07	PSY 24	Feeling why one should get educated when the age is so much
39.	2.07	INS 49	Providing too much information within a short time

(Table Contd...)

1	2	3	4
40.	2.07	COM 67	Getting newly married
41.	2.06	INS 41	The instructor is unable to explain clearly
42.	2.05	ECO 2	Busy with farm work
43.	2.05	INS 52	Teaching aids are not available at the right time
44.	2.05	COM 61	Good friends are not available at the centre
45.	2.04	INS 53	The absence of audio-visual aids useful for instruction
46.	2.03	ECO 1	No immediate financial benefit by education
47.	2.03	PSY 26	Feeling shy during conversation with others
48.	2.03	INS 43	The instructor is negligent
49.	2.02	PER 72	The other learners are mocking because of my backwardness in learning
50.	2.01	INS 40	There is no teaching experience to the instructor
51.	2.01	COM 63	Co-educational centre
52.	2.00	INS 45	The instruction is not relevant to the learners
53.	2.00	COM 60	I am not permitted to go with my friends
54.	1.98	SOC 13	There are some fights in the village
55.	1.98	COM 58	There is no encouragement from the village elders
56.	1.97	PER 69	Quarrelling with other learners
57.	1.96	PER 75	The instructor is male
58.	1.95	PSY 27	Learners calling by nicknames
59.	1.94	SOC 10	Personal position is at stake in the society
60.	1.91	ECO 5	My family is economically backward
61.	1.91	COM 65	The time of the programme is short
62.	1.90	PSY 28	The fellow learners do not listen to the thoughts and ideas
63.	1.89	PER 70	Getting the marriage age
64.	1.86	SOC 12	The instructor and the learners are not friendly
65.	1.86	INS 42	The instructor does not treat all the learners equally

(Table Contd...)

1	*2*	*3*	*4*
66.	1.86	PER 51	The instructors use difficult language, pictures and symbols
67.	1.85	PER 14	Many learners belong to the upper caste
68.	1.84	PER 71	The other learners are much older
			Less Significant
69.	1.82	PER 9	The instructor utilises the learners for his personal work
70.	1.82	PER 37	The centre is not well maintained
71.	1.75	PER 32	Looking after the children
72.	1.74	PER 7	The instructor does not belong to my place
73.	1.74	PER 8	The instructor does not belong to my caste
74.	1.74	PER 73	Getting discouraged after working hard for sometime to get educated and feeling that this attempt is useless
75.	1.71	PER 33	Other family members do not co-operate in matters of education
76.	1.70	PER 67	Getting newly married
77.	1.69	PER 39	The instructor is not well versed with this teaching
78.	1.67	PRO 25	Feeling that education is only for wealthy people
79.	1.64	PRO 15	There are some learners with bad behaviour in the centre
80.	1.57	PRO 3	Owners and landlords do not permit for attending centres

ECO: Economic Problems area
INS: Instructor related Problems area
SOC: Social Problems area
COM: Community related Problems area
PSY: Psychological Problems area
PER: Personal Problems area
FAM: Familial Problems area
PRO: Programme related Problems

There are 27 very significant problems (Rank Order 1-27), 41 significant problems (Rank Order 28-68) and 12 less significant problems (Rank Order 69-80).

The problem area-wise distribution of very significant, significant and less significant problems is summarized and presented in Table 4.38. By looking at the problems, area in the Table 4.37, the exact problem may be located.

Table 4.38: Showing the Very Significant, Significant and Less Significant Problems as Problems area-wise indicated by OC Caste Group Drop-outs

Problem Areas	*Very Significant*	*Significant*	*Less Significant*	*Total*
Economic Problems (ECO)	1	4	1	6
Social Problems (SOC)	2	4	4	10
Psychological Problems (PSY)	8	5	1	14
Familial Problems (FAM)	3	1	2	6
Instructor related Problems (INS)	7	12	2	21
Community related Problems (COM)	1	7	-	8
Personal Problems (PER)	2	8	2	12
Programme related Problems (PRO)	3	-	-	3
Total	**27**	**43**	**7**	**80**

Problems of Agriculture Group Drop-outs

The very significant, significant and less significant problems of other caste group drop-outs are presented in the Table 4.39.

Table 4.39: Showing the Very Significant, Significant and Less Significant Problems in the case of Agriculture Group Drop-outs

Rank Order	*Mean Difficulty*	*Problem Area and Sl. No. in the Rating Scale*	*Problem*
1	*2*	*3*	*4*
			Very Significant
1.	2.42	INS 46	The instructor lacks good vice and fluency
2.	2.42	PSY 23	Easily getting tired
3.	2.40	PSY 18	The instructor fails to enthuse the learners to participate
4.	2.32	INS 47	The instructor fails to enthuse the learners to participate
5.	2.29	FAM 35	There are none else at home

(Table Contd...)

1	*2*	*3*	*4*
6.	2.25	PSY 19	Unwilling to get educated
7.	2.24	PSY 29	Feeling that studying at the centre is a waste
8.	2.23	PRO 80	The centre is at a distance
9.	2.22	COM 2	Good friends are not available at the centre
10.	2.22	SOC 16	Attending functions and going to movies
11.	2.20	PER 68	Due to ill-health
12.	2.20	FAM 36	Unable to go to the centre because of heavy work
13.	2.18	PER 76	Lack of knowledge abut this programme
14.	2.18	INS 50	The instructor does not reveal in learner's progress
15.	2.18	FAM 31	Other family members refuse permission to attend during nights
16.	2.17	COM 60	I am not permitted to go with my friends
17.	2.17	PSY 28	The fellow learners do not listen to the thoughts and ideas
18.	2.16	PRO 78	Minimum amenities are not found at the centre (air/ventilation)
19.	2.16	ECO 6	There are no specific working hours in different professions
			Significant
20.	2.12	INS 49	Providing too much information within a short time
21.	2.11	PSY 24	Feeling why one should get educated when the age is so much
22.	2.10	INS 55	The lessons are not according to the requirements and tastes
23.	2.10	ECO 4	There is no immediate use by getting educated
24.	2.09	INS 54	Primer and follow up books are not in order
25.	2.08	PRO 79	The centre is started at inconvenient place/having much sounds and bad smell
26.	2.08	PER 72	The other learners are mocking because of my backwardness in learning
27.	2.08	COM 64	No one else visits the centre except the instructor

(Table Contd...)

1	2	3	4
28.	2.08	INS 56	The books are difficult to learn
29.	2.08	PSY 22	Feeling that others would mock
30.	2.08	PSY 21	Feeling shy to go to the centre
31.	2.07	PSY 20	Feeling that the age to study has passed
32.	2.06	PER 71	The other learners are much older
33.	2.06	COM 63	Co-educational centre
34.	2.06	SOC 10	Personal position is at stake in the society
35.	2.05	ECO 2	Busy with farm work
36.	2.04	COM 62	The time of the centre is inconvenient
37.	2.04	COM 58	There is no encouragement from the village elders
38.	2.04	INS 38	The instructor is not punctual to the centre
39.	2.04	SOC 11	Some co-learners have enmity in the centre
40.	2.04	INS 52	Teaching aids are not available at the right time
41.	2.03	PSY 26	Feeling shy during conversation with other
42.	2.03	PSY 17	There is no understanding between the learners and the instructor
43.	2.02	PSY 30	Feeling that learning at home instead of at the centre is better
44.	2.01	PER 75	The instructor is male
45.	2.00	PER 74	The other learners also are average in learning
46.	2.00	INS 48	Instruction is limited only to literacy
47.	2.00	INS 40	There is no teaching experience to the instructor
48.	2.00	FAM 32	Looking after the children
49.	1.99	INS 44	The instructor does not accept criticism with open heart
50.	1.98	INS 42	The instructor does not treat all the learners equally
51.	1.98	SOC 8	The instructor does not belong to my caste
52.	1.97	COM 59	Friends do not go to the centre
53.	1.97	INS 53	The absence of audio-visual aids useful for instruction
54.	1.97	FAM 34	The time of the centre is the supper time

(Table Contd...)

1	2	3	4
55.	1.97	PSY 27	Learners calling by nicknames
56.	1.96	PER 77	The relevant lessons are not taught at the centre
57.	1.95	COM 65	The time of the programme is short
58.	1.95	SOC 9	The instructor utilises the learners for his personal work
59.	1.93	INS 57	The instructional methods specified by the government are not liked
60.	1.92	INS 39	The instructor is not well-versed with his teaching
61.	1.91	ECO 1	No immediate financial benefit by education
62.	1.90	INS 51	The instructor uses difficult language, pictures and symbols
63.	1.89	INS 43	The instructor is negligent
64.	1.88	PER 70	Getting the marriage age
65.	1.88	INS 41	The instructor is unable to explain clearly
66.	1.85	SOC 14	Many learners belong to the upper caste
67.	1.85	SOC 7	The instructor does not belong to my place
			Less Significant
68.	1.83	SOC 15	There are some learners with bad behaviour in the centre
69.	1.82	PER 66	Becoming a slave to bad habits
70.	1.80	INS 37	The centre is not well maintained
71.	1.78	SOC 12	The instructor and the learner are not friendly
72.	1.77	INS 45	The instructor is not relevant to the learners
73.	1.75	ECO 5	My family is economically backward
74.	1.75	PSY 25	Feeling that education is only for wealthy people
75.	1.74	SOC 3	There are some fights in the village
76.	1.73	FAM 33	Other family members do not co-operate in matters of education
77.	1.65	PER 73	Getting discouraged after working hard for sometime to get educated and feeling that this attempt is useless

(Table Contd...)

1	2	3	4
78.	1.63	PER 69	Quarrelling with other learners
79.	1.53	ECO 3	Owners and landlords do not permit for attending centre
80.	1.53	PER 67	Getting newly married

ECO: Economic Problems area
SOC: Social Problems area
PSY: Psychological Problems area
FAM: Familial Problems area
INS: Instructor related Problems area
COM: Community related Problems area
PER: Personal Problems area
PRO: Programme related Problems

There are 19 very significant problems (Rank Order 1-19), 48 significant problems (Rank Order 20-67) and 13 less significant problems (Rank Order 68-80).

The problem area-wise distribution of very significant, significant and less significant problems is summarized and presented in Table 4.40. By looking at the problems-area in the Table 4.39, the exact problem may be located.

Table 4.40: Showing the Very Significant, Significant and Less Significant Problems as Problems area-wise indicated by Agriculture Group Drop-outs

Problem Areas	*Very Significant*	*Significant*	*Less Significant*	*Total*
Economic Problems (ECO)	1	3	2	6
Social Problems (SOC)	1	6	3	10
Psychological Problems (PSY)	5	8	1	14
Familial Problems (FAM)	3	2	1	6
Instructor related Problems (INS)	3	16	2	21
Community related Problems (COM)	2	6	-	8
Personal Problems (PER)	2	6	4	12
Programme related Problems (PRO)	2	1	-	3
Total	**19**	**48**	**13**	**80**

Problems of Labour Group Drop-outs

The very significant, significant and less significant problems of other caste group drop-outs are presented in Table 3.41.

Table 4.41: Showing the Very Significant, Significant and Less Significant Problems in the case of Labour Group Drop-outs

Rank Order	*Mean Difficulty*	*Problem Area and Sl. No. in the Rating Scale*	*Problem*
1	2	3	4
			Very Significant
1.	2.43	PSY 30	Feeling that learning at home instead of at the centre is better
2.	2.43	PRO 80	The centre is at a distance
3.	2.42	INS 56	The books are difficult to learn
4.	2.41	PSY 20	Feeling that the age to study has passed
5.	2.36	PER 75	The instructor is male
6.	2.31	COM 60	I am not permitted to go with my friends
7.	2.27	ECO 6	There are no specific working hours in different professions
8.	2.24	INS 52	Teaching aids are not available at the right time
9.	2.24	INS 48	Instruction is limited only to literacy
10.	2.23	PER 70	Getting the marriage age
11.	2.20	PSY 19	Unwilling to get educated
12.	2.19	COM 62	The time of the centre is inconvenient
13.	2.17	FAM 35	There are none else at home
14.	2.16	FAM 34	The time of the centre is the supper time
15.	2.16	FAM 33	Other family members do not co-operate in matters of education
16.	2.16	PSY 22	Feeling that others would mock
17.	2.16	ECO 1	No immediate financial benefit by education
18.	2.15	INS 46	The instructor lacks good voice and fluency
19.	2.15	PSY 23	Easily getting tired

(Table Contd...)

1	*2*	*3*	*4*
20.	2.14	PER 77	The relevant lessons are taught at the centre
			Significant
21.	2.13	COM 59	Friends do not go to the centre
22.	2.13	SOC 10	Personal position is at stake in the society
23.	2.12	INS 41	The instructor is unable to explain clearly
24.	2.11	INS 51	The instructor uses difficult languages, pictures and symbols
25.	2.11	PSY 28	The fellow learners do not listen to the thoughts and ideas
26.	2.11	ECO 5	My family is economically backward
27.	2.10	INS 50	The instructor does not reveal in learner's progress
28.	2.10	ECO 2	Busy with farm work
29.	2.08	INS 53	The absence of audio-visual aids useful for instruction
30.	2.08	INS 45	The instruction is not relevant to the learners
31.	2.08	FAM 36	Unable to go to the centre because of heavy work
32.	2.07	INS 49	Providing too much information within a short time
33.	2.05	PER 76	Lack of knowledge about this programme
34.	2.05	COM 58	There is no-encouragement from the village elders
35.	2.05	INS 57	The instructional methods used by the instructor are not liked
36.	2.05	FAM 31	Other family members refuse permission to attend during nights
37.	2.05	SOC 12	The instructor and the learners are not friends
38.	2.04	PER 72	The other learners are mocking because of my backwardness in learning
39.	2.04	INS 55	The lessons are not according to the requirements and tastes

(Table Contd...)

1	2	3	4
40.	2.02	PER 66	Becoming a slave to bad habits
41.	2.02	PSY 29	Feeling that studying at the centre is waste
42.	2.02	PSY 17	There is no understanding between the learner and the instructor
43.	2.02	ECO 4	There is no immediate use by getting educated
44.	2.01	COM 63	Co-educational centre
45.	2.00	INS 54	Primer and follow-up books are not in order
46.	2.00	PSY 18	The learner is not able to answer to the instructor
47.	1.99	PRO 79	The centre is started at inconvenient place/having much sounds and bad smell
48.	1.99	PRO 47	The instructor fails to enthuse the learners to participate
49.	1.99	INS 42	The instructor does not treat all the learners equally
50.	1.97	PRO 78	Minimum amenities are not found at the centre (air/ventilation)
51.	1.95	PER 73	Getting discouraged after working hard for sometime to get educated and feeling that this attempt is useless
52.	1.95	SOC 14	Many learners belong to the upper caste
53.	1.94	PER 68	Due to ill-health
54.	1.93	INS 43	The instructor is negligent
55.	1.91	PSY 27	Easily getting tired
56.	1.91	PSY 21	Feeling shy to go to the centre
57.	1.90	PSY 24	Feeling why one should get educated when the age is so much
58.	1.89	COM 64	No one else visits the centre except the instructor
59.	1.89	INS 40	There is no teaching experience to the instructor
60.	1.89	SOC 7	The instructor does not belong to my place

(Table Contd...)

1	2	3	4
61.	1.88	PSY 26	Feeling shy during conversation with others
62.	1.87	COM 65	The time of the programme is short
63.	1.86	SOC 16	Attending functions and going to movies
64.	1.84	INS 37	The centre is not well maintained
65.	1.83	INS 44	The instructor does not accept criticism with open heart
			Less Significant
66.	1.82	PER 71	The other learners are much older
67.	1.82	COM 61	Good friends are not available at the centre
68.	1.80	INS 39	The instructor is not well versed with his teaching
69.	1.77	PSY 25	Feeling that education is only for wealthy people
70.	1.75	PER 67	Getting newly married
71.	1.74	PER 74	The other learners also are average in learning
72.	1.73	ECO 3	Owners and landlords do not permit for attending centres
73.	1.72	SOC 15	There are some learners with bad behaviour in the centre
74.	1.71	PER 69	Quarrelling with other learners
75.	1.71	FAM 32	Looking after the children
76.	1.63	SOC 13	There are some fights in the village
77.	1.63	SOC 11	Some co-learners have enmity in the centre
78.	1.57	INS 38	The instructor is not punctual to the centre
79.	1.57	SOC 9	The instructor utilises the learners for his personal work
80.	1.54	SOC 8	The instructor does not belong to my caste

ECO: Economic Problems area
SOC: Social Problems area
PSY: Psychological Problems area
FAM: Familial Problems area
INS: Instructor related Problems area
COM: Community related Problems area
PER: Personal Problems area
PRO: Programme related Problems

There are 20 very significant problems (Rank Order 1-20), 44 significant problems (Rank Order 21-64) and 4 less significant problems (Rank Order 65-80).

The problem area-wise distribution of very significant, significant and less significant problems is summarized and presented in Table 4.42. By looking at the problems-area in the Table 4.41, the exact problem may be located.

Table 4.42: Showing the Very Significant, Significant and Less Significant Problems as Problems area-wise indicated by Labour Group Drop-outs

Problem Areas	*Very Significant*	*Significant*	*Less Significant*	*Total*
Economic Problems (ECO)	2	3	1	6
Social Problems (SOC)	-	5	5	10
Psychological Problems (PSY)	5	8	1	14
Familial Problems (FAM)	3	2	1	6
Instructor related Problems (INS)	4	14	3	21
Community related Problems (COM)	2	5	1	8
Personal Problems (PER)	3	5	4	12
Programme related Problems (PRO)	1	2	-	3
Total	**20**	**44**	**16**	**80**

Problems of Other Group Drop-outs

The very significant, significant and less significant problems of other group drop-outs are presented in the Table 4.43.

Table 4.43: Showing the Very Significant, Significant and Less Significant Problems in the case of Other Group Drop-outs

Rank Order	*Mean Difficulty*	*Problem Area and Sl. No. in the Rating Scale*	*Problem*
1	2	3	4
			Very Significant
1.	2.43	INS 53	The absence of audio-visual aids useful for instruction
2.	2.43	COM 59	Friends do not go to the centre
3.	2.43	INS 45	The instruction is not relevant to the learners
4.	2.43	PSY 23	Easily getting tired
5.	2.42	PER 66	Becoming a slave to bad habits
6.	2.42	PSY 22	Feeling that others would mock
7.	2.42	SOC 12	The instructor and the learners are not friendly
8.	2.42	FAM 31	Other family members refuse permission to attend during nights
9.	2.41	SOC 8	The instructor does not belong to my caste
10.	2.40	FAM 34	The time of the centre is the supper time
11.	2.39	PRO 78	Minimum amenities are not found at the centre
12.	2.39	PSY 25	Feeling that education is only for wealthy people
13.	2.36	INS 48	Instruction is limited only to literacy
14.	2.36	INS 43	The instructor is negligent
15.	2.35	PER 74	The other learners also are average in learning
16.	2.35	COM 62	The time of the centre is inconvenient
17.	2.33	PER 77	The relevant lesson are not taught at the centre
18.	2.33	INS 56	The books are difficult to learn
19.	2.32	SOC 16	Attending functions and going to movies
20.	2.30	PER 72	The other learners are mocking because of my backwardness in learning

(Table Contd...)

1	2	3	4
21.	2.30	PSY 18	The learner is not able to answer to the instructor
22.	2.29	INS 55	The lessons are not according to the requirements or tastes
23.	2.29	INS 47	The instructor fails to enthuse the learners to participate
24.	2.29	SOC 7	The instructor does not belong to my place
25.	2.29	ECO 6	There are no specific working hours in different professions
26.	2.27	INS 52	Teaching aids are not available at the right time
27.	2.27	INS 39	The instructor is not well versed with his teaching
28.	2.27	FAM 35	There are none else at home
29.	2.27	COM 64	No one else visits the centre except the instructor
30.	2.25	INS 42	The instructor does not treat all the learners equally
31.	2.23	PER 69	Quarrelling with other learners
32.	2.23	PER 68	Due to ill-health
33.	2.23	INS 51	The instructor uses difficult language, pictures and symbols
34.	2.22	PSY 26	Feeling shy during conversation with others
35.	2.22	SOC 11	Some co-learners have enmity in the centre
36.	2.20	PER 71	The other learners are much older
37.	2.20	COM 63	Co-educational centre
38.	2.20	COM 58	There is no encouragement from the village elders
39.	2.20	INS 46	The instructor lacks good voice and fluency
40.	2.20	PSY 30	Feeling that learning at home instead of at the centre is better
41.	2.19	INS 50	The instructor does not reveal in learner's progress
42.	2.19	PSY 29	Feeling that studying at the centre is a waste
43.	2.19	PSY 27	Learners calling by nicknames
44.	2.19	PSY 20	Feelings that the age to study has passed
45.	2.17	PRO 79	The centre is started at inconvenient place having much sounds and bad smell

(Table Contd...)

1	*2*	*3*	*4*
46.	2.17	INS 38	The instructor is not punctual to the centre
47.	2.17	PSY 17	There is no understanding between the learner and the instructor
48.	2.15	SOC 14	Many learners belong to the upper caste
49.	2.15	SOC 10	Personal position is at stake in the society
			Significant
50.	2.13	PER 70	Getting the marriage age
51.	2.10	PER 76	Lack of knowledge about this programme
52.	2.09	PSY 19	Unwilling to get educated
53.	2.09	PER 67	Getting newly married
54.	2.07	PSY 21	Feeling shy to go to the centre
55.	2.07	SOC 15	There are some learners with bad behaviour in the centre
56.	2.05	PER 75	The instructor is male
57.	2.05	COM 60	I am not permitted to go with my friends
58.	2.05	PSY 24	Feeling why one should get educated when the age is so much
59.	2.04	INS 57	The instructional methods used by the instructor are not liked
60.	2.04	INS 44	The instructor does not accept criticism with open heart
61.	2.03	SOC 9	The instructor utilises the learners for his personal work
62.	2.02	COM 61	Good friends are not available at the centre
63.	2.00	COM 65	The time of the programme is short
64.	2.00	FAM 36	Unable to go to the centre because of heavy work
65.	1.97	PRO 80	The centre is at a distance
66.	1.96	ECO 3	Owners and landlords do not permit for attending centres
67.	1.95	INS 37	The centre is not well maintained
68.	1.92	INS 41	The instructor is unable to explain clearly
69.	1.92	ECO 1	No immediate financial benefit by education
70.	1.90	ECO 2	Busy with farm work
71.	1.89	FAM 33	Other family members do not co-operate in matters of education

(Table Contd...)

1	2	3	4
72.	1.89	ECO 4	There is no immediate use by getting educated
73.	1.88	PSY 28	The fellow learners do not listen to the thoughts and ideas
74.	1.86	FAM 32	Looking after the children
75.	1.86	ECO 5	My family is economically backward
76.	1.84	INS 54	Primer and follow-up books are not in order
			Less Significant
77.	1.79	PER 73	Getting discouraged after working hard for sometime to get educated and feeling that this attempt is useless
78.	1.79	INS 49	Providing too much information within a short time
79.	1.79	INS 40	There is no teaching experience to the instructor
80.	1.70	SOC 13	There are some fights in the village

ECO: Economic Problems area
INS: Instructor related Problems area
SOC: Social Problems area
COM: Community related Problems area
PSY: Psychological Problems area
PER: Personal Problems area
FAM: Familial Problems area
PRO: Programme related Problems

There are 49 very significant problems (Rank Order 1-49), 27 significant problems (Rank Order 50-76) and 4 less significant problems (Rank Order 77-80).

The problem area-wise distribution of very significant, significant and less significant problems is summarized and presented in Table 4.44. By looking at the problems-area in the Table 4.43, the exact problem may be located.

Table 4.44: Showing the Very Significant, Significant and Less Significant Problems as Problems area-wise indicated by Other Group Drop-outs

Problem Areas	*Very Significant*	*Significant*	*Less Significant*	*Total*
1	2	3	4	5
Economic Problems (ECO)	1	5	-	6

(Table Contd...)

1	2	3	4	5
Social Problems (SOC)	7	2	1	10
Psychological Problems (PSY)	10	4	-	14
Familial Problems (FAM)	3	3	-	6
Instructor related Problems (INS)	14	5	2	21
Community related Problems (COM)	5	3	-	8
Personal Problems (PER)	7	4	1	12
Programme related Problems (PRO)	2	1	-	3
Total	**49**	**27**	**4**	**80**

Problems of Rs. 20,000 and below Annual Income Group Drop-outs

The very significant, significant and less significant problems of Rs.20,000 and below annual income group dropouts are presented in Table 4.45.

Table 4.45: Showing the Very Significant, Significant and Less Significant Problems in the case of Rs. 20,000 and below Income Group Drop-outs

Rank Order	*Mean Difficulty*	*Problem Area and Sl. No. in the Rating Scale*	*Problem*
1	2	3	4
			Very Significant
1.	2.43	FAM 36	Unable to go to the centre because of heavy work
2.	2.42	PRO 80	The centre is at a distance
3.	2.41	PSY 23	Easily getting tired
4.	2.39	INS 56	The books are difficult to learn
5.	2.35	PER 76	Lack of knowledge about this programme
6.	2.31	PSY 20	Feeling that the age to study has passed
7.	2.30	INS 48	Instruction is limited only to literacy
8.	2.30	INS 52	Teaching aids are not available at the right time

(Table Contd...)

1	2	3	4
9.	2.29	COM 62	The time of the centre is inconvenient
10.	2.28	PSY 19	Unwilling to get educated
11.	2.27	PSY 18	The learner is not able to answer to the instructor
12.	2.27	FAM 35	There are none else at home
13.	2.27	COM 60	I am not permitted to go with my friends
14.	2.26	INS 53	The absence of audio-visual aids useful for instruction
15.	2.26	COM 58	There is no encouragement from the village elders
16.	2.26	INS 47	The instructor fails to enthuse the learners to participate
17.	2.23	INS 46	The instructor lacks good voice and fluency
18.	2.20	SOC 12	The instructor and the learners are not friendly
19.	2.19	ECO 6	There are no specific working hours in different professions
20.	2.19	COM 63	Co-educational centre
21.	2.15	PSY 29	Feeling that studying at the centre is waste
22.	2.15	PER 66	Becoming a slave to bad habits
23.	2.14	SOC 8	The instructor does not belong to my caste
24.	2.14	PSY 28	The fellow learners do not listen to the thoughts and ideas
25.	2.14	COM 59	Friends do not go to the centre
			Significant
26.	2.12	PSY 22	Feeling that others would mock
27.	2.12	PSY 24	Feeling why one should get educated when the age is so much
28.	2.12	FAM 34	The time of the centre is the supper time
29.	2.12	INS 50	The instructor does not reveal in learner's progress
30.	2.12	PER 75	The instructor is male
31.	2.12	PRO 79	The centre is started at inconvenient place/having much sounds and bad smell

(Table Contd...)

1	2	3	4
32.	2.11	ECO 2	Busy with farm work
33.	2.11	ECO 4	There is no immediate use by getting educated
34.	2.11	SOC 10	Personal position is at stake in the society
35.	2.11	FAM 31	Other family members refuse permission to attend during nights
36.	2.10	INS 55	The lessons are not according to the requirements and tastes
37.	2.09	SOC 14	Many learners belong to the upper caste
38.	2.08	PER 71	The other learners are much older
39.	2.07	PSY 26	Feeling shy during conversation with other
40.	2.07	INS 54	Primer and follow-up books are not in order
41.	2.07	PER 70	Getting the marriage age
42.	2.06	PRO 78	Minimum amenities are not found at the centre (air/ventilation)
43.	2.05	PSY 21	Feeling shy to go to the centre
44.	2.04	INS 42	The instructor does not treat all the learners equally
45.	2.03	PSY 27	Learners calling by nicknames
46.	2.03	INS 43	The instructor is negligent
47.	2.03	PER 72	The other learners are mocking because of my backwardness in learning
48.	2.02	INS 40	There is no teaching experience to the instructor
49.	2.02	INS 45	The instruction is not relevant to the learners
50.	2.02	COM 61	Good friends are not available at the centre
51.	2.02	PER 77	The relevant lessons are not taught at the centre
52.	2.01	PSY 17	There is no understanding between the learner and the instructor
53.	2.01	INS 49	Providing too much information within a short time
54.	1.99	INS 39	The instructor is not well versed with his teaching

(Table Contd...)

1	2	3	4
55.	1.98	ECO 5	My family is economically backward
56.	1.98	SOC 16	Attending functions and going to movies
57.	1.98	PSY 30	Feeling that learning at home instead of at the centre is better
58.	1.97	SOC 7	The instructor does not belong to my place
59.	1.95	PER 68	Due to ill-health
60.	1.92	SOC 9	The instructor utilises the learners for his personal work
61.	1.92	INS 44	The instructor does not accept criticism with open heart
62.	1.91	INS 51	The instructor uses difficult language, pictures and symbols
63.	1.90	ECO 1	No immediate financial benefit by education
64.	1.90	COM 64	No one else visits the centre except the instructor
65.	1.89	ECO 3	Owners and landlords do not permit for attending centres
66.	1.88	SOC 15	There are some learners with bad behaviour in the centre
67.	1.87	FAM 33	Other family members do not co-operate in matters of education
68.	1.86	PSY 25	Feeling that education is only for wealthy people
69.	1.86	PER 74	The other learners also are average in learning
70.	1.84	INS 41	The instructor is unable to explain clearly
			Less Significant
71.	1.82	INS 37	The centre is not well maintained
72.	1.80	COM 65	The time of the programme is short
73.	1.76	INS 57	The instructional methods used by the instructor are not liked
74.	1.76	INS 38	The instructor is not punctual to the centre
75.	1.75	SOC 11	Some co-learners have enmity in the centre

(Table Contd...)

1	2	3	4
76.	1.73	PER 73	Getting discouraged after working hard for sometime to get educated and feeling that this attempt is useless
77.	1.71	FAM 32	Looking after the children
78.	1.70	SOC 13	There are some fights in the village
79.	1.62	PER 67	Getting newly married
80.	1.60	PER 69	Quarrelling with other learners

ECO: Economic Problems area
SOC: Social Problems area
PSY: Psychological Problems area
FAM: Familial Problems area
INS: Instructor related Problems area
COM: Community related Problems area
PER: Personal Problems area
PRO: Programme related Problems

There are 25 very significant problems (Rank Order 1-25), 45 significant problems (Rank Order 26-70) and 10 less significant problems (Rank Order 71-80).

The problem area-wise distribution of very significant, significant and less significant problems is summarized and presented in Table 4.46. By looking at the problems' area in the Table 4.44, the exact problem may be located.

Table 4.46: Showing the Very Significant, Significant and Less Significant Problems as Problems area-wise indicated by Rs. 20,000 and below Income Group Drop-outs

Problem Areas	*Very Significant*	*Significant*	*Less Significant*	*Total*
Economic Problems (ECO)	1	5	-	6
Social Problems (SOC)	2	6	2	10
Psychological Problems (PSY)	6	8	-	14
Familial Problems (FAM)	2	3	1	6
Instructor related Problems (INS)	5	12	3	21
Community related Problems (COM)	2	2	1	8
Personal Problems (PER)	-	7	3	12
Programme related Problems (PRO)	1	2	-	3
Total	**25**	**45**	**10**	**80**

Problems of Rs. 21-30 thousands Annual Income Group Drop-outs

The very significant, significant and less significant problems of Rs. 21-30 thousand annual income group drop-outs are presented in Table 4.47.

Table 4.47: Showing the Very Significant, Significant and Less Significant Problems in the case of Rs. 21-30 thousands Income Group Dropouts

Rank Order	*Mean Difficulty*	*Problem Area and Sl. No. in the Rating Scale*	*Problem*
1	2	3	4
			Very Significant
1.	2.40	PER 68	Due to ill-health
2.	2.34	INS 46	The instructor lacks good voice and fluency
3.	2.32	INS 51	The instructor uses difficult languages, pictures and symbols
4.	2.32	ECO 6	There are no specific working hours in different professions
5.	2.27	PSY 22	Feeling that others would mock
6.	2.26	PSY 18	The learner is not able to answer to the instructor
7.	2.26	INS 50	The instructor does not reveal in learner's progress
8.	2.26	COM 59	Friends do not go to the centre
9.	2.25	COM 60	I am not permitted to go with my friends
10.	2.24	PSY 19	Unwilling to get educated
11.	2.21	FAM 36	Unable to go to the centre because of heavy work
12.	2.20	INS 56	The books are difficult to learn
13.	2.19	FAM 31	Other family members refuse permission to attend during night
14.	2.18	PRO 78	Minimum amenities are not found at the centre (air/ventilation)

(Table Contd...)

1	2	3	4
15.	2.18	PSY 23	Easily getting tired
16.	2.17	COM 64	No one else visits the centre except the instructor
17.	2.17	PSY 21	Feeling shy to go to the centre
18.	2.17	INS 45	The instruction is not relevant to the learners
19.	2.16	INS 47	The instructor fails to enthuse the learners to participate
20.	2.15	COM 61	Good friends are not available at the centre
21.	2.14	INS 55	The lessons are not according to the requirements and tastes
22.	2.14	SOC 16	Attending functions and going to movies
23.	2.14	FAM 35	There are none else at home
24.	2.14	PER 77	The relevant lessons are not taught at the centre
			Significant
25.	2.13	SOC 11	Some co-learners have enmity in the centre
26.	2.13	INS 42	The instructor does not treat all the learners equally
27.	2.13	INS 48	Instruction is limited only to literacy
28.	2.12	PER 74	The other learners also are average in learning
29.	2.11	FAM 32	Looking after the children
30.	2.11	SOC 10	Personal position is at stake in the society
31.	2.11	PSY 20	Feeling that the age to study has passed
32.	2.10	INS 57	The instructional methods used by the instructor are not liked
33.	2.10	FAM 34	The time of the centre is the supper time
34.	2.09	FAM 62	The time of the centre is inconvenient
35.	2.09	PER 72	The other learners are mocking because of my backwardness in learning
36.	2.08	PSY 17	There is no understanding between the learner and the instructor
37.	2.06	SOC 7	The instructor does not belong to my place

(Table Contd...)

1	2	3	4
38.	2.06	INS 41	The instructor is unable to explain clearly
39.	2.06	COM 63	Co-educational centre
40.	2.06	PER 75	The instructor is male
41.	2.05	PSY 28	The fellow learners do not listen to the thoughts and ideas
42.	2.05	INS 49	Providing too much information within a short time
43.	2.05	PER 70	Getting the marriage age
44.	2.05	PER 71	The other learners are much older
45.	2.04	PRO 80	The centre is at a distance
46.	2.04	FAM 33	Other family members do not co-operate in matters of education
47.	2.04	INS 44	The instructor does not accept criticism with open heart
48.	2.04	INS 54	Primer and follow up books are not in order
49.	2.03	SOC 8	The instructor does not belong to my caste
50.	2.02	PRO 79	The centre is started at inconvenient place/having much sounds and bad smell
51.	2.00	PSY 29	Feeling that studying at the centre is a waste
52.	2.00	PSY 24	Feeling why one should get educated when the age is so much
53.	1.99	ECO 1	No immediate financial benefit by education
54.	1.98	INS 52	Teaching aids are not available at the centre
55.	1.96	INS 38	The instructor is not punctual to the centre
56.	1.95	PSY 27	Learners calling by nicknames
57.	1.94	PER 76	Lack of knowledge about this programme
58.	1.94	INS 39	The instructor is not well versed with his teaching
59.	1.94	COM 65	The time of the programme is short

(Table Contd...)

1	2	3	4
60.	1.92	ECO 2	Busy with farm work
61.	1.91	ECO 4	There is no immediate use by getting educated
62.	1.91	PSY 26	Feeling shy during conversation with others
63.	1.91	PSY 30	Feeling that learning at home instead of at the centre is better
64.	1.91	INS 43	The instructor is negligent
65.	1.91	PER 67	Getting newly married
66.	1.91	PER 73	Getting discouraged after working hard for sometime to get educated and feeling that this attempt is useless
67.	1.90	SOC 15	There are some learners with bad behaviour in the centre
68.	1.90	PER 69	Quarrelling with other learners
69.	1.86	ECO 5	My family is economically backward
70.	1.86	SOC 12	The instructor and the learners are not friendly
71.	1.86	INS 40	There is no teaching experience to the instructor
72.	1.84	COM 58	There is no encouragement from the village elders
73.	1.84	SOC 14	Many learners belong to the upper caste
			Less Significant
74.	1.82	SOC 9	The instructor utilises the learners for his personal work
75.	1.82	INS 37	The centre is not well maintained
76.	1.81	PSY 25	Feeling that education is only for wealthy people
77.	1.81	PER 66	Becoming a slave to bad habits
78.	1.76	INS 53	The absence of audio-visual aids useful for instruction
79.	1.63	SOC 13	There are some fights in the village
80.	1.59	ECO 3	Owners and landlords do not permit for attending the centres

ECO: Economic Problems area
INS: Instructor related Problems area
SOC: Social Problems area
COM: Community related Problems area
PSY: Psychological Problems area
PER: Personal Problems area
FAM: Familial Problems area
PRO: Programme related Problems

There are 24 very significant problems (Rank Order 1-24), 49 significant problems (Rank Order 25-73) and 7 less significant problems (Rank Order 74-80).

The problem area-wise distribution of very significant, significant and less significant problems is summarized and presented in Table 4.48. By looking at the problems area in the Table 4.47, the exact problem may be located.

Table 4.48: Distribution of Very Significant, Significant and Less Significant Problems as Problems area-wise indicated by Rs. 21-30 thousands Income Group Drop-outs

Problem Areas	*Very Significant*	*Significant*	*Less Significant*	*Total*
Economic Problems (ECO)	1	4	1	6
Social Problems (SOC)	1	7	2	10
Psychological Problems (PSY)	5	8	1	14
Familial Problems (FAM)	3	3	-	6
Instructor related Problems (INS)	7	12	2	21
Community related Problems (COM)	4	4	-	8
Personal Problems (PER)	2	9	1	12
Programme related Problems (PRO)	1	2	-	3
Total	**24**	**49**	**7**	**80**

Problems of Rs. 31 thousand and above Annual Income Group Drop-outs

The very significant, significant and less significant problems of Rs. 31 thousand and above annual income group drop-outs are presented in Table 4.49.

Table 4.49: Showing the Very Significant, Significant and Less Significant Problems in the case of Rs. 31 thousands and above Income Group Drop-outs

Rank Order	*Mean Difficulty*	*Problem Area and Sl. No. in the Rating Scale*	*Problem*
1	2	3	4
			Very Significant
1.	2.43	PSY 23	Easily getting tired
2.	2.43	FAM 31	Other family members refuse permission to attend during nights
3.	2.43	PSY 29	Feeling that studying at the centre is waste
4.	2.42	SOC 16	Attending functions and going to movies
5.	2.42	INS 57	The instructional methods used by the instructor are not liked
6.	2.40	FAM 35	There are none else at home
7.	2.40	PER 72	The other learners are mocking because of my backwardness in learning
8.	2.36	PER 75	The instructor is male
9.	2.31	INS 36	Unable to go to the centre because of heavy work
10.	2.30	COM 65	The time of the programme is short
11.	2.28	ECO 1	No immediate financial benefit by education
12.	2.28	PSY 22	Feeling that others would mock
13.	2.28	COM 64	No one else visits the centre except the instructor
14.	2.27	PRO 78	Minimum amenities are not found at the centre (air/ventilation)
15.	2.24	SOC 8	The instructor does not belong to my caste
16.	2.22	INS 38	The instructor is not punctual to the centre
17.	2.22	PER 77	The relevant lessons are not taught at the centre
18.	2.21	PER 66	Becoming a slave to bad habits
19.	2.16	INS 41	The instructor is unable to explain clearly
20.	2.15	PSY 17	There is no understanding between the learner and the instructor

(Table Contd...)

1	2	3	4
21.	2.15	PSY 18	The learner is not able to answer to the instructor
22.	2.15	PSY 25	Feeling that education is only for wealthy people
23.	2.15	INS 43	The instructor is negligent
			Significant
24.	2.13	PSY 26	Feeling shy during conversation with other
25.	2.13	FAM 34	The time of the centre is the supper time
26.	2.13	INS 55	The lessons are not according to the requirements and tastes
27.	2.12	ECO 6	There are no specific working hours in different professions
28.	2.12	PSY 20	Feeling that the age to study has passed
29.	2.12	PSY 30	Feeling that learning at home instead of at the centre is better
30.	2.12	INS 47	The instructor fails to enthuse the learners to participate
31.	2.10	SOC 13	There are some fights in the village
32.	2.10	INS 52	Teaching aids are not available at the right time
33.	2.07	ECO 2	Busy with farm work
34.	2.07	SOC 11	Some co-learners have enmity in the centre
35.	2.07	INS 49	Providing too much information within a short time
36.	2.07	PER 74	The other learners also are average in learning
37.	2.06	COM 58	There is no encouragement from the village elders
38.	2.06	PER 69	Quarrelling with other learners
39.	2.04	ECO 4	There is no immediate use by getting educated
40.	2.04	SOC 10	Personal position is at stake in the society
41.	2.03	PRO 79	The centre is started at inconvenient place/having much sounds and bad smell
42.	2.01	PER 68	Due to ill-health
43.	2.01	PSY 28	The fellow learners do not listen to the thoughts and ideas
44.	2.01	FAM 36	Unable to go to the centre because of heavy work

(Table Contd...)

1	2	3	4
45.	2.01	INS 50	The instructor does not reveal in learner's progress
46.	2.00	PSY 27	Learners calling by nicknames
47.	2.00	PER 70	Getting the marriage age
48.	1.98	COM 59	Friends do not go to the centre
49.	1.95	INS 37	The centre is not well maintained
50.	1.93	INS 56	The books are difficult to learn
51.	1.93	COM 62	The time of the centre is inconvenient
52.	1.90	SOC 12	The instructor and the learners are not friendly
53.	1.89	PSY 19	Unwilling to get educated
54.	1.87	PER 76	Lack of knowledge about this programme
55.	1.87	INS 39	The instructor is not well versed with the teaching
56.	1.86	INS 45	The instruction is not relevant to the learners
57.	1.86	COM 61	Good friends are not available at the centre
58.	1.84	INS 42	The instructor does not treat all the learners equally
59.	1.84	INS 44	The instructor does not accept criticism with open heart
60.	1.84	COM 60	I am not permitted to go with my friends
			Less Significant
61.	1.83	PSY 24	Feeling why one should get educated when the age is so much
62.	1.83	INS 48	Instruction is limited only to literacy
63.	1.83	PER 67	Getting newly married
64.	1.80	FAM 32	Looking after the children
65.	1.80	INS 51	The instructor uses difficult language, pictures and symbols
66.	1.80	PRO 80	The centre is at a distance
67.	1.78	INS 53	The absence of audio-visual aids useful for instruction
68.	1.78	SOC 14	Many learners belong to the upper caste
69.	1.77	ECO 5	My family is economically backward
70.	1.77	COM 63	Co-educational centre
71.	1.75	INS 40	There is no teaching experience to the instructor

(Table Contd...)

1	2	3	4
72.	1.74	INS 54	Primer and follow-up books are not in order
73.	1.72	PSY 21	Feeling shy to go to the centre
74.	1.71	FAM 33	Other family members do not co-operate in matters of education
75.	1.71	PER 71	The other learners are much older
76.	1.69	SOC 7	The instructor does not belong to my place
77.	1.63	SOC 9	The instructor utilises the learners for his personal work
78.	1.63	PER 73	Getting discouraged after working hard for sometime to get educated and feeling that this attempt is useless
79.	1.52	SOC 15	There are some learners with bad behaviour in the centre
80.	1.54	ECO 3	Owners and landlords do not permit for attending centres

ECO: Economic Problems area
INS: Instructor related Problems area
SOC: Social Problems area
COM: Community related Problems area
PSY: Psychological Problems area
PER: Personal Problems area
FAM: Familial Problems area
PRO: Programme related Problems

There are 23 very significant problems (Rank Order 1-23), 37 significant problems (Rank Order 24-60) and 20 less significant problems (Rank Order 61-80).

The problem area-wise distribution of very significant, significant and less significant problems is summarized and presented in Table 4.50. By looking at the problems-area in the Table 4.49, the exact problem may be located.

Table 4.50: Distribution of Very Significant, Significant and Less Significant Problems as Problems area-wise indicated by Rs. 31 thousands and above Income Group Drop-outs

Problem Areas	*Very Significant*	*Significant*	*Less Significant*	*Total*
1	2	3	4	5
Economic Problems (ECO)	1	3	2	6

(Table Contd...)

1	2	3	4	5
Social Problems (SOC)	2	4	4	10
Psychological Problems (PSY)	6	6	2	14
Familial Problems (FAM)	2	2	2	6
Instructor related Problems (INS)	5	11	5	21
Community related Problems (COM)	2	5	1	8
Personal Problems (PER)	4	5	3	12
Programme related Problems (PRO)	1	1	1	3
Total	23	37	20	80

Problems of Drop-outs with 1-2 months attendance in the Centre

The very significant, significant and less significant problems of dropouts with 1-2 months attendance in the centre are presented in Table 4.51.

Table 4.51: Showing the Very Significant, Significant and Less Significant Problems in the case of Drop-outs with 1-2 months Attendance in the Centre

Rank Order	*Mean Difficulty*	*Problem Area and Sl. No. in the Rating Scale*	*Problem*
1	2	3	4
			Very Significant
1.	2.43	PRO 80	The centre is at a distance
2.	2.41	INS 47	The instructor fails to enthuse the learners to participate
3.	2.37	PSY 23	Easily getting tired
4.	2.33	PSY 19	Unwilling to get educated
5.	2.32	ECO 6	There are no specific working hours in different professions
6.	2.31	PSY 20	Feeling that the age to study has passed
7.	2.30	INS 46	The instructor lacks good voice and fluency
8.	2.29	INS 56	The books are difficult to learn

(Table Contd...)

1	2	3	4
9.	2.28	COM 60	I am not permitted to go with my friends
10.	2.28	FAM 35	There are none else at home
11.	2.28	PSY 18	The learner is not able to answer to the instructor
12.	2.27	INS 55	The lessons are not according to the requirements and tastes
13.	2.26	INS 52	Teaching aids are not available at the right time
14.	2.23	INS 48	Instruction is limited only to literacy
15.	2.21	COM 63	Co-educational centre
16.	2.21	COM 61	Good friends are not available at the centre
17.	2.20	INS 54	Primer and follow-up books are not in order
18.	2.20	SOC 16	Attending functions and going to movies
19.	2.18	PRO 78	Minimum amenities are not found at the centre (air/ventilation)
20.	2.17	PRO 79	The centre is started at inconvenient place/having much sounds and bad smell
21.	2.16	FAM 34	The time of the centre is the supper time
22.	2.15	PSY 28	The fellow learners do not listen to the thoughts and ideas
23.	2.14	PER 75	The instructor is male
24.	2.14	COM 58	There is no encouragement from the village elders
25.	2.14	PSY 29	Feeling that studying at the centre is waste
26.	2.14	PSY 26	Feeling shy during conversation with others
			Significant
27.	2.12	PER 71	The other learners are much older
28.	2.12	COM 62	The time of the centre is inconvenient
29.	2.12	INS 50	The instructor does not reveal in learner's progress
30.	2.11	COM 36	Unable to go to the centre because of heavy work

(Table Contd...)

1	2	3	4
31.	2.11	PSY 22	Feeling that others would mock
32.	2.10	INS 39	The instructor is no well versed with his teaching
33.	2.09	PER 66	Becoming a slave to bad habits
34.	2.09	INS 45	The instruction is not relevant to the learners
35.	2.09	INS 42	The instructor does not treat all the learners equally
36.	2.09	FAM 31	Other family members refuse permission to attend during nights
37.	2.09	SOC 9	The instructor utilises the learners for his personal work
38.	2.09	INS 49	Providing too much information within a short time
39.	2.08	INS 43	The instructor is negligent
40.	2.08	PER 77	The relevant lessons are not taught at the centre
41.	2.07	PER 76	Lack of knowledge about this programme
42.	2.07	COM 59	Friends do not go to the centre
43.	2.06	PER 68	Due to ill-health
44.	2.05	PSY 27	Learners calling by nicknames
45.	2.05	SOC 10	Personal position is at stake in the society
46.	2.05	ECO 4	There is no immediate use by getting educated
47.	2.02	SOC 8	The instructor does not belong to my caste
48.	2.01	PER 70	Getting the marriage age
49.	2.00	PER 72	The other learners are mocking because of my backwardness in learning
50.	2.00	PSY 24	Feeling why one should get educated when the age is so much
51.	1.99	PSY 17	There is no understanding between the learner and the instructor
52.	1.99	ECO 1	No immediate financial benefit by education
53.	1.99	INS 53	The absence of audio-visual aids useful for instruction

(Table Contd...)

1	2	3	4
54.	1.98	ECO 5	My family is economically backward
55.		COM 64	No one else visits the centre except the instructor
56.	1.97	PSY 30	Feeling that learning at home instead of at the centre is better
57.	1.97	PSY 21	Feeling shy to go to the centre
58.	1.97	SOC 15	There are some learners with bad behaviour in the centre
59.	1.96	INS 57	The instructional methods used by the instructor are not liked
60.	1.96	SOC 12	The instructor and the learner are not friendly
61.	1.95	ECO 2	Busy with farm work
62.	1.94	INS 44	The instructor does not accept criticism with open heart
63.	1.92	INS 57	The instructional methods used by the instructor are not liked
64.	1.92	SOC 14	Many learners belong to the upper caste
65.	1.90	INS 41	The instructor is unable to explain clearly
66.	1.90	FAM 33	Other family members do not co-operate in matters of education
67.	1.90	PSY 25	Feeling that education is only for wealthy people
68.	1.90	SOC 11	Some co-learners have enmity in the centre
69.	1.89	INS 38	The instructor is not punctual to the centre
70.	1.89	FAM 32	Looking after the children
71.	1.89	SOC 7	The instructor does not belong to my place
72.	1.87	ECO 3	Owners and landlords do not permit for attending centres
73.	1.85	PER 74	The other learners also are average in learning
			Less Significant
74.	1.82	PER 69	Quarrelling with other learners
75.	1.81	PER 67	Getting newly married

(Table Contd...)

1	2	3	4
76.	1.76	COM 65	The time of the programme is short
77.	1.76	INS 40	There is no teaching experience to the instructor
78.	1.74	INS 37	The centre is not well maintained
79.	1.65	PER 73	Getting discouraged after working hard for sometime to get educated and feeling that this attempt is useless
80.	1.60	SOC 13	There are some fights in the village

ECO: Economic Problems area
INS: Instructor related Problems area
SOC: Social Problems area
COM: Community related Problems area
PSY: Psychological Problems area
PER: Personal Problems area
FAM: Familial Problems area
PRO: Programme related Problems

There are 26 very significant problems (Rank Order 1-26), 47 significant problems (Rank Order 27-73) and 7 less significant problems (Rank Order 74-80).

The problem area-wise distribution of very significant, significant and less significant problems is summarized and presented in Table 4.52. By looking at the problems-area in the Table 4.51, the exact problem may be located.

Table 4.52: Distribution of Very Significant, Significant and Less Significant Problems as Problems area-wise indicated by Dropouts 1-2 Months Attendance Groups in the Centre

Problem Areas	*Very Significant*	*Significant*	*Less Significant*	*Total*
Economic Problems (ECO)	1	5	-	6
Social Problems (SOC)	1	8	1	10
Psychological Problems (PSY)	7	7	-	14
Familial Problems (FAM)	2	4	-	6
Instructor related Problems (INS)	7	2	2	21
Community related Problems (COM)	4	3	1	8
Personal Problems (PER)	1	8	3	12
Programme related Problems (PRO)	3	-	-	3
Total	**26**	**47**	**7**	**80**

Problems of Drop-outs with 2-4 months attendance in the Centre

The very significant, significant and less significant problems of dropouts with 2-4 months attendance in the centre are presented in the Table 4.53.

Table 4.53: Showing the Very Significant, Significant and Less Significant Problems in the case of Drop-outs with 2-4 months attendance in the Centre

Rank Order	*Mean Difficulty*	*Problem Area and Sl. No. in the Rating Scale*	*Problem*
1	2	3	4
			Very Significant
1.	2.32	PER 68	Due to ill-health
2.	2.31	COM 65	The time of the programme is short
3.	2.30	PSY 23	Easily getting tired
4.	2.29	PRO 78	Minimum amenities are not found at the centre (air/ventilation)
5.	2.29	PSY 29	Feeling that studying at the centre is waste
6.	2.27	INS 50	The instructor does not reveal in learner's progress
7.	2.26	FAM 31	Other family members refuse permission to attend during nights
8.	2.25	PSY 22	Feeling that others would mock
9.	2.23	INS 48	Instruction is limited only to literacy
10.	2.22	ECO 2	Busy with farm work
11.	2.20	SOC 14	Many learners belong to the upper caste
12.	2.20	SOC 10	Personal position is at stake in the society
13.	2.19	COM 64	No one else visits the centre except the instructor
14.	2.19	INS 49	Providing too much information within a short time
15.	2.19	PSY 18	The learner is not able to answer to the instructor

(Table Contd...)

1	2	3	4
16.	2.18	PER 72	The other learners are mocking because of my backwardness in learning
17.	2.18	PER 70	Getting the marriage age
18.	2.18	COM 59	Friends do not go to the centre
19.	2.16	FAM 34	The time of the centre is the supper time
20.	2.15	FAM 36	Unable to go to the centre because of heavy work
21.	2.14	PER 76	Lack of knowledge about this programme
22.	2.14	INS 40	There is no teaching experience to the instructor
			Significant
23.	2.13	INS 51	The instructor uses difficult language, pictures and symbols
24.	2.13	PSY 21	Feeling shy to go to the centre
25.	2.13	PSY 20	Feeling that the age to study has passed
26.	2.12	PRO 80	The centre is at a distance
27.	2.12	INS 57	The instructional methods used by the instructor are not liked
28.	2.11	COM 62	The time of the centre is inconvenient
29.	2.11	FAM 35	There are none else at home
30.	2.10	ECO 6	There are no specific working hours in different professions
31.	2.09	INS 56	The books are difficult to learn
32.	2.09	INS 45	The instruction is not relevant to the learners
33.	2.08	COM 58	There is no encouragement from the village elders
34.	2.07	COM 63	Co-educational centre
35.	2.07	INS 53	The absence of audio-visual aids useful for instruction
36.	2.07	INS 46	The instructor lacks good voice and fluency
37.	2.07	PSY 19	Unwilling to get educated
38.	2.07	SOC 12	The instructor and the learner are not friends
39.	2.06	PSY 24	Feeling why one should get educated when the age is so much

(Table Contd...)

1	2	3	4
40.	2.06	ECO 1	No immediate financial benefit by education
41.	2.04	PER 77	The relevant lessons are not taught at the centre
42.	2.04	COM 60	I am not permitted to go with my friends
43.	2.03	PER 66	Becoming a slave to bad habits
44.	2.03	INS 41	The instructor is unable to explain clearly
45.	2.03	SOC 11	Some co-learners have enmity in the centre
46.	2.02	SOC 8	The instructor does not belong to my caste
47.	2.00	PRO 79	The centre is started at inconvenient place/having much sounds and bad smell
48.	2.00	PER 73	Getting discouraged after working hard for sometime to get educated and feeling that this attempt is useless
49.	2.00	PSY 28	The fellow learners do not listen to the thoughts and ideas
50.	2.00	PSY 17	There is no understanding between the learners and the instructor
51.	2.00	SOC 13	There are some fights in the village
52.	2.00	ECO 4	There is no immediate use by getting educated
53.	1.98	INS 54	Primer and follow-up books are not in order
54.	1.97	SOC 7	The instructor does not belong to my place
55.	1.96	PER 75	The instructor is male
56.	1.96	PER 74	The other learners also are average in learning
57.	1.96	INS 42	The instructor does not treat all the learners equally
58.	1.96	PSY 26	Feeling shy during conversation with others
59.	1.96	PSY 25	Feeling that education is only for wealthy people
60.	1.96	SOC 16	Attending functions and going to movies

(Table Contd...)

1	2	3	4
61.	1.95	INS 52	Teaching aids are not available at the right time
62.	1.93	PSY 30	Feeling that learning at home instead of at the centre is better
63.	41.92	FAM 33	Other family members do not co-operate in matters of education
64.	1.91	INS 44	The instructor does not accept criticism with open heart
65.	1.90	INS 47	The instructor fails to enthuse the learners to participate
66.	1.89	PER 71	The other learners are much older
67.	1.88	INS 38	The instructor is not punctual to the centre
68.	1.87	INS 55	The lessons are not according to the requirements and tastes
69.	1.87	INS 43	The instructor is negligent
70.	1.86	ECO 5	My family is economically backward
			Less Significant
71.	1.81	PER 69	Quarrelling with other learners
72.	1.81	COM 61	Good friends are not available at the centre
73.	1.81	INS 37	The centre is not well maintained
74.	1.80	INS 39	The instructor is not well versed with his teaching
75.	1.79	FAM 32	Looking after the children
76.	1.77	SOC 15	There are some learners with bad behaviour in the centre
77.	1.68	PSY 27	Learners calling by nicknames
78.	1.67	SOC 9	The instructor utilises the learners for his personal work
79.	1.65	PER 67	Getting newly married
80.	1.55	ECO 3	Owners and landlords do not permit for attending centres

ECO: Economic Problems area
INS: Instructor related Problems area
SOC: Social Problems area
COM: Community related Problems area
PSY: Psychological Problems area
PER: Personal Problems area
FAM: Familial Problems area
PRO: Programme related Problems

There are 22 very significant problems (Rank Order 1-22), 48 significant problems (Rank Order 23-70) and 10 less significant problems (Rank Order 71-80).

The problem area-wise distribution of very significant, significant and less significant problems is summarized and presented in Table 4.54. By looking at the problems area in the Table 4.53, the exact problem may be located.

Table 4.54: Distribution of Very Significant, Significant and Less Significant Problems as Problems area-wise indicated by Drop-outs 2-4 Months Attendance Groups in the Centre

Problem Areas	*Very Significant*	*Significant*	*Less Significant*	*Total*
Economic Problems (ECO)	1	4	1	6
Social Problems (SOC)	2	6	2	10
Psychological Problems (PSY)	4	9	1	14
Familial Problems (FAM)	3	2	1	6
Instructor related Problems (INS)	4	15	2	21
Community related Problems (COM)	3	4	1	8
Personal Problems (PER)	4	6	2	12
Programme related Problems (PRO)	1	2	-	3
Total	**22**	**48**	**10**	**80**

Problems of Drop-outs with 4-6 months attendance in the Centre

The very significant, significant and less significant problems of drop-outs with 4-6 months attendance in the centre are presented in Table 4.55.

Table 4.55: Showing the Very Significant, Significant and Less Significant Problems in the case of Drop-outs with 4-6 months Attendance in the Centre

Rank Order	*Mean Difficulty*	*Problem Area and Sl. No. in the Rating Scale*	*Problem*
1	2	3	4
			Very Significant
1.	2.43	INS 46	The instructor lacks good voice and fluency
2.	2.42	SOC 8	The instructor does not belong to my caste
3.	2.40	PER 75	The instructor is male
4.	2.40	PSY 23	Easily getting tired
5.	2.39	INS 56	The books are difficult to learn
6.	2.36	FAM 35	There are none else at home
7.	2.35	FAM 31	Other family members refuse permission to attend during nights
8.	2.34	PSY 27	Learners calling by nicknames
9.	2.32	PER 74	The other learners also are average in learning
10.	2.31	COM 59	Friends do not go to the centre
11.	2.31	PSY 22	Feeling that others would mock
12.	2.30	COM 62	The time of the centre is inconvenient
13.	2.28	PER 72	The other learners are mocking because of my backwardness in learning
14.	2.28	PSY 17	There is no understanding between the learner and the instructor
15.	2.25	PER 77	The relevant lessons are not taught at the centre
16.	2.25	PSY 18	The learner is not able to answer to the instructor
17.	2.23	COM 60	I am not permitted to go with my friends
18.	2.21	PER 76	Lack of knowledge about this programme
19.	2.21	INS 52	Teaching aids are not available at the right time

(Table Contd...)

1	*2*	*3*	*4*
20.	2.21	INS 47	The instructor fails to enthuse the learners to participate
21.	2.20	INS 54	Primer and follow-up books are not in order
22.	2.20	ECO 6	There are no specific working hours in different professions
23.	2.18	SOC 16	Attending functions and going to movies
24.	2.17	INS 55	The lessons are not according to the requirements and tastes
			Significant
25.	2.12	SOC 7	The instructor does not belong to my place
26.	2.11	INS 37	The centre is not well maintained
27.	2.11	PSY 20	Feeling that the age to study has passed
28.	2.11	PSY 19	Unwilling to get educated
29.	2.10	PRO 80	The centre is at a distance
30.	2.10	FAM 36	Unable to go to the centre because of heavy work
31.	2.09	INS 51	The instructor uses difficult language, pictures and symbols
32.	2.07	PSY 28	The fellow learners do not listen to the thoughts and ideas
33.	2.07	PSY 21	Feeling shy to go to the centre
34.	2.06	INS 50	The instructor does not reveal in learner's progress
35.	2.06	SOC 12	The instructor and the learner are not friends
36.	2.05	PSY 30	Feeling that learning at home instead of at the centre is better
37.	2.05	PSY 24	Feeling why one should get educated when the age is so much
38.	2.05	SOC 10	Personal position is at stake in the society
39.	2.04	COM 61	Good friends are not available at the centre
40.	2.04	INS 43	The instructor is negligent
41.	2.04	INS 42	The instructor does not treat all the learners equally
42.	2.04	INS 41	The instructor is unable to explain clearly

(Table Contd...)

1	2	3	4
43.	2.03	COM 64	No one else visits the centre except the instructor
44.	2.03	INS 44	The instructor does not accept criticism with open heart
45.	2.00	INS 38	The instructor is not punctual to the centre
46.	2.00	PSY 29	Feeling that studying at the centre is a waste
47.	1.97	PER 68	Due to ill-health
48.	1.97	FAM 34	The time of the centre is the supper time
49.	1.95	INS 53	The absence of audio-visual aids useful for instruction
50.	1.95	FAM 32	Looking after the children
51.	1.95	ECO 2	Busy with farm work
52.	1.94	PRO 79	The centre is started at inconvenient place/having much sounds and bad smell
53.	1.94	PER 70	Getting the marriage age
54.	1.93	PER 71	The other learners are much older
55.	1.93	COM 58	There is no encouragement from the village elders
56.	1.93	ECO 1	No immediate financial benefit by education
57.	1.92	PER 66	Becoming a slave to bad habits
58.	1.92	FAM 33	Other family members do not co-operate in matters of education
59.	1.90	INS 45	The instruction is not relevant to the learners
60.	1.89	INS 48	Instruction is limited only to literacy
61.	1.89	SOC 11	Some co-learners have enmity in the centre
62.	1.88	INS 40	There is no teaching experience to the instructor
63.	1.87	PRO 78	Minimum amenities are not found at the centre (air/ventilation)
64.	1.87	COM 63	Co-educational centre
65.	1.87	PSY 26	Feeling shy during conversation with other

(Table Contd...)

1	2	3	4
66.	1.86	INS 39	The instructor is not well versed with his teaching
67.	1.82	PER 67	Getting newly married
			Less Significant
68.	1.78	ECO 5	My family is economically backward
69.	1.76	PSY 25	Feeling that education is only for wealthy people
70.	1.73	PER 73	Getting discouraged after working hard for sometime to get educated and feeling that this attempt is useless
71.	1.71	COM 65	The time of the programme is short
72.	1.71	INS 49	Providing too much information within a short time
73.	1.70	ECO 4	There is no immediate use by getting educated
74.	1.69	SOC 15	There are some learners with bad behaviour in the centre
75.	1.69	ECO 3	Owners and landlords do not permit for attending centre
76.	1.68	PER 69	Quarrelling with other learners
77.	1.64	SOC 14	Many learners belong to the upper caste
78.	1.55	SOC 9	The instructor utilises the learners for his personal work
79.	1.54	SOC 13	There are some fights in the village
80.	1.53	INS 57	The instructional methods used by the instructor are not liked

ECO: Economic Problems area *INS:* Instructor related Problems area
SOC: Social Problems area *COM:* Community related Problems area
PSY: Psychological Problems area *PER:* Personal Problems area
FAM: Familial Problems area *PRO:* Programme related Problems

There are 24 very significant problems (Rank Order 1-24), 43 significant problems (Rank Order 25-67) and 13 less significant problems (Rank Order 68-80).

The problem area-wise distribution of very significant, significant and less significant problems is summarized and presented in Table 4.56. By looking at the problems area in the Table 4.55, the exact problem may be located.

Table 4.56: Distribution of Very Significant, Significant and Less Significant Problems as Problems area-wise indicated by Drop-outs 4-6 Months Attendance Groups in the Centre

Problem Areas	*Very Significant*	*Significant*	*Less Significant*	*Total*
Economic Problems (ECO)	1	2	3	6
Social Problems (SOC)	2	4	4	10
Psychological Problems (PSY)	5	8	1	14
Familial Problems (FAM)	2	4	-	6
Instructor related Problems (INS)	6	13	2	21
Community related Problems (COM)	3	4	1	8
Personal Problems (PER)	5	5	2	12
Programme related Problems (PRO)	-	3	-	3
Total	24	43	13	80

Analysis of Very Significant Problems

The rating scale covered 80 problems. The problems of 22 groups of drop-outs including total drop-outs were studied and classified as very significant problems, significant problems and less significant problems. The very significant problems of 22 groups were further analysed for two purposes.

- To find out the group/groups which have maximum number of very significant problems, if the number of problems is more, the difficulty experienced by the group is more.
- To find out the very significant problems which were experienced by maximum number of groups, if the number of groups is more, the difficulty of the problem is more in general. If there is no group which experienced the problem, then it is not a very significant problem to any group. It may be a significant or less significant problem to one group or the other. This analysis is done to see whether the 80 problems were very significant problems to one group or the other.

- Among 22 groups of drop-outs, the rank order of the groups which experienced the very significant problems and the percentage of total problems (80) are given in table 4.57.

Table 4.57: Showing the Rank Order of the Group which experienced the Very Significant Problems

Rank Order	*No. of problems experienced and % to total problems*		*Drop-out Group*
1.	49	61.25	Other (Occupation)
2.	39	48.75	36 years and above (Age)
3.	30	37.50	Previous schooling (Education)
4.	30	37.50	B.C. Caste (Caste)
5.	28	35.00	Males (Sex)
6.	27	33.75	OC Caste (Caste)
7.	26	32.50	20 years and below (Age)
8.	26	32.50	1-2 months attendance (Attendance in the centre)
9.	25	31.25	Unmarried (Marital Status)
10.	25	31.25	Rs. 20 thousands and below annual income (Income)
11.	24	30.00	Rs. 21-30 thousands annual income (Income)
12.	24	30.00	4-6 months attendance (Attendance in the centre)
13.	23	28.75	Rs. 31 thousand and above annual income (Income)
14.	23	28.75	2-4 months attendance (Attendance in the centre)
15.	23	28.75	SC/ST caste (Caste)
16.	22	27.50	Married (Marital Status)
17.	21	26.25	21-35 years (Age)
18.	21	26.25	Total drop-outs
19.	20	25.00	Females
20.	20	25.00	Labour (Occupation)
21.	19	23.75	Agriculture (Occupation)
22.	18	22.50	No schooling (Education)

Among 22 groups of drop-outs, the 'other' occupation group (other than agriculture and labour) has highest number of very significant problems, followed by 36 years age group, previous schooling group and B.C. caste group. The 'no schooling' group has lowest number of very significant problems, followed by agriculture (occupation) group, labour (occupation) group and females. The range of very significant problems felt by different groups of drop-outs vary from 49 (61.25%) to 18 (22.5%). The number of very significant problems of total drop-outs is 21 (26.25%) of total problems.

Among very significant problems, the rank order of the very significant problems as indicated by the number of groups of dropouts which felt the problems is given. The list also indicates the problems which are not at all felt as very significant problem by any group.

Table 4.58: Showing the Rank Order of the Very Significant Problems felt by the Groups of Dropouts

Rank Order	*No. of problems experienced and % to total problems*	*Very Significant problems (S. No. in the rating scale)*	*Drop-out Group*
1	2	3	4
1.	22	86.36	23
2.	19	86.34	6, 18, 35, 46
3.	17	77.27	56
4.	16	72.73	22
5.	15	68.18	19, 31, 60
6.	14	63.64	20, 29, 47, 78, 80
7.	13	59.01	16, 59
8.	12	54.55	8, 48, 52, 62, 76
9.	11	50.00	50, 75
10.	10	45.45	17, 72, 77
11.	9	40.91	10, 28, 34, 36, 55, 63, 68
12.	8	36.36	64

(Table Contd...)

1	2	3	4
13.	7	31.82	58, 61
14.	6	27.27	12, 30, 42, 51, 57, 66, 70, 74, 79
15.	5	22.73	2, 14, 26, 53, 54
16.	4	18.18	21, 25, 45, 65, 71
17.	3	13.64	1, 27, 32, 38, 39, 43, 49, 69
18.	2	9.09	4, 15, 24, 33, 40, 41, 44
19.	1	4.55	7, 11, 37
20.	0	0	3, 5, 9, 13, 67, 73

Among very significant problems, the problem which was felt as very significant problem by all the 22 groups of drop-outs is S.No. 23 (Easily getting tired) followed by problems Nos. are 6. There are no specific working hours in different professions, 18. The learner is not able to answer to the instructor, 35. There are none else at home and 46. The instructor lacks good voice and fluency. The problem 23 is also the No. 1 very significant problem of total drop-outs. The 24 problems which are felt as very significant problems by 50% of drop-outs groups are 23, easily getting tired.

6. There are no specific working hours in different professions.
18. The learner is not able to answer to the instructor.
35. There are no else at home.
46. The instructor lacks good voice and fluency.
56. The books are difficult to learn.
22. Feeling that others would mock.
19. Unwilling to get educated.
31. Other family members refuse permission to attend during, nights.
60. I am not permitted to go with my friends.
20. Feeling that the age to study has passed.
29. Feeling that studying at the centre is a waste.
47. The instructor fails to enthuse the learners to participate.

78. Minimum amenities are not found at the centre (air/ ventilation).
80. The centre is at a distance.
16. Attending functions and going to movies.
59. Friends do not go to the centre.
8. The instructor does not belong to my caste.
48. Instruction is limited only to literacy.
52. Teaching aids are not available at the right time.
62. The time of the centre is inconvenient.
76. Lack of knowledge about this programme.
50. The instructor does not personally reveal any development.
75. The instructor is male.

All the 21 problems found to be very significant problems for total drop-outs group are also found to be very significant problems by 50% of the drop-outs groups.

All the 80 problems were found to be very significant problems to one group or the other, except the 6 problems—S.No. in the rating scale 3, 5, 9, 13, 67 and 73 which are not at all very significant problems for any group.

3. Owners and landlords do not permit for attending centres.
5. My family is economically backward.
9. The instructor utilises the learners for his personal work.
13. There are some fights in the village.
67. Getting newly married.
73. Getting discouraged after working hard for some time to get educated and feeling that this attempt is useless.

SUM-UP

The problems of 22 groups of drop-outs were identified and presented in Tables 4.03 to 4.34.

The study covered as many as 80 problems of drop-outs. If all the drop-outs say that the difficulty level of a problem is 'Not at all', then the average difficulty score will be 1. The study revealed that the lowest minimum average difficult score is 1.53. Therefore, all the 80 problems are the problems of drop-outs.

A perusal of the difficult levels of the problems experienced by different groups of drop-outs reveals that the problems have varying levels of difficulty and that there are some groups of problems with same difficulty level (vide Tables 4.01, 4.02 and 4.14 to 4.34).

1. The hypothesis-2, "The problems of drop-outs are various and varied" is proved.
2. The hypothesis-3, "The problems of drop-outs have varying levels of difficult/effect" is proved.
3. The hypothesis-4, "There are some groups of problems which have same difficult level effect" is also supported.

PART-III

Differential Effects of Different Problem Areas on Different Drop-outs

The effect of difficulty of each problem of drop-outs on their sex, education, marital status, age, caste, occupation, annual income and attendance in centres are presented. In other words, the similarities and differences in the difficulty level or effect of each problem between the different categories of drop-outs are detailed. The effect is the extent or degree of the difficulty (mean difficulty) of the problem felt by different categories of drop-outs. The categories covered in the study include the following :

1. Sex—male and female
2. Education—previous schooling and no schooling
3. Marital status—married and unmarried
4. Age—20 years and below, 21-35 years and 36 years and above
5. Caste—SC/ST, BC and other castes

6. Occupation—agriculture, labour and others
7. Income—Rs. 20,000 and below, Rs. 21-30 thousands and 31 thousands and above per annum
8. Attendance in the centre—1-2 months, 2-4 months and 4-6 months

Effect of Problems on the Sex of the Drop-outs

1. The effect of the difficulty of the problems experienced by the male and female dropouts is the same on 60 problems shown in Table 4.59.

Table 4.59: Showing no difference in the effect of problems between Male and Female Drop-outs

S. No. of problem in the rating scale	*Problem*	*Male N = 28*		*Female N = 172*		*'t' value*	*Significant*
		Mean	*SD*	*Mean*	*SD*		
1	2	3	4	5	6	7	8
ECO 1	No immediate financial benefit by education	1.96	1.26	2.05	1.36	0.66	NS
ECO 2	Busy with farm work	2.10	1.36	1.94	1.39	1.16	NS
ECO 3	Owners and landlords to not permit	1.65	1.33	1.74	1.43	0.65	NS
ECO 4	There is no immediate use by getting education	2.08	1.32	1.96	1.27	0.89	NS
ECO 5	My family is economically backward	1.99	1.38	1.78	1.34	1.52	NS
ECO 6	There are no specific working hours in different professions	2.19	1.34	2.27	1.30	0.56	NS
SOC 7	The instructor does not belong to my place	1.98	1.35	1.93	1.38	0.40	NS
SOC 8	The instructor does not belong to my caste	2.20	1.40	2.01	1.41	1.29	NS
SOC 9	The instructor utilises the learners for his personal work	1.85	1.39	1.83	1.38	0.13	NS
SOC 12	The instructor and the learner are not friends	1.97	1.38	2.10	1.41	9.09	NS

(Table Contd...)

1	2	3	4	5	6	7	8
SOC 14	Many learners belong to the upper caste	2.01	1.34	1.86	1.53	1.04	NS
SOC 15	There are some learners with bad behaviour in the centre	1.90	1.37	1.77	1.42	0.88	NS
SOC 16	Attending functions and going to movies	2.18	1.39	2.03	1.38	1.09	NS
PSY 17	There is no understanding between the learner and the instructor	2.11	1.32	1.99	1.32	0.89	NS
PSY 18	The learner is not able to answer to the instructor	2.25	1.28	2.25	1.36	0.00	NS
PSY 19	Unwilling to get education	2.28	1.30	2.09	1.24	1.52	NS
PSY 20	Feeling that the age to study has passed	2.18	1.21	2.24	1.29	0.44	NS
PSY 21	Feeling shy to go to the centre	2.05	1.38	2.03	1.43	0.15	NS
PSY 22	Feeling that others would mock	2.24	1.34	2.15	1.39	0.6	NS
PSY 23	Easily getting tired	2.39	1.16	2.31	1.24	0.58	NS
PSY 25	Feeling that education is only for wealthy people	1.97	1.37	1.79	1.36	1.32	NS
PSY 26	Feeling shy during conversation with others	2.02	1.38	2.02	1.36	0.19	NS
PSY 27	Learners calling by nicknames	2.00	1.37	1.99	1.42	0.07	NS
PSY 28	The fellow learners do not listen to the thoughts and ideas	2.17	1.35	1.97	1.34	1.45	NS
PSY 29	Feeling that studying at the centre is a waste	2.11	1.34	2.22	1.34	0.78	NS
PSY 30	Feeling that learning at home instead of at the centre is better	2.00	1.33	1.95	1.36	0.29	NS
FAM 31	Other family members refuse permission to attend during nights	2.10	1.39	1.33	1.32	1.68	NS
FAM 32	Looking after the children	1.88	1.33	1.86	1.33	0.18	NS
FAM 33	Other family members do not co-operate in matters of education	1.83	1.31	2.01	1.35	1.29	NS
FAM 34	The time of the centre is the supper time	2.07	1.27	2.18	1.36	0.83	NS
FAM 35	There is none else at home	2.29	1.40	2.18	1.32	0.85	NS

(Table Contd...)

1	2	3	4	5	6	7	8
FAM 36	Unable to go to the centre because of heavy work	2.05	0.29	2.21	1.27	1.21	NS
INS 39	The instructor is not well-versed with his teaching	2.04	1.34	1.83	1.47	1.48	NS
INS 40	There is no teaching experience to the instructor	2.02	1.34	1.78	1.32	1.79	NS
INS 42	The instructor does not treat all the learners equally	2.11	1.34	1.94	1.44	1.21	NS
INS 43	The instructor is negligent	2.03	1.34	1.96	1.47	0.52	NS
INS 45	The instruction is not relevant to the learners	2.00	1.36	2.12	1.26	0.91	NS
INS 46	The instructor lacks good voice and fluency	2.23	1.23	2.36	1.21	1.03	NS
INS 48	Instruction is limited only to literacy	2.18	1.33	2.13	1.37	0.37	NS
INS 51	The instructor uses difficult language, pictures and symbols	2.05	1.18	2.03	1.27	0.14	NS
INS 53	The absence of audio-visual aids useful for instruction	2.02	1.24	1.97	1.21	0.39	NS
INS 55	The lessons are not according to the requirements and taste	2.13	1.30	2.11	1.26	0.11	NS
INS 56	The books are difficult to learn	2.30	1.31	2.18	1.34	0.87	NS
INS 57	The instructional methods specified by the government are not liked	2.04	1.24	1.93	1.35	0.90	NS
COM 58	There is no encouragement from the village elders	1.97	1.24	2.21	1.37	1.79	NS
COM 59	Friends do not go to the centre	2.16	1.37	2.16	1.32	0.00	NS
COM 60	I am not permitted to go with my friends	2.14	1.28	2.26	1.42	0.82	NS
COM 61	Good friends are not available at the centre	2.00	1.30	2.11	1.33	0.87	NS
COM 62	The time of the centre is inconvenient	2.07	1.23	2.27	1.22	1.64	NS
COM 64	No one else visits the centre except the instructor	2.03	1.31	2.09	1.33	0.46	NS
COM 65	The time of the programme is short	1.92	1.24	1.94	1.37	0.13	NS
PER 66	Becoming a slave to bad habits	2.02	1.41	2.05	1.50	0.21	NS

(Table Contd…)

1	2	3	4	5	6	7	8
PER 67	Getting newly married	1.80	1.31	1.70	1.36	0.72	NS
PER 69	Quarrelling with other learners	1.77	1.28	1.81	1.39	0.31	NS
PER 70	Getting the marriage age	2.10	1.36	1.98	1.36	0.84	NS
PER 71	The other learners are much older	2.07	1.35	1.93	1.32	0.99	NS
PER 72	The other learner are mocking because of backwardness in learning	2.18	1.35	1.53	1.29	1.18	NS
PER 75	The instructor is male	2.10	1.29	2.19	1.46	0.69	NS
PER 76	Lack of knowledge about this programme	2.16	1.32	2.07	1.23	0.70	NS
PER 77	The relevant lessons are not taught at the centre	2.17	1.29	2.00	1.30	1.29	NS

PSY: Psychological Problems area *FAM:* Familial Problems area

SOC: Social Problems area *INS:* Instructor related Problems area

PER: Personal Problems area *COM:* Community related Problems area

ECO: Economic Problems area

2. In the case of the following 17 problems, the effect or difficulty experienced by male drop-outs is higher, compared to female drop-outs as shown in Table 4.60.

Table 4.60: Showing Problems on which the effect experienced by Males is Higher than the Females

S. No. of problem in the rating scale	*Problem*	*Male N = 228*		*Female N = 172*		*'t' value*	*Significant*
		Mean	*SD*	*Mean*	*SD*		
1	2	3	4	5	6	7	8
SOC 10	Personal position is at a stake in the society	2.25	1.29	1.90	1.41	2.62	@
SOC 11	Some learners have enmity in the centre	2.01	1.38	1.75	1.46	2.31	@@
SOC 13	There are some fights in the village	1.81	1.32	1.54	1.31	2.06	@@

(Table Contd...)

1	2	3	4	5	6	7	8
INS 37	The centre is not well maintained	2.00	1.31	1.63	1.25	2.87	@
INS 38	The instructor is not punctual to the centre	2.03	1.36	1.76	1.29	1.99	@@
INS 41	The instructor is unable to explain clearly	2.11	1.29	1.78	1.30	2.53	@@
INS 44	The instructor does not accept criticism with open heart	2.09	1.31	1.76	1.29	2.45	@@
INS 47	The instructor fails to enthuse the learners to participate	2.43	1.27	1.90	1.30	4.14	@
INS 49	Providing too much information within a short time	2.18	1.42	1.84	1.28	2.47	@@
INS 50	The instructor does not personally reveal any development	2.34	1.35	1.91	1.29	3.15	@
INS 52	Teaching aids are not available at the right time	2.26	1.28	2.00	1.32	1.99	@@
INS 54	Related primary teaching books are not in order	2.16	1.28	1.81	1.42	2.56	@@
PER 68	Due to ill-health	2.26	1.36	1.94	1.37	2.28	@@
PER 73	Getting discouraged after working hard to get educated and feeling that this attempt is useless	2.00	1.26	1.53	1.22	4.04	@
PER 74	The other learners also are average in learning	2.20	1.29	1.70	1.26	3.84	@
PRO 78	Minimum amenities are not found at the centre (air/ventilation)	2.26	1.29	2.00	1.35	1.97	@@
PRO 79	The centre is started at inconvenient place/environment with sounds and bad smell	2.24	1.28	1.84	1.25	3.14	@

@ Significant at 0.01 level — @@ Significant at 0.05 level

SOC: Social Problems area — PER: Personal Problems area

INS: Instructor related Problems area — PRO: Programme related problems

3. The effect or difficulty felt by female drop-outs is higher than the male dropouts with regard to the following three problems shown in Table 4.61.

Table 4.61: Showing the problems on which the effect experienced by Females is Higher than the Males

S.No.of problem in the rating scale	Problem	Male N = 228		Female N = 172		't' value	Significant
		Mean	SD	Mean	SD		
PSY 24	Feeling why one should get educated when the age is so much	1.87	1.32	2.24	1.20	2.88	@
COM 63	The centre is co-educated	1.91	1.38	2.29	1.28	2.75	@
PRO 80	The centre is at a distance	2.05	1.26	2.39	1.29	3.79	@

@ Significant at 0.01 level

PSY: Psychological Problems *COM:* Community related Problems

PRO: Programme related problems

4. The hypothesis-5(i) that "there is no difference in the effect of problems between male drop-outs and female drop-outs" is proved in the case of 60 problems shown in Table 4.59 and not in the case of remaining 20 problems (17+3) found in Tables 4.60 and 4.61.

Effect of Problems on the Educational Status of the Drop-outs

The dropouts from the TLC centres are divided into two categories on the basis of their educational level

1. Those who never entered the formal educational system earlier and joined the TLC centres for the first time and dropped. They are treated as 'no schooling' drop-outs.
2. Those who joined formal educational institutions, studied primary classes (I to V), dropped from the institutions, rejoined TLC centres and dropped. They are treated as 'previous schooling' drop-outs.

1. The drop-outs with 'previous schooling' and 'no schooling' experienced 'no difference' in difficulty or effect in the case of the following 73 problems shown in Table 4.62.

Table 4.62: Showing 'No Difference' in the effect of problems between 'No Schooling' and 'Previous Schooling' Drop-outs

S. No. of problem in the rating scale	*Problem*	*Male N = 228*		*Female N = 172*		*'t' value*	*Significant*
		Mean	*SD*	*Mean*	*SD*		
1	2	3	4	5	6	7	8
ECO 1	No immediate financial benefit by education	2.07	1.28	1.90	1.33	1.27	NS
ECO 2	Busy with farm work	2.04	1.37	2.20	1.38	0.13	NS
ECO 3	Owners and landlords to not permit for attending centres	1.59	1.32	1.82	1.43	1.66	NS
ECO 4	There is no immediate use by getting education	2.10	1.30	1.92	1.30	1.35	NS
ECO 5	My family is economically backward	1.89	1.32	1.91	1.43	0.16	NS
ECO 6	There are no specific working hours in different professions	2.26	1.32	2.18	1.34	0.55	NS
SOC 7	The instructor does not belong to my place	1.87	1.34	2.08	1.38	1.51	NS
SOC 8	The instructor does not belong to my caste	2.17	1.35	2.05	1.48	0.85	NS
SOC 9	The instructor utilises the learners for his personal work	1.93	1.37	1.71	1.40	1.53	NS
SOC 10	Personal position is at stake in the society	2.18	1.36	2.00	1.34	1.33	NS
SOC 11	Some learners have enmity in the centre	1.97	1.36	1.90	1.80	0.05	NS
SOC 12	The instructor and the learner are not friends	1.93	1.38	2.15	1.47	1.55	NS
SOC 13	There are some fights in the village	1.73	1.31	1.64	1.33	0.70	NS
SOC 14	Many learners belong to the upper caste	1.89	1.35	2.20	1.52	0.92	NS
SOC 15	There are some learners with bad behaviour in the centre	1.79	1.43	1.91	1.34	0.84	NS

(Table Contd...)

1	2	3	4	5	6	7	8
SOC 16	Attending functions and going to movies	2.20	1.38	2.01	1.39	1.30	NS
PSY 17	There is no understanding between the learner and the instructor	2.16	1.34	1.92	1.28	1.73	NS
PSY 18	The learner is not able to answer to the instructor	2.27	1.29	2.21	1.35	0.43	NS
PSY 19	Unwilling to get education	2.15	1.32	2.27	1.22	0.94	NS
PSY 20	Feeling that the age to study has passed	2.31	1.26	2.08	1.20	1.81	NS
PSY 21	Feeling shy to go to the centre	2.13	1.38	1.93	1.43	1.37	NS
PSY 22	Feeling that others would mock	2.24	1.39	2.15	1.33	0.05	NS
PSY 23	Easily getting tired	2.35	1.13	2.36	1.27	0.03	NS
PSY 24	Feeling why one should get educated when the age is so much	1.98	1.21	2.09	1.37	0.89	NS
PSY 25	Feeling that education is only for wealthy people	1.89	1.38	1.89	1.35	0.00	NS
PSY 26	Feeling shy during conversation with others	2.05	1.39	1.99	1.35	0.41	NS
PSY 27	Learners calling by nicknames	1.93	1.33	2.09	1.39	1.18	NS
PSY 29	Feeling that studying at the centre is a waste	2.26	1.35	2.02	1.31	1.76	NS
PSY 30	Feeling that learning at home instead of at the centre is better	2.03	1.38	1.91	1.29	0.02	NS
FAM 31	Other family members refuse permission to attend during nights	2.09	1.39	2.35	1.31	1.84	NS
FAM 32	Looking after the children	1.92	1.39	2.35	1.24	0.80	NS
FAM 33	Other family members do not co-operate in matters of education	1.98	1.29	1.18	1.38	1.26	NS
FAM 34	The time of the centre is the supper time	2.21	1.26	1.18	1.37	1.61	NS
FAM 35	There is none else at home	2.26	1.37	2.00	1.36	0.24	NS
FAM 37	The centre is not well maintained	1.79	1.25	2.12	1.35	0.86	NS
INS 39	The instructor is not well-versed with his teaching	1.95	1.40	1.91	1.41	0.09	NS

(Table Contd...)

1	2	3	4	5	6	7	8
INS 40	There is no teaching experience to the instructor	1.95	1.31	1.96	1.36	0.58	NS
INS 41	The instructor is unable to explain clearly	2.00	1.26	1.93	1.37	0.51	NS
INS 43	The instructor is negligent	2.00	1.40	1.39	1.39	0.02	NS
INS 44	The instructor does not accept criticism with open heart	1.95	1.22	1.94	1.44	0.06	NS
INS 45	The instruction is not relevant to the learners	2.23	1.22	2.17	1.41	0.42	NS
INS 46	The instructor lacks good voice and fluency	2.31	1.20	2.24	1.25	0.58	NS
INS 47	The instructor fails to enthuse the learners to participate	2.12	1.28	1.95	1.36	1.22	NS
INS 48	Instruction is limited only to literacy	2.11	1.35	2.22	1.33	0.83	NS
INS 49	Providing too much information within a short time	1.97	1.32	2.11	1.43	0.99	NS
INS 50	The instructor does not reveal in learners progress	2.12	1.28	2.21	1.42	0.644	NS
INS 52	Teaching aids are not available at the right time	2.24	1.27	2.02	1.34	1.66	NS
INS 53	The absence of audio-visual aids useful for instruction	2.02	1.23	1.98	1.22	0.31	NS
INS 54	Related primary teaching books are not in order	2.12	1.35	1.8	1.33	1.95	NS
INS 55	The lessons are not according to the requirements and taste	2.22	1.25	1.95	1.31	1.84	NS
INS 56	The books are difficult to learn	2.34	1.22	2.13	1.43	1.54	NS
COM 58	There is no encouragement from the village elders	2.05	1.35	2.11	1.24	0.41	NS
COM 59	Friends do not go to the centre	2.06	1.32	2.29	1.37	1.74	NS
COM 60	I am not permitted to go with my friends	2.19	1.40	2.19	1.26	0.01	NS
COM 61	Good friends are not available at the centre	2.03	1.33	2.06	1.30	0.18	NS
COM 62	The time of the centre is inconvenient	2.19	1.23	2.12	1.24	0.55	NS
COM 63	The centre is co-educated	2.13	1.35	1.99	1.35	1.06	NS
COM 64	No one else visits the centre except the instructor	2.12	1.28	1.97	1.37	1.13	NS

(Table Contd...)

1	2	3	4	5	6	7	8
PER 66	Becoming a slave to bad habits	2.04	1.43	2.02	1.47	0.12	NS
PER 67	Getting newly married	1.70	1.30	1.84	1.37	0.99	NS
PER 68	Due to ill-health	2.17	1.46	2.07	1.25	0.72	NS
PER 69	Quarrelling with other learners	1.86	1.27	1.68	1.39	1.37	NS
PER 70	Getting the marriage age	2.07	1.36	2.02	1.37	0.32	NS
PER 71	The other learners are much older	2.05	1.32	1.95	1.36	0.68	NS
PER 72	The other learners are mocking because of backwardness in learning	2.19	1.32	2.01	1.33	1.33	NS
PER 73	Getting discouraged after working hard to get educated and feeling that this attempt is useless	1.84	1.25	1.70	1.29	1.05	NS
PER 74	The other learners also are average in learning	2.03	1.28	1.93	1.32	0.75	NS
PER 75	The instructor is male	2.08	1.38	2.21	1.35	0.98	NS
PER 76	Lack of knowledge about this programme	2.08	1.26	2.18	1.31	0.80	NS
PER 77	The relevant lessons are not taught at the centre	2.18	1.30	1.98	1.27	1.52	NS
PER 78	Minimum amenities are not found at the centre (air/ventilation)	2.24	1.33	2.02	1.31	1.57	NS
PRO 79	The centre is started at inconvenient place/environment with sounds and bad smell	2.13	1.31	1.98	1.23	1.13	NS
PRO 80	The centre is a distance	2.27	1.24	2.24	1.36	0.22	NS

NS: Not-Significant

SOC: Social Problems area *INS:* Instructor related Problems area

PER: Personal Problems area *COM:* Community related Problems area

ECO: Economic Problems area *PRO:* Problem related Problems

2. The "previous schooling" drop-outs felt more difficulty than the 'no schooling' drop-outs on 7 problems indicated in the Table 4.63.

Table 4.63: Showing the problem on which the effect experienced by 'Previous Schooling' Drop-outs is more than the 'No Schooling' Drop-outs

S. No. of problem in the rating scale	*Problem*	*Male N = 228*		*Female N = 172*		*'t' value*	*Significant*
		Mean	*SD*	*Mean*	*SD*		
PSY 28	The fellow learners do not listen to the thoughts and ideas	2.22	1.37	1.91	1.30	2.28	NS
FAM 36	Unable to go to the centre because of heavy work	2.27	1.29	1.91	1.25	2.80	NS
INS 38	The instructor is not punctual to the centre	2.03	1.34	1.74	1.31	2.15	NS
INS 42	The instructor does not treat all the learners equally	2.18	1.46	1.85	1.25	2.13	NS
INS 51	The instructor uses difficult language, pictures and symbols	2.17	1.24	1.86	1.16	2.55	NS
INS 57	The instructional methods specified by the government are not liked	2.20	1.30	1.72	1.23	3.69	NS
COM 65	The time of the programme is short	2.03	1.31	1.67	1.23	3.57	NS

@ Significant at 0.01 level @@ Significant at 0.05 level

PSY: Psychological Problems *INS:* Instructor related Problems area

FAM: Familial Problems *COM:* Community related Problems area

3. There are no problems where the no schooling felt more difficulty (effects is more) than the previous schooling drop-outs.

4. The hypothesis-5(ii) that "there is no difference in the effect of problems between the drop-outs with previous schooling and with no schooling is proved in the case of 73 problems shown in Table 4.62 and not in the case of 7 problems found in the Table 4.63.

Effect of the problems on marital status of the drop-outs

1. There is exists 'no difference' between married drop-outs and unmarried drop-outs on the difficulty/effect felt in respect of the following 65 problems shown in Table 4.64.

Table 4.64: Showing the problems on which there is no difference in the effect of problems between Married and Unmarried Drop-outs

S.No. of problem in the rating scale	Problem	Male N = 228		Female N = 172		't' value	Significant
		Mean	SD	Mean	SD		
1	2	3	4	5	6	7	8
ECO 1	No immediate financial benefit by education	2.02	1.28	1.96	1.33	0.49	NS
ECO 3	Owners and landlords do not permit	1.75	1.34	1.59	1.41	1.12	NS
ECO 4	There is no immediate use by getting education	2.03	1.31	2.02	1.29	0.09	NS
ECO 5	My family is economically backward	1.94	1.38	1.83	1.35	0.78	NS
ECO 6	There are no specific working hours in different professions	2.26	1.30	2.17	1.36	0.63	NS
SOC 7	The instructor does not belong to my place	1.96	1.31	1.96	1.44	0.00	NS
SOC 8	The instructor does not belong to my caste	2.02	1.42	2.25	1.38	1.60	NS
SOC 9	The instructor utilises the learners for his personal work	1.91	1.41	1.74	1.34	1.21	NS
SOC 10	Personal position is at stake in the society	2.18	1.37	1.99	1.33	1.35	NS
SOC 11	Some learners have enmity in the centre	1.97	1.43	1.89	1.41	0.57	NS
SOC 12	The instructor and the learner are not friends	2.03	1.44	2.01	1.31	0.13	NS
SOC 13	There are some fights in the village	1.61	1.26	1.81	1.40	1.46	NS
SOC 14	Many learners belong to the upper caste	1.97	1.37	1.91	1.51	0.44	NS
SOC 15	There are some learners with bad behaviour in the centre	1.86	1.40	1.83	1.38	0.19	NS
PSY 17	There is no understanding between the learner and the instructor	2.00	1.28	2.14	1.37	0.99	NS

(Table Contd...)

1	2	3	4	5	6	7	8
PSY 18	The learner is not able to answer to the instructor	2.26	1.34	2.23	1.28	0.19	NS
PSY 19	Unwilling to get education	2.25	1.29	1.13	1.26	0.89	NS
PSY 20	Feeling that the age to study has passed	2.25	1.20	2.15	1.30	0.76	NS
PSY 21	Feeling shy to go to the centre	2.15	1.41	1.88	1.39	1.86	NS
PSY 22	Feeling that others would mock	2.27	1.35	2.10	1.37	1.20	NS
PSY 23	Easily getting tired	2.42	1.21	2.27	1.17	1.21	NS
PSY 24	Feeling why one should get educated when the age is so much	2.05	1.30	2.00	1.26	0.33	NS
PSY 27	Learners calling by nicknames	1.91	1.33	2.12	1.31	1.49	NS
PSY 28	The fellow learners do not listen to the thoughts and ideas	2.15	1.36	2.00	1.33	1.09	NS
PSY 29	Feeling that studying at the centre is a waste	2.23	1.27	2.04	1.43	1.36	NS
PSY 30	Feeling that learning at home instead of at the centre is better	2.05	1.36	1.88	1.32	1.22	NS
FAM 31	Other family members refuse permission to attend during nights	2.25	1.39	2.12	1.33	0.90	NS
FAM 33	Other family members do not co-operate in matters of education	1.80	1.34	2.06	1.29	1.93	NS
FAM 34	The time of the centre is the supper time	2.12	1.23	2.11	1.42	0.06	NS
FAM 35	There is none else at home	2.15	1.34	2.38	1.38	1.63	NS
FAM 36	Unable to go the centre because of heavy work	2.11	1.32	2.13	1.23	0.13	NS
FAM 37	The centre is not well maintained	1.87	1.28	1.80	1.33	0.49	NS
INS 39	The instructor is not well-versed with his teaching	1.94	1.40	1.97	1.41	0.20	NS
INS 40	There is no teaching experience to the instructor	1.90	1.35	1.94	1.21	0.27	NS
INS 41	The instructor is unable to explain clearly	2.04	1.29	1.87	1.32	1.31	NS
INS 42	The instructor does not treat all the learners equally	2.00	1.36	2.10	1.43	0.71	NS
INS 43	The instructor is negligent	1.93	1.41	2.11	1.37	1.29	NS
INS 45	The instruction is not relevant to the learners	2.09	1.32	1.98	1.32	0.80	NS

(Table Contd...)

1	2	3	4	5	6	7	8
INS 46	The instructor lacks good voice and fluency	2.23	1.25	2.36	1.19	1.03	NS
INS 48	Instruction is limited only to literacy	2.18	1.40	2.12	1.26	0.47	NS
INS 49	Providing too much information within a short time	2.09	1.34	1.95	1.41	1.04	NS
INS 50	The instructor does not reveal in learners progress	2.16	1.29	2.14	1.27	0.14	NS
INS 51	The instructor uses difficult languages, pictures and symbols	2.10	1.18	1.95	1.27	1.27	NS
INS 52	Teaching aids are not available at the right time	2.08	1.26	2.25	1.35	1.24	NS
INS 53	The absence of audio-visual aids useful for instruction	1.95	1.21	2.07	1.25	0.92	NS
INS 54	Related primary teaching books are not in order	2.00	1.38	2.02	1.31	0.14	NS
INS 55	The lessons are not according to the requirements and taste	2.16	1.27	2.06	1.29	0.81	NS
INS 56	The books are difficult to learn	2.27	1.31	2.22	1.33	0.37	NS
COM 58	There is no encouragement from the village elders	2.05	1.32	2.11	1.29	0.39	NS
COM 59	Friends do not go to the centre	2.08	1.34	2.27	1.35	1.40	NS
COM 62	The time of the centre is inconvenient	2.18	1.26	2.13	1.14	0.35	NS
COM 65	The time of the programme is short	1.98	1.30	1.87	1.29	0.85	NS
PER 66	Becoming a slave to bad habits	2.04	1.46	2.03	1.43	0.10	NS
PER 67	Getting newly married	1.77	1.34	1.74	1.32	0.22	NS
PER 68	Due to ill-health	2.13	1.38	2.11	1.35	0.12	NS
PER 69	Quarrelling with other learners	1.85	1.36	1.69	1.27	1.22	NS
PER 71	The other learners are much older	2.01	1.38	2.00	1.26	0.07	NS
PER 72	The other learner are mocking because of my backwardness in learning	2.02	1.31	2.26	1.345	1.81	NS
PER 73	Getting discouraged after working hard to get educated and feeling that this attempt is useless	1.80	1.26	1.75	1.28	0.41	NS
PER 75	The instructor is male	2.05	1.34	2.20	1.40	1.48	NS

(Table Contd...)

1	2	3	4	5	6	7	8
PER 76	Lack of knowledge about this programme	2.02	1.34	2.27	1.18	1.93	NS
PER 77	The relevant lessons are not taught at the centre	2.09	1.26	2.11	1.34	0.10	NS
PER 78	Minimum amenities are not found at the centre (air/ventilation)	2.08	1.31	2.24	1.24	1.20	NS
PRO 79	The centre is started at inconvenient place/environment with sounds and bad smell	2.06	1.32	2.08	1.22	0.09	NS
PRO 80	The centre is a distance	2.24	1.29	2.28	1.30	0.27	NS

NS: Not-Significant

ECO: Economic problems

PSY: Psychological problems

INS: Instructor related Problems area

PRO: Programme related problems

SOC: Social Problems area

FAM: Familial Problems

PER: Personal Problems area

COM: Community related Problems area

ECO: Economic Problems area

PRO: Problem related Problems

2. The exact experienced by married drop-outs is higher than that of the unmarried drop-outs on 7 problems noted in Table 4.65.

Table 4.65: Showing the problems on which the effect experienced by Married Drop-outs is higher than the Unmarried Drop-outs

S. No. of problem in the rating scale	*Problem*	*Male N = 228*		*Female N = 172*		*'t' value*	*Significant*
		Mean	*SD*	*Mean*	*SD*		
1	2	3	4	5	6	7	8
ECO 1	Busy with farm work	2.15	1.33	1.86	1.41	2.11	@@
PSY 25	Feeling that education is only for wealthy people	2.06	1.34	1.64	1.37	3.00	@
FAM 32	Looking after the children	2.00	1.35	1.69	1.29	2.28	@@
INS 38	The instructor is not punctual to the centre	2.04	1.34	1.72	1.31	2.30	@@

(Table Contd...)

1	2	3	4	5	6	7	8
INS 57	The instructional methods specified by the government are not liked	2.15	1.29	1.77	1.26	2.90	@
COM 64	No one else visits the centre except the instructor	2.16	1.30	1.89	1.34	2.03	@@
PER 74	The other learners also are average in learning	2.11	1.24	1.80	1.36	2.34	@@

@ Significant at 0.01 level
@@ Significant at 0.05 level
ECO: Economic problems
INS: Instructor related Problems area
PSY: Psychological problems
COM: Community related Problems area
FAM: Familial Problems
PER: Personal Problems area

3. The effect felt by the unmarried drop-outs is greater than that of the married drop-outs on 8 problems found in Table 4.66.

Table 4.66: Showing the problems on which the effect experienced by Unmarried Drop-outs is higher than the Married Drop-outs

S.No. of problem in the rating scale	*Problem*	*Male N = 228*		*Female N = 172*		*'t' value*	*Significant*
		Mean	*SD*	*Mean*	*SD*		
1	2	3	4	5	6	7	8
SOC 16	Attending functions and going to movies	2.00	1.42	2.30	1.32	2.14	@@
PSY 2	Feeling shy during conversation with others	1.86	1.36	2.27	1.36	2.95	@
INS 44	The instructor does not accept criticism with open heart	1.80	1.38	2.16	1.33	2.70	@
INS 47	The instructor fails to enthuse the learners to participate	2.08	1.31	2.38	1.28	2.29	@@
COM 60	I am not permitted to go with my friends	2.05	1.34	2.41	1.31	2.67	@
COM 61	Good friends are not available at the centre	1.87	1.28	2.30	1.32	3.19	@

(Table Contd...)

1	2	3	4	5	6	7	8
COM 63	The centre is co-educated	1.89	1.38	2.34	1.26	3.31	@
PER 70	Getting the marriage age	1.84	1.39	2.35	1.26	3.71	@

@ Significant at 0.01 level @@ Significant at 0.05 level

SOC: Social problems INS: Instructor related Problems area

PSY: Psychological problems COM: Community related Problems area

PER: Personal Problems area

4. The hypothesis-5(iii) that "there is no difference in the effect of problems between married drop-outs and unmarried drop-outs" is proved in respect of 65 problems shown in Table 4.64 and not in respect of 15 problems (7+8) shown in Tables 4.65 and 4.66 respectively.

Effect of Problems on the Age of the Dropouts

There exists 'no difference' in the effect experienced among the drop-outs of different age groups namely below 20 years, 21-35 years, and 36 years and above age groups on 65 problems noted in the Table 4.67.

Table 4.67: Showing the problems on which there is no difference in the effect of problems among drop-outs of different age groups

S. No. of problem in the rating scale	*Problem*	*Group-1 20 years and below N = 34*		*Group-2 21-35 years N = 191*		*Group-3 36 years and above N = 75*		*'F' Value*	*Significant*
		Mean	*SD*	*Mean*	*SD*	*Mean*	*SD*		
1	2	3	4	5	6	7	8	9	10
ECO 1	No immediate financial benefit by education	2.00	1.38	1.95	1.26	2.12	1.29	0.41	NS
ECO 2	Busy with farm work	1.89	1.41	2.00	1.32	2.40	1.38	3.42	
ECO 3	Owners and landlords to not permit for attending centres	1.57	1.43	1.70	1.23	1.86	1.50	1.10	NS

(Table Contd...)

1	2	3	4	5	6	7	8	9	10
ECO 4	There is not immediate use by getting education	2.11	1.58	1.92	1.29	2.14	1.38	1.20	NS
ECO 5	My family is economically backward	1.72	1.33	1.99	1.40	2.00	1.31	1.76	NS
ECO 6	There are no specific working hours in different professions	2.14	1.34	1.54	1.34	2.40	1.27	0.86	NS
SOC 7	The instructor does not belong to my place	2.08	1.46	1.82	1.32	2.09	1.28	1.93	NS
SOC 8	The instructor does not belong to my caste	2.28	1.36	1.98	1.44	2.17	1.40	1.77	NS
SOC 9	The instructor utilises the learners for his personal work	1.68	1.31	1.86	1.41	2.06	1.44	1.85	NS
SOC 10	Personal position is at stake in the society	2.03	1.35	2.02	1.38	2.38	1.27	1.99	NS
SOC 11	Some learners have enmity in the centre	1.88	1.48	2.20	1.38	1.90	1.41	0.33	NS
SOC 12	The instructor and the learner are not friends	1.94	1.41	2.00	1.40	2.25	1.49	1.21	NS
SOC 13	There are some fights in the village	1.66	1.37	1.69	1.31	1.77	1.24	0.167	NS
SOC 14	Many learners belong to the upper caste	1.87	1.51	1.98	1.36	2.28	1.41	2.43	NS
SOC 15	There are some learners with bad behaviour in the centre	1.80	1.38	1.89	1.48	1.82	1.20	0.15	NS

(Table Contd...)

1	2	3	4	5	6	7	8	9	10
PSY 19	Unwilling to get education	2.18	1.25	2.16	1.34	2.34	1.14	0.57	NS
PSY 20	Feeling that the age to study has passed	2.18	1.29	2.10	1.21	2.42	1.22	2.98	NS
PSY 21	Feeling shy to go to the centre	1.82	1.34	2.21	1.40	2.02	1.48	3.11	NS
PSY 22	Feeling that others would mock	2.06	1.37	2.28	1.40	2.25	1.23	1.03	NS
PSY 23	Easily getting tired	2.29	1.19	2.33	1.92	2.43	1.24	1.10	NS
PSY 24	Feeling why one should get educated when the age is so much	2.04	1.32	2.08	1.25	1.88	1.41	0.68	NS
PSY 25	Feeling that education is only for wealthy people	1.73	1.35	1.89	1.40	2.18	1.25	2.28	NS
PSY 26	Feeling shy during conver-sation with others	2.10	1.32	2.03	1.40	1.86	1.32	0.72	NS
PSY 27	Learners calling by nick-names	2.04	1.29	1.94	1.42	2.05	1.33	0.27	NS
PSY 29	Feeling that studying at the centre is a waste	2.04	1.45	2.20	1.27	2.25	1.30	0.77	NS
PSY 30	Feeling that learning at home instead of at the centre is better	1.88	1.36	1.95	1.31	2.22	1.39	1.61	NS
FAM 31	Other family members refuse permission to attend during nights	2.05	1.34	2.25	1.35	2.33	1.43	1.22	NS
FAM 33	Other family members do not co-operate in matters of education	2.05	1.33	1.75	1.33	2.04	1.28	2.44	NS

(Table Contd...)

1	2	3	4	5	6	7	8	9	10
FAM 34	The time of the centre is the supper time	2.10	1.45	2.01	1.25	2.42	1.14	2.67	NS
FAM 35	There are none else at home	2.35	1.41	2.15	1.39	2.29	1.20	0.94	NS
FAM 36	Unable to go to the centre because of heavy work	2.13	1.25	2.00	1.26	2.41	1.36	2.74	NS
FAM 37	The centre is not well maintained	1.82	1.40	1.81	1.25	1.97	1.24	0.43	NS
FAM 38	The instructor is not punctual to the centre	1.66	1.32	2.00	1.35	2.13	1.28	2.82	
INS 39	The instructor is not well-versed with his teaching	1.99	1.43	1.89	1.44	2.06	1.26	0.48	NS
INS 40	There is no teaching experience to the instructor	1.86	1.31	1.90	1.33	2.06	1.28	0.57	NS
INS 41	The instructor is unable to explain clearly	1.86	1.36	1.98	1.25	2.13	1.34	1.02	NS
INS 42	The instructor does not treat all the learners equally	2.14	1.43	1.86	1.37	2.32	1.29	3.50	NS
INS 43	The instructor is negligent	2.03	1.33	1.95	1.45	2.08	1.38	0.24	NS
INS 44	The instructor does not accept criticism with open heart	2.11	1.41	1.77	1.28	2.10	1.18	3.35	
INS 45	The instruction is not relevant to the learners	2.02	2.32	2.08	1.20	2.00	1.36	0.15	NS
INS 46	The instructor lacks good voice and fluency	2.35	1.18	2.30	1.20	2.10	1.35	1.06	NS
INS 47	The instructor fails to enthuse the learners to participate	2.39	1.32	2.08	1.28	2.18	1.32	2.25	NS

(Table Contd...)

1	2	3	4	5	6	7	8	9	10
INS 49	Providing too much information within a short time	1.94	1.46	2.09	1.32	2.06	1.41	0.51	NS
INS 50	The instructor does not reveal in learners, progress	2.10	1.27	2.21	1.32	2.10	1.51	0.36	NS
INS 51	The instructor uses difficult languages, pictures and symbols	2.00	1.28	2.00	1.19	2.22	1.18	1.01	NS
INS 52	Teaching aids are not available at the right time	2.34	1.36	2.00	1.32	2.24	1.08	1.02	NS
INS 54	Related primary teaching books are not in order	1.97	1.35	2.07	1.28	1.92	1.27	0.46	NS
INS 55	The lessons are not according to the requirements and taste	1.96	1.28	2.24	1.28	2.10	1.26	1.93	NS
INS 56	The books are difficult to learn	2.22	1.40	2.40	1.26	2.16	1.34	0.38	NS
COM 58	There is no encouragement from the village elders	2.05	1.28	2.15	1.29	1.94	1.38	0.70	NS
COM 59	Friends do not go to the centre	2.23	1.38	2.20	1.35	1.92	1.24	1.51	NS
COM 62	The time of the centre is inconvenient	2.21	1.19	2.07	1.20	2.28	1.37	0.90	NS
COM 64	No one else visits the centre except the instructor	1.87	1.33	2.08	1.29	2.32	1.34	2.83	
COM 65	The time of the programme is short	1.81	2.29	2.28	1.30	2.02	1.29	0.93	NS
PER 66	Becoming a slave to bad habits	2.05	1.41	2.43	1.46	2.13	1.48	0.25	NS
PER 68	Due to ill-health	2.11	2.36	2.04	1.37	2.34	1.39	2.28	NS
PER 69	Quarrelling with other learners	1.68	1.28	2.41	1.29	1.86	1.50	0.62	NS

(Table Contd...)

1	2	3	4	5	6	7	8	9	10
PER 71	The other learners are much older	2.00	1.27	1.89	1.36	2.33	1.33	2.98	NS
PER 72	The other learner are mocking because of backwardness in learning	2.34	1.34	2.00	1.33	1.01	1.23	2.87	NS
PER 73	Getting discouraged after working hard to get educated and feeling that this attempt is useless	1.84	1.30	1.73	1.23	1.81	1.32	0.31	NS
PER 75	The instructor is male	2.25	1.34	2.08	1.42	2.09	1.26	0.66	NS
PER 77	The relevant lessons are not taught at the centre	2.08	1.33	2.18	1.32	1.93	1.15	1.02	NS
PER 78	Minimum amenities are not found at the centre (air/ventilation)	2.14	1.32	2.16	1.31	2.12	1.39	0.03	NS
PRO 79	The centre is started at inconvenient place/ environment with sounds and bad smell	2.08	1.22	1.94	1.27	2.37	1.36	3.08	NS
PRO 80	The centre is at a distance	2.40	1.25	2.15	1.35	2.29	1.19	1.51	NS

NS: Not-Significant

ECO: Economic problems — *SOC:* Social Problems area

PSY: Psychological problems — *FAM:* Familial Problems

INS: Instructor related Problems area — *PER:* Personal Problems area

PRO: Programme related problems — *COM:* Community related Problems area

ECO: Economic Problems area — *PRO:* Problem related Problems

2. **There exists difference in the effect of problems among drop-outs belonging to different age groups on 15 problems, the details of which are shown in Table 4.68.**

a. **The effect experienced by "20 years and below age group" is higher than the "21-35 age group" on 8 problems indicated below:**

16. Attending functions and going to movies
17. There is no understanding between the learner and the instructor.
53. The absence of audio-visual aids useful for instruction.
60. I am not permitted to go with my friends.
61. Good friends are not available at the centre.
63. The centre is co-educated
70. Getting the marriage age
76. Lack of knowledge about this programme

b. **The effect is more on "21-35 age group" than that of "20 years and below age group" with regard to only one problem i.e.**

57. The instructional methods specified by the government are not liked.

c. **The "20 years and below age group" experienced more effect in the case of 3 problems shown below compared to the age group "36 years and above".**

60. I am not permitted to go with my friends.
61. Good friends are not available at the centre.
62. The centre is co-educated.

d. **The "36 years and above age group" felt more effect on 8 problems noted below compared to "20 years and below age group".**

16. Attending functions and going to movies.
18. The learner is not able to answer to the instructor.
28. The fellow learners do not listen to the thoughts and ideas.
32. Looking after the children.
48. Instruction is limited only to literacy.
57. The instructional methods specified by the government are not liked.

67. Getting newly married.
74. The other learners also are average in learning.

e. The "36 years and above age group" felt more effect compared to "21-35 years age group" on the following 7 problems :

17. There is no understanding between the learner and the instructor.
18. The learner is not able to answer to the instructor.
28. The fellow learners do not listen to the thoughts and ideas.
48. Instruction is limited only to literacy.
53. The absence of audio-visual aids useful for instruction.
67. Getting newly married.
76. Lack of knowledge about this programme.

3. Looking at the effect of each problem experienced by different age groups, the following problem-wise conclusions are drawn.

Problem 16: "Attending functions and going to movies"

- This problem is more with 20 years below age group compared to 21-35 years age group.
- It is more with 36 years and above age group than 20 years below age group.
- There is no difference between 21-35 age years group and 36 years above age group.

Problem 17: There is no understanding between the learner and the instructor

- This problem is more with 20 years below age group compared to 21-35 years age group.
- There is no difference between 20 years below and 36 years above age groups.
- It is more with 36 years and above age group than 21-35 years age group.

Problem 18: The learner is not able to answer to the instructor

- There is no difference in effect between 20 years below and 21-35 years age group.
- The effect is more with 36 years and above age group than 20 years below age group.
- The effect is high with 36 years and above age group than 21-35 years age group.

Problem 28: The fellow learners do not listen to the thoughts and ideas

- This problem has no difference between 20 years below age group and 21-35 years age group.
- It is more with 36 years and above age group than 20 years below age group.
- There is difference between 21-35 years and 36 years and above age group. It is high with 36 and above age group than 21-35 years age group.

Problem 32: Looking after the children

- This problem has no difference between 20 years and below, and 21-35 years age group.
- It is more with 36 years and above age group compared to 20 years below age group.
- There is no difference between 21-35 years and 36 years and above age group.

Problem 48: Instruction is limited only to literacy

- The difficulty felt by 20 years and below age group and 21-35 years age group is the same.
- It is more with 36 years and above age compared to 20 years and below age group.
- It is higher with 36 years and above age group than 21-35 years age group.

Problem 53: The absence of audio-visual aids useful for instruction

- This problem is more with 20 years below age group compared to 21-35 years age group.

- There is no difference between 20 years below and 36 years above age groups.
- It is more with 36 years and above age group than 20 years below age group.

Problem 57: The instructional methods specified by the government are not liked

- This problem is more with 21-35 years age group compared to 20 years below age group.
- It is more with 36 years and above age group than 20 years below age group.
- There is no difference between 21-35 years and 36 years and above age group.

Problem 60: I am not permitted to go with my friends

- It is greater with 20 years below age group than 21-35 years age group.
- This problem is higher with 20 years below age group than 36 years and above age group.
- There is no difference between 21-35 years age group and 36 years and above age group.

Problem 61: Good friends are not available at the centre

- This problem is more with 20 years below age group compared to 21-35 years age group.
- It is more with 20 years below age group than 36 years and above age group.
- There is no difference between 21-35 years and 36 years and above age groups.

Problem 63: The centre is co-educated

- This problem is more with 20 years below age group compared to 21-35 years age group.
- It is more with 20 years below age group than 36 years and above age group.

- There is no difference between 21-35 years and 36 years and above age groups.

Problem 67: Getting newly married

- There is no difference in the difficulty experienced between 20 years below age group and 21-35 years age group.
- It is more with 36 years and above age group compared to 20 years below age group.
- The difficulty felt by 36 years and above age group is higher than 21-35 years age group.

Problem 70: Getting the marriage age

- This problem is more with 20 years below age group compared to 21-35 years age group.
- There is no difference between 20 years below and 36 years above age groups.
- There is no difference between 21-35 years age group and 36 years and above age group.

Problem 74: The other learners are also average in learning

- This problem has no difference between 20 years below age group and 21-35 years age group.
- It is more with 36 and above group compared to 20 years below age group.
- There is no difference between 21-35 years age group and 36 years and above age groups.

Problem 76: Lack of knowledge about this programme

- This problem is more with 20 years below age group compared to 21-35 years age group.
- There is no difference between 20 years below and 36 years above age groups.
- It is more with 36 years and above age group than 21-35 years age group.

The hypothesis 5(iv) that "there is no difference in the effect of problems among drop-outs in the age groups of 20 years and below; 21-35 years; and 36 years and above" is proved in the case of 65 problems noted in Table 4.67 and not in the case of 15 problems found in Table 4.68.

Table 4.68: Showing the problems on which differential effects exist among drop-outs of different age groups

S.No. of problem in the rating scale	*Problem*	*Group-1 20 years and below*		*Group-2 21-35 years*		*Group-3 36 years and above*		*'F' value*	*Significance*	*'t' values*		
		Mean	*SD*	*Mean*	*SD*	*Mean*	*SD*			*Group 1-2*	*Group 2-3*	*Group 1-3*
1	*2*	*3*	*4*	*5*	*6*	*7*	*8*	*9*	*10*	*11*	*12*	*13*
SOC 16	Attending functions and going to movies	2.23	1.34	1.92	1.41	2.41	1.32	4.06	@@	2.02@@	0.90NS	2.62@
PSY 17	There is no understanding between the learner and the instructor	2.17	1.43	1.80	1.18	2.42	1.29	9.07	@	2.02@@	4.15@	1.74NS
PSY 18	The learner is not able to answer to the instructor	2.24	1.30	2.10	1.32	2.43	11.28	4.26	@@	0.97NS	2.96@	2.06@@
PSY 28	The fellow learners do not listen to the thoughts and ideas	2.10	1.36	1.90	1.36	2.43	1.20	5.94	@@	1.29NS	3.69@	2.36@@

(Table Contd...)

1	2	3	4	5	6	7	8	9	10	11	12	13
FAM 32	Looking after the children	1.65	1.22	1.89	1.41	2.22	1.24	4.49	@@	1.58^{NS}	1.91^{NS}	3.20$^{@}$
INS 48	Instruction is limited only to literacy	2.11	1.31	2.03	1.33	2.43	1.37	4.47	@@	0.50^{NS}	2.90$^{@}$	2.36$^{@@}$
INS 53	The absence of audio-visual aids useful for instruction	2.17	1.24	1.75	1.19	2.33	1.18	8.28	@	3.10$^{@}$	3.59$^{@}$	0.88^{NS}
INS 57	The instructional methods specified by the government are not liked	1.64	1.23	2.23	1.31	2.02	1.23	8.24	@	4.09$^{@}$	1.19^{NS}	2.13$^{@@}$
COM 60	I am not permitted to go with my friends	2.41	1.37	2.05	1.33	2.08	1.24	4.22	@@	2.74$^{@}$	0.16^{NS}	2.12$^{@@}$
COM 61	Good friends are not available at the centre	2.39	1.30	1.83	2.28	1.97	1.32	7.42	@	3.82$^{@}$	0.75^{NS}	2.23$^{@@}$
COM 63	The centre is co-educated	2.32	1.23	1.82	1.39	2.28	1.36	6.44	@@	3.38$^{@}$	2.43$^{@@}$	0.21^{NS}
PER 67	Getting newly married	1.78	1.32	1.60	1.33	2.13	1.30	4.26	@@	1.18^{NS}	2.93$^{@}$	1.85^{NS}
PER 70	Getting the marriage age	2.32	1.24	1.87	1.37	2.02	1.47	4.45	@@	3.11$^{@}$	0.77^{NS}	1.50^{NS}
PER 74	The other learners also average in learning	1.75	1.38	2.04	1.26	2.29	1.18	4.46	@@	1.92^{NS}	1.53^{NS}	2.98$^{@}$
PER 76	Lack of knowledge about this programme	2.38	1.15	1.86	1.36	2.32	1.17	7.71	@	3.70$^{@}$	2.70$^{@@}$	0.40^{NS}

@: Significant at 0.01 level   @@: Significant at 0.05 level

SOC: Social Problems area   *INS:* Instructor related Problems area

PSY: Psychological problems   *COM:* Community related Problems area

FAM: Familial Problems   *PER:* Personal Problems area

Effect of Problems on the Caste of the Drop-outs

1. There exists 'no difference' in the difficulty level/effect experienced among drop-outs of different caste groups namely SC/ST, B.C. and OC on 67 problems noted in Table 4.69.

Table 4.69: Showing the problems on which there is no difference in the effect of problems among dropouts of different caste groups

S. No. of problem in the rating scale	*Problem*	*SC/ST N = 169*		*BC N = 177*		*OC N = 144*		*'F' Value*	*Significant*
		Mean	*SD*	*Mean*	*SD*	*Mean*	*SD*		
1	2	3	4	5	6	7	8	9	10
ECO 1	No immediate financial benefit by education	2.00	1.38	1.96	1.23	2.03	1.26	0.81	NS
ECO 2	Busy with farm work	2.03	1.47	2.03	1.29	2.05	1.30	0.06	
ECO 3	Owners and landlords do not permit for attending centres	1.76	1.42	1.81	1.33	1.57	1.32	2.24	NS
ECO 4	There is no immediate use by getting education	2.07	1.28	1.91	1.25	2.08	1.39	0.67	NS
ECO 5	My family is economically backward	1.95	1.40	1.82	1.39	1.91	1.29	0.35	NS
ECO 6	There are no specific working hours in different professions	2.30	1.32	2.17	1.27	2.17	1.39	0.49	NS
SOC 7	The instructor does not belong to my place	2.08	1.32	2.09	1.37	1.74	1.40	2.12	NS
SOC 9	The instructor utilises the learners for his personal work	1.81	1.42	1.90	1.41	1.82	1.31	0.17	NS
SOC 10	Personal position is at a stake in the society	2.18	1.42	2.14	1.28	1.94	1.31	1.10	NS
SOC 12	The instructor and the learner are not friends	2.00	1.50	2.22	1.36	1.86	1.34	1.82	NS

(Table Contd...)

1	2	3	4	5	6	7	8	9	10
SOC 13	There are some fights in the village	1.59	1.32	1.56	1.20	1.98	1.40	3.77	NS
SOC 14	Many learners belong to the upper caste	2.00	1.42	1.97	1.44	1.85	1.43	0.41	NS
SOC 16	Attending functions and going to movies	2.03	1.44	2.07	1.59	2.29	1.39	1.30	NS
PSY 18	The learner is not able to answer to the instructor	2.11	1.38	2.43	1.27	2.25	1.26	2.10	
PSY 19	Unwilling to get education	2.12	1.22	2.34	1.31	2.18	1.32	1.01	NS
PSY 20	Feeling that the age to study has passed	2.28	1.29	2.12	1.25	2.19	1.17	0.55	NS
PSY 21	Feeling shy to go to the centre	1.98	1.40	2.06	1.41	2.11	1.42	0.28	NS
PSY 22	Feeling that others would mock	2.26	1.35	1.95	1.32	2.37	1.41	2.99	NS
PSY 23	Easily getting tired	2.40	1.20	2.32	1.24	2.32	1.14	2.23	NS
PSY 24	Feeling why one should get educated when the age is so much	1.98	1.23	2.05	1.34	2.07	1.30	0.18	NS
PSY 25	Feeling that education is only for wealthy people	1.98	1.41	1.98	1.29	1.67	1.36	2.05	NS
PSY 26	Feeling shy during conversation with others	1.94	1.32	2.14	1.39	2.03	1.43	0.76	NS
PSY 27	Learners calling by nick-names	2.04	1.40	1.98	1.25	1.95	1.41	0.145	NS
PSY 29	Feeling that studying at the centre is a waste	2.14	1.37	1.98	1.33	2.35	1.38	2.30	NS
FAM 31	Other family members refuse permission to attend during nights	2.18	1.44	12.28	1.32	2.18	1.30	0.26	NS
FAM 33	Other family members do not co-operate in matters of education	1.91	1.34	2.11	1.36	1.71	1.25	2.63	NS
FAM 34	The time of the centre is the supper time	2.02	1.23	2.29	1.40	2.08	1.32	1.42	NS

(Table Contd...)

1	2	3	4	5	6	7	8	9	10
FAM 36	Unable to go to the centre because of heavy work	2.07	1.34	2.07	1.25	2.24	1.22	0.70	NS
FAM 37	The centre is not well maintained	1.70	1.27	2.07	1.41	1.82	1.18	2.88	NS
FAM 38	The instructor is not punctual to the centre	1.78	1.41	1.94	1.30	2.08	1.24	1.81	NS
INS 40	There is no teaching experience to the instructor	1.75	1.33	2.06	1.29	2.01	1.36	2.28	NS
INS 41	The instructor is unable to explain clearly	1.90	1.41	1.99	1.20	2.06	1.26	0.49	NS
INS 42	The instructor does not treat all the learners equally	2.25	1.47	1.91	1.32	1.86	1.30	3.39	NS
INS 43	The instructor is negligent	1.94	1.37	2.07	1.43	2.03	1.40	0.35	NS
INS 44	The instructor does not accept criticism with open heart	1.89	1.36	1.88	1.30	2.10	1.26	1.07	NS
INS 45	The instruction is not relevant to the learners	1.97	1.37	2.22	1.32	2.00	1.23	1.38	NS
INS 46	The instructor lacks good voice and fluency	2.12	1.31	2.40	1.16	2.41	1.14	2.60	NS
INS 47	The instructor fails to enthuse the learners to participate	2.14	1.37	2.07	1.26	2.43	1.23	2.58	NS
INS 48	Instruction is limited only to literacy	2.20	1.39	1.94	1.38	2.32	1.22	2.37	NS
INS 49	Providing too much information within a short time	2.03	1.48	2.00	1.30	2.07	1.28	0.09	NS
INS 50	The instructor does not reveal in learners, progress	2.10	1.28	2.05	1.37	2.35	1.39	1.81	NS
INS 51	The instructor uses difficult languages, pictures and symbols	2.18	1.08	2.01	1.36	1.86	1.25	2.31	NS
INS 52	Teaching aids are not available at the right time	2.10	1.35	2.33	1.35	2.05	1.17	1.59	NS

(Table Contd...)

1	2	3	4	5	6	7	8	9	10
INS 53	The absence of audio-visual aids useful for instruction	1.86	1.18	2.11	1.18	2.04	1.33	1.18	
INS 54	Related primary teaching books are not in order	2.05	1.42	1.80	1.33	2.15	1.25	2.16	NS
INS 55	The lessons are not according to the requirements and taste	2.11	1.39	2.05	1.20	2.21	1.18	0.50	NS
INS 56	The books are difficult to learn	2.16	1.38	2.43	1.31	2.11	1.21	3.28	NS
INS 57	The instructional methods specified by the government are not liked	1.71	1.28	2.10	1.18	2.19	1.38	3.48	NS
COM 58	There is no encouragement from the village elders	2.05	1.32	2.20	1.31	1.98	1.27	0.87	NS
COM 59	Friends do not go to the centre	2.12	1.38	2.26	1.32	2.11	1.32	0.47	NS
COM 60	I am not permitted to go with my friends	2.24	1.21	2.32	1.28	2.00	1.35	1.85	NS
COM 61	Good friends are not available at the centre	1.98	1.23	2.14	1.43	2.05	1.32	0.52	
COM 62	The time of the centre is inconvenient	2.19	1.21	2.19	1.26	2.07	1.24	0.36	NS
COM 63	The centre is co-educated	2.22	1.46	1.92	1.12	2.01	1.38	1.88	NS
COM 64	No one else visits the centre except the instructor	1.91	1.40	2.10	1.24	2.21	1.26	1.87	NS
COM 65	The time of the programme is short	1.89	1.34	2.02	1.21	1.91	1.33	0.38	NS
PER 66	Becoming a slave to bad habits	1.82	1.48	2.29	1.30	2.10	1.49	3.82	NS
PER 67	Getting newly married	1.65	1.32	1.98	1.21	1.70	1.37	2.25	NS
PER 70	Getting the marriage age	2.15	1.37	2.05	1.34	1.89	1.35	1.28	NS
PER 72	The other learners are mocking because of my backwardness in learning	2.22	1.34	2.05	1.30	2.02	1.28	0.92	NS

(Table Contd...)

1	2	3	4	5	6	7	8	9	10
PER 73	Getting discouraged after working hard to get educated and feeling that this attempt is useless	1.78	1.37	1.82	1.29	1.74	1.13	0.10	NS
PER 74	The other learners also are average in learning	1.89	1.34	1.97	1.28	2.15	1.25	1.42	NS
PER 75	The instructor is male	2.20	1.39	2.23	1.29	1.96	1.40	1.35	NS
PER 76	Lack of knowledge about this programme	2.02	1.35	2.25	1.27	2.14	1.17	1.15	NS
PER 77	The relevant lessons are not taught at the centre	2.16	1.27	2.00	1.28	2.10	1.35	0.50	NS
PRO 79	The centre is started at inconvenient place/ environment with sounds and bad smell	1.94	1.34	2.12	1.70	2.21	1.35	1.66	NS
PRO 80	The centre is at a distance	2.36	1.28	2.12	1.23	2.25	1.36	2.26	NS

NS: Not-Significant

ECO: Economic problems

SOC: Social Problems area

PSY: Psychological problems

FAM: Familial Problems

INS: Instructor related Problems area

COM: Community related Problems area

PER: Personal Problems area

PRO: Programme related problems

2. There exists differences among drop-outs belonging to different caste groups on 13 problems, the details of which are shown in Table 4.70.

a. The difficulty experienced by "BC caste group" is higher than the "SC/ST caste group" on 8 problems indicated below:

11. Some learners have enmity in the centre.
15. There are some learners with bad behaviour in the centre.
28. The fellow learners do not listen to the thoughts and ideas.
32. Looking after the children.
39. The instructor is not well versed with his teaching.
68. Due to ill-health.

71. The other learners are much older.
78. Minimum amenities are not found at the centre (air/ventilation).

b. **The effect is more on "SC/ST caste group" than that of "BC caste group" with regard to only 2 problems i.e.,**

17. There is no understanding between the learner and the instructor,
69. Quarrelling with other learners.

c. **The "OC caste group" experienced more difficulty in the case of 3 problems shown below compared to "SC/ST caste group".**

11. Some learners have enmity in the centre.
30. Feeling that learning at home instead of at the centre is better.
35. There is none else at home.

d. **The "BC caste group" felt more difficulty on 7 problems noted below compared to "OC caste group".**

8. The instructor does not belong to his caste.
15. There are some learners with bad behaviour in the centre.
28. The fellow learners do not listen to the thoughts and ideas.
32. Looking after the children.
39. The instructor is not well-versed with his teaching.
68. Due to ill-health.
78. Minimum amenities are not found at the centre (air/ventilation).

e. **The "OC caste group" felt more difficulty compared to "BC caste group" on the following 5 problems :**

17. There is no understanding between the learner and the instructor.
30. Feeling that learning at home instead of at the centre is better.
35. There is none else at home.
69. Quarrelling with other learners.

78. Minimum amenities are not found at the centre (air/ventilation).

3. Perusing at the difficulty level of each problem experienced by different caste groups, the following problem-wise conclusions are drawn:

Problem 8: The instructor does not belong to his caste

- This problem has no difference between "SC/ST caste group" and "BC caste group".
- There is no difference between "SC/ST caste" and "OC caste" group.
- It is more with "BC caste" group compared to "OC caste" group.

Problem 11: Some learners have enmity in the centre

- This problem is more with "BC caste group" compared to "SC/ST caste group".
- It is more with "OC caste group" than "SC/ST caste group".
- There is no difference between "BC caste group" and "OC caste group".

Problem 15: There are some learners with bad behaviours in the centre

- This problem is more with "BC caste group" compared to "SC/ST caste group".
- There is no difference between "SC/ST caste group" and "OC caste group".
- It is more with "BC caste group "compared to "OC caste group".

Problem 17: There is no understanding between the learner and the instructor

- This problem is more with "SC/ST caste group" compared to "BC caste group".
- This problem has no difference between "SC/ST caste group" and "OC caste group".
- It is high with "BC caste group", compared to "OC caste group".

- It is more with "OC caste group" than "BC caste group".

Problem 28: The fellow learners do not listen to the thoughts and ideas

- This problem is more with "BC caste group" than "SC/ST caste group".
- There is no difference between "SC/ST caste group" and "OC caste group".
- It is high with "BC caste compared to "OC caste group".

Problem 30: Feeling that learning at home instead of at the centre is better

- This problem has no difference between "BC caste group" and "SC/ST caste group".
- It is more with "OC caste group" compared to "SC/ST caste group".
- This is more with "OC caste group" than the "BC caste group".

Problem 32: Looking after the children

- This problem is more with "BC caste group" compared to "SC/ST caste group".
- There is no difference between "SC/ST caste group" and "OC caste group".
- It is more with "BC caste group" than the "OC caste group".

Problem 35: There is none else at home

- There is no difference between "SC/ST caste group" and "BC caste group".
- It is more with "OC caste group" compared to "SC/ST caste group".
- This problem is more with "OC caste group" than the "BC caste group".

Problem 39: The instructor is not well-versed with his teaching

- This problem is more with "BC caste group" compared to "SC/ST caste group".
- There is no difference between "SC/ST and OC caste group".

- It is more with "BC caste group" than the "OC caste group".

Problem 68: Due to ill-health

- This problem is more with "BC caste group" compared to "SC/ST caste group".
- This problem has no difference between "SC/ST caste" and "OC caste" as groups.
- It is more with "BC caste group" compared to "OC caste group".

Problem 69: Quarrelling with other learners

- This is more with "SC/ST caste group" compared to "BC caste group".
- There is no difference between "SC/ST caste" and "OC caste group".
- This problem is more with "OC caste group" than "BC caste group".

Problem 71: The other learners are much older

- This problem is more with "BC caste group" compared to "SC/ST caste group".
- There is no difference between "SC/ST caste group" and "OC caste groups".

Problem 78: Minimum amenities are not found at the centre (air/ventilation)

- This problem is more with "BC caste group" compared to "SC/ST caste group".
- There is no difference between "SC/ST and OC caste groups".
- This problem is high with "OC caste group" compared to "BC caste group".

4. The hypothesis 5(v) that "there is no difference in the effect of problems among drop-outs belonging to different castes—scheduled caste/scheduled tribe; backward class, and other castes" is proved in the case of 67 problems found in the Table 4.69 and not in the case of 13 problems founding the Table 4.70.

Table 4.70: Showing the problems on which differential effects exist among dropouts of different caste groups

S.No. of problem in the rating scale	Problem	Group-1 SC/ST		Group-2 BC		Group-3 OC		'F' Value	Significance	't' values		
		Mean	SD	Mean	SD	Mean	SD			Group 1-2	Group 2-3	Group 1-3
1	2	3	4	5	6	7	8	9	10	11	12	13
SOC 8	The instructor does not belong to the caste	2.14	1.40	2.35	1.32	1.74	1.47	3.97	@@	1.29[NS]	2.80[@]	1.74[NS]
SOC 11	Some learners have enmity in the centre	1.63	1.37	2.19	1.42	2.14	1.43	6.98	@	3.31[@]	0.30[@]	2.94[@]
SOC 15	There are some learners with bad behaviour in the centre	1.72	1.34	2.23	1.40	1.64	1.40	6.38	@@	3.08[@]	3.16[@]	0.43[NS]
PSY 17	There is no understanding between the learner and the instructor	2.17	1.35	1.76	1.35	2.20	1.19	4.38	@@	2.57[@@]	2.62[@]	0.15[NS]
PSY 28	The fellow learners do not listen to the thoughts and ideas	1.98	1.36	2.41	1.31	1.90	1.33	5.11	@@	2.69[@]	2.97[@]	0.52[NS]
PSY 30	Feeling that learning at home instead of at the centre is better	1.79	1.34	1.90	1.37	2.34	1.26	6.08	@@	0.69[NS]	2.53[@@]	3.52[@]

(Table Contd...)

1	2	3	4	5	6	7	8	9	10	11	12	13
FAM 32	Looking after the children	1.66	1.24	2.29	1.46	1.75	1.23	8.47	@	$3.76^{@}$	$3.02^{@}$	0.57^{NS}
FAM 35	There is none else at home	2.17	1.34	2.02	1.47	2.43	1.23	5.21	@@	0.89^{NS}	$3.10^{@}$	$2.60^{@}$
FAM 39	The instructor is not well-versed with his teaching	1.80	1.32	2.43	1.45	1.69	1.36	10.19	@	$3.73^{@}$	$4.01^{@}$	0.68^{NS}
PER 68	Due to ill-health	1.86	1.38	2.43	1.19	2.07	1.43	9.20	@	$4.52^{@}$	$2.75^{@}$	1.25^{NS}
PER 69	Quarrelling with other learners	1.85	1.38	1.55	1.18	1.97	1.34	3.91	@@	$2.24^{@@}$	$2.75^{@}$	0.69^{NS}
PER 71	The other learners are much older	1.91	1.36	2.32	1.27	1.84	1.32	4.67	@@	$2.63^{@}$	$2.83^{@}$	0.42^{NS}
PRO 78	Minimum amenities are not found at the centre (air/ventilation)	1.92	1.27	2.37	1.29	2.25	1.38	4.60	@@	$2.94^{@}$	0.69^{NS}	$2.04^{@@}$

@: Significant at 0.01 level   @@: Significant at 0.05 level

SOC: Social Problems area   *INS:* Instructor related Problems area

PSY: Psychological problems   *PER:* Personal Problems

FAM: Familial Problems   *PRO:* Programme related Problems

Effect of Problems on the Occupation of the Drop-outs

1. There exists 'no difference' in the difficulty level/effect experienced among drop-outs of different caste groups namely agriculture, labour and others on 68 problems noted in Table 4.71.

Table 4.71: Showing the problems on which there is no difference in the effect of problems among drop-outs of different occupation groups

S.No. of problem in the rating scale	*Problem*	*Agriculture*		*Labour*		*Others*		*'F' Value*	*Significant*
		Mean	*SD*	*Mean*	*SD*	*Mean*	*SD*		
1	2	3	4	5	6	7	8	9	10
ECO 1	No immediate financial benefit by education	1.91	1.23	2.16	1.41	1.92	1.26	1.54	NS
ECO 2	Busy with farm work	2.05	1.34	2.10	1.41	1.90	1.37	0.56	
ECO 3	Owners and land-lords do not permit	1.53	1.29	1.73	1.51	1.96	1.29	2.90	NS
ECO 4	There is no immediate use by getting education	2.10	1.31	2.02	1.21	1.89	1.43	0.75	NS
ECO 5	My family is economically backward	1.76	1.43	2.11	1.29	1.86	1.32	2.66	NS
ECO 6	There are no specific working hours in different professions	2.16	1.38	2.27	1.28	2.29	1.27	0.39	NS
SOC 7	The instructor does not belong to my place	1.85	1.37	1.89	1.38	2.29	1.29	3.26	NS
SOC 8	The instructor does not belong to my caste	1.98	1.48	1.54	1.40	2.41	1.21	2.72	NS
SOC 10	Personal position is at a stake in the society	2.06	1.28	2.13	1.45	2.15	1.34	0.18	NS

(Table Contd...)

1	*2*	*3*	*4*	*5*	*6*	*7*	*8*	*9*	*10*
SOC 13	There are some fights in the village	1.74	1.44	1.63	1.23	1.70	1.20	0.23	NS
SOC 14	Many learners belong to the upper caste	1.85	1.44	1.95	1.42	2.15	1.39	2.25	NS
SOC 15	There are some learners with bad behaviour in the centre	1.83	1.40	1.72	1.37	2.07	1.40	·1.59	NS
SOC 16	Attending functions and going to movies	2.22	1.44	1.86	1.41	2.32	1.17	3.64	NS
PSY 17	There is no understanding between the learner and the instructor	2.03	1.29	2.02	1.35	2.17	1.33	0.41	NS
PSY 18	The learner is not able to answer to the instructor	2.40	1.28	2.00	1.29	2.30	1.38	3.80	
PSY 19	Unwilling to get education	2.25	1.25	2.20	1.19	2.09	1.46	0.44	NS
PSY 20	Feeling that the age to study has passed	2.07	1.24	2.41	1.23	2.19	1.24	2.96	NS
PSY 21	Feeling shy to go to the centre	2.08	1.38	1.91	1.41	2.07	1.47	0.25	NS
PSY 22	Feeling that others would mock	2.08	1.37	2.16	1.33	2.42	1.37	3.03	NS
PSY 23	Easily getting tired	2.42	1.19	2.15	1.22	2.43	1.12	3.30	NS
PSY 24	Feeling why one should get educated when the age is so much	2.11	1.27	1.90	1.31	2.05	1.27	1.07	NS
PSY 26	Feeling shy during conversation with others	2.03	1.35	1.88	1.39	2.22	1.38	1.56	NS
PSY 27	Learners calling by nick-names	1.97	1.40	1.91	1.38	2.19	1.23	1.10	NS
PSY 28	The fellow learners do not listen to the thoughts and ideas	2.17	1.36	2.11	1.39	1.88	1.23	1.34	NS
PSY 29	Feeling that studying at the centre is a waste	2.24	1.32	2.02	1.39	2.19	1.29	1.12	NS

(Table Contd...)

1	2	3	4	5	6	7	8	9	10
PSY 30	Feeling that learning at home instead of at the centre is better	2.02	1.32	2.43	1.36	2.20	1.34	2.56	NS
FAM 31	Other family members refuse permission to attend during nights	2.18	1.34	2.05	1.43	2.42	1.28	2.44	NS
FAM 32	Looking after the children	1.97	1.33	1.71	1.29	1.86	1.36	1.82	NS
FAM 34	The time of the centre is the supper time	2.29	1.30	2.16	1.30	2.40	1.25	3.40	NS
FAM 35	There is none else at home	1.97	1.33	2.17	1.41	2.27	1.25	0.32	NS
FAM 36	Unable to go the centre because of heavy work	2.20	1.30	2.08	1.31	2.00	1.20	0.84	NS
FAM 37	The centre is not well maintained	1.80	1.30	1.84	1.26	1.95	1.36	0.38	NS
FAM 39	The instructor is not well-versed with his teaching	1.92	1.44	1.80	1.37	2.27	1.35	3.02	NS
INS 40	There is no teaching experience to the instructor	2.00	1.32	1.89	1.37	1.79	1.30	0.96	NS
INS 41	The instructor is unable to explain clearly	1.88	1.30	2.12	1.23	1.92	1.44	1.38	NS
INS 42	The instructor does not treat all the learners equally	1.98	1.40	1.99	3.35	2.25	1.42	1.15	NS
INS 43	The instructor is negligent	1.89	1.37	1.93	1.45	2.36	1.32	3.61	NS
INS 44	The instructor does not accept criticism with open heart	1.99	1.33	1.83	1.35	2.04	1.21	0.82	NS
INS 46	The instructor lacks good voice and fluency	2.42	1.21	2.15	1.29	2.20	1.13	2.13	NS
INS 47	The instructor fails to enthuse the learners to participate	2.32	1.36	1.99	1.32	2.29	1.10	2.77	NS

(Table Contd...)

1	*2*	*3*	*4*	*5*	*6*	*7*	*8*	*9*	*10*
INS 48	Instruction is limited only to literacy	2.00	1.34	2.24	1.35	2.36	1.33	2.47	NS
INS 49	Providing too much information within a short time	2.12	1.26	2.07	1.56	1.79	1.24	1.66	NS
INS 50	The instructor does not reveal in learners progress	2.18	1.38	2.10	1.31	2.19	1.32	0.17	NS
INS 51	The instructor uses difficult languages, pictures and symbols	1.90	1.21	2.11	1.17	2.23	1.29	2.57	NS
INS 52	Teaching aids are not available at the right time	2.03	1.34	2.24	1.33	2.27	1.15	1.45	NS
INS 53	The absence of audio-visual aids useful for instruction	1.97	1.23	2.08	1.27	2.43	1.09	0.45	
INS 54	Related primary teaching books are not in order	2.09	1.22	2.00	1.52	1.84	1.33	0.96	NS
INS 55	The lessons are not according to the requirements and taste	2.10	1.21	2.04	1.34	2.29	1.32	1.04	NS
INS 56	The books are difficult to learn	2.08	1.28	2.42	1.36	2.33	1.30	2.67	NS
INS 57	The instructional methods specified by the government are not liked	1.93	1.30	2.05	1.29	2.04	1.27	0.40	NS
COM 58	There is no encouragement from the village elders	2.04	1.30	2.05	1.37	2.20	1.20	0.46	NS
COM 60	I am not permitted to go with my friends	2.17	1.32	2.31	1.43	2.05	1.22	0.94	NS
COM 61	Good friends are not available at the centre	2.22	1.36	1.82	1.18	2.02	1.37	3.56	
COM 62	The time of the centre is inconvenient	2.04	1.17	2.19	1.37	2.35	1.10	1.84	NS
COM 63	The centre is co-educated	2.06	1.37	2.01	1.37	2.20	1.26	0.50	NS

(Table Contd...)

1	2	3	4	5	6	7	8	9	10
COM 64	No one else visits the centre except the instructor	2.08	1.32	1.89	1.34	2.26	1.26	2.02	NS
COM 65	The time of the programme is short	1.95	1.29	1.87	1.34	2.00	1.24	0.27	NS
PER 67	Getting newly married	1.53	1.29	1.75	1.34	2.08	1.38	3.45	NS
PER 68	Due to ill-health	2.20	1.40	1.94	1.41	2.23	1.23	1.75	NS
PER 70	Getting the marriage age	1.88	1.33	2.23	1.42	2.13	1.29	2.77	NS
PER 71	The other learners are much older	2.06	1.33	1.82	1.39	2.20	1.22	2.23	NS
PER 72	The other learner are mocking because of my backwardness in learning	2.08	1.33	2.04	1.39	2.30	1.28	1.12	NS
PER 73	Getting discouraged after working hard to get educated and feeling that this attempt is useless	1.65	1.29	1.95	1.33	1.79	1.09	2.22	NS
PER 75	The instructor is male	2.01	1.33	2..6	1.40	2.05	1.37	2.68	NS
PER 76	Lack of knowledge about this programme	2.18	1.29	2.05	1.30	2.10	1.05	0.39	NS
PER 77	The relevant lessons are not taught at the centre	1.96	1.25	2.14	1.30	2.33	1.34	2.50	NS
PRO 78	Minimum amenities are not found at the centre (air/ventilation)	2.16	1.38	1.97	1.28	2.39	1.24	2.57	NS
PRO 79	The centre is started at inconvenient place/ environment with sounds and bad smell	2.08	1.35	1.99	1.27	2.17	1.13	0.55	NS

NS: Not-Significant

ECO: Economic problems
COM: Community related Problems area
SOC: Social Problems area
PER: Personal Problems area
PSY: Psychological problems
PRO: Programme related problems
FAM: Familial Problems
INS: Instructor related Problems area

2. There exists differences among drop-outs belonging to different occupation groups on 12 problems, the details of which are shown in Table 4.72.

a. The difficulty experienced by "agriculture group" is higher than the labour group on 3 problems indicated below :

9. The instructor utilises the learners for his personal work
11. Some learners have enmity in the centre.
38. Other family members do not co-operate in matters of education.

b. The effect is more on "labour group" than that of "agriculture group" with regard to only 2 problems i.e.,

33. Other family members do not co-operate in matter of education.
45. The instruction is not relevant to the learners.

c. The "others group" experienced more difficulty in the case of 6 problems shown below compared to "agriculture group".

12. The instructor and the learner are not friends.
25. Feeling that education is only for wealthy people.
59. Providing too much information within a short time.
66. Becoming a slave to bad habits.
69. Quarrelling with other learners.
74. The other learners also are average in learning.

d. The "others group" felt more difficulty on 10 problems noted below compared to "labour groups".

9. The instructor utilises the learners for his personal work.
11. Some learners have enmity in the centre
12. The instructor and the learner are not friends.
25. Feeling that education is only for wealthy people.
38. The instructor is not punctual in the centre.

45. The instructor is not relevant to the learners.
59. Providing too much information within a short time.
66. Becoming a slave to bad habits.
69. Quarrelling with other learners.
74. The other learners also are average in learning.

3. A glance through the difficulty level, of each problem experienced by different occupation groups, would reveal the following problem-wise differences.

Problem 9: The instructor utilises the learners for his personal work

- This problem is high with agriculture group compared to labour group.
- There is no difference between agriculture group and other groups.
- It is more with other group than that of labour group.

Problem 11: Some learners have enmity in the centre

- This problem is more with "agriculture group" compared to "labour group".
- This problem has no difference between two groups i.e., agriculture and other groups.
- It is greater with other group compared to labour group.

Problem 12: The instructor and the learner are not friends

- This problem has no difference between agriculture group and labour groups.
- It is more with "Other group" compared to agriculture groups.
- This is high with "Other group" compared to labour groups.

Problem 25: Feeling that education is only for wealthy people

- This problem has no difference between two groups i.e., agriculture and labour groups.

- It is more with "Other group" than that of agriculture group.
- It is more with others, compared to labour groups.

Problem 33: Other family members do not co-operate in matters of education

- It is high with "Labour group" than that of agriculture group.
- This problem has no difference between "agriculture group and other group".
- There is no difference between "labour group and other group".

Problem 38: The instructor is not punctual to the centre

- This problem is more with agriculture group compared to labour group.
- There is no difference between agriculture and other groups.
- This is more with "other group" than that of labour group.

Problem 45: The instructor is not relevant to the learners

- This problem is greater with "labour group" compared to "agriculture group".
- There is no difference between agriculture group and other group.
- It is high with other group, compared to labour group.

Problem 59: Providing too much information within a short time

- This problem has no difference between 'agriculture' and labour groups.
- It is more with 'other group' compared to 'agriculture group'.
- It is enroll with 'other group' than that of labour group.

Problem 66: Becoming a slave to bad habits

- There is no difference between 'agriculture group' and labour group.

- This problem is more with 'other group' compared to 'agriculture group'.
- It is more with 'other group' than that of 'labour group'

Problem 74: The other learners also are average in learning

- This problem has no difference between 'agriculture group' and 'labour group'.
- This problem is more with 'other group' compared to 'agriculture group'.
- It is more with 'other group' than that of 'labour group'.

Problem 80: The centre is at a distance

- There is no difference between 'agriculture group' and labour group.
- This problem has no difference between two groups i.e., 'agriculture group' and 'other groups'.
- It is more with 'labour group' compared to other group.

4. The hypothesis 5(vi) that "there is no difference in the effect of problems among drop-outs belonging to different occupations—agriculture, labour and others is proved in the case of 68 problems found in Table 4.71 and not in the case of 12 problems found in Table 4.72.

Table 4.72: Showing the problems on which differential effects exist among dropouts of different occupation groups

S.No. of problem in the rating scale	Problem	Group-1 Agriculture		Group-2 Labour		Group-3 Others		'F' value	Significance	't' values		
		Mean	SD	Mean	SD	Mean	SD			Group 1-2	Group 2-3	Group 1-3
1	2	3	4	5	6	7	8	9	10	11	12	13
SOC 9	The instructor utilises the learners for his personal work	1.95	1.36	1.57	1.39	2.03	1.32	4.07	@@	2.43@@	2.48@@	0.45NS
SOC 11	Some learners have enmity in the centre	2.04	1.42	1.63	1.43	2.22	1.33	5.33	@@	2.46@@	3.08@	0.01NS
SOC 12	The instructor and the learner are not friends	1.78	1.40	2.05	1.52	2.42	1.17	7.75	@	1.64NS	2.47@@	4.43@
PSY 25	Feeling that education is only for wealthy people	1.75	1.34	1.77	1.42	2.42	1.23	7.23	@	0.08NS	3.43@	3.95@
FAM 33	Other family members do not co-operate in the matters of educations	1.73	1.28	2.16	1.29	1.89	1.43	4.06	@@	2.91@	1.41NS	0.86NS
INS 38	The instructor is not punctual to the centre	2.04	1.35	1.57	1.30	1.89	1.28	7.21	@	3.19@	3.39@	0.75NS

(Table Contd...)

1	2	3	4	5	6	7	8	9	10	11	12	13
INS 45	The instruction is not relevant to the learners	1.77	1.26	2.08	1.34	2.43	1.24	11.55	@	2.04$^{@@}$	2.88$^{@}$	4.97$^{@}$
COM 59	Providing too much information with a short time	1.97	1.41	2.13	1.32	2.43	1.15	63.81	@	1.04^{NS}	2.87$^{@}$	3.96$^{@}$
PER 66	Becoming a slave to bad habits	1.82	1.39	2.02	1.55	2.43	1.26	7.16	@	1.17^{NS}	2.67$^{@}$	4.14$^{@}$
PER 69	Quarrelling with other learners	1.63	1.32	1.71	1.32	2.23	1.24	6.36	@@	0.55^{NS}	2.93$^{@}$	3.69$^{@}$
PER 74	The other learners are average in learning	2.00	1.40	1.74	1.24	2.35	1.06	5.81	@@	1.72^{NS}	3.87$^{@}$	2.26$^{@@}$
PRO 80	The centre is at a distance	2.23	1.30	2.42	1.22	1.97	1.32	3.94	@@	1.65^{NS}	2.79$^{@}$	1.50^{NS}

@: Significant at 0.01 level

@@: Significant at 0.05 level

SOC: Social Problems area

INS: Instructor related Problems area

PSY: Psychological problems

PER: Personal Problems

FAM: Familial Problems

PRO: Programme related Problems

COM: Community related Problems

Effect of problems on the Annual Income of the Drop-outs

1. There exists 'no difference' in the difficulty level among drop-outs of different income groups namely Rs. 20,000 and below, Rs. 21-30 thousands and Rs. 31 thousands and above per annum on 70 problems noted in Table 4.73.

Table 4.73: Showing the problems on which there is no difference in the effect of problems among drop-outs of different income groups

S. No. of problem in the rating scale	*Problem*	*Rs. 20,000 and below N = 188*		*Rs. 21-30 thousands N = 146*		*Rs. 31 thousands and N = 166*		*'F' value*	*Significant*
		Mean	*SD*	*Mean*	*SD*	*Mean*	*SD*		
1	2	3	4	5	6	7	8	9	10
ECO 1	No immediate financial benefit by education	1.90	1.39	1.99	1.28	2.28	1.08	2.06	NS
ECO 2	Busy with farm work	2.11	1.47	1.92	1.26	2.07	1.29	0.82	NS
ECO 4	There is no immediate use by getting education	2.11	1.23	1.91	1.37	2.04	1.35	0.95	NS
ECO 5	My family is economically backward	1.98	1.36	1.86	1.42	1.77	1.26	0.68	NS
ECO 6	There are no specific working hours in different professions	2.19	1.33	2.32	1.29	2.12	1.39	0.62	NS
SOC 7	The instructor does not belong to my place	1.97	1.42	2.06	1.29	1.69	1.34	1.64	NS
SOC 8	The instructor does not belong to my caste	2.14	1.42	2.03	1.38	2.24	1.43	0.55	NS
SOC 9	The instructor utilises the learners for his personal work	1.92	1.41	1.82	1.44	1.63	1.18	1.07	NS
SOC 10	Personal position is at a stake in the society	2.11	1.39	2.11	1.37	2.04	1.23	0.07	NS
SOC 11	Some learners have enmity in the centre	1.75	1.45	2.13	1.36	2.07	1.42	3.20	NS
SOC 12	The instructor and the learner are not friends	2.20	1.47	1.86	1.33	1.90	1.45	2.62	NS

(Table Contd...)

1	2	3	4	5	6	7	8	9	10
SOC 14	Many learners belong to the upper caste	2.09	1.46	1.84	1.39	1.78	1.39	1.69	NS
SOC 15	There are some learners with bad behaviour in the centre	1.88	1.36	1.90	1.48	1.62	1.29	1.06	NS
SOC 16	Attending functions and going to movies	1.98	1.34	2.14	1.42	2.42	1.39	2.87	NS
PSY 17	There is no under-standing between the learner and the instructor	2.01	1.37	2.08	1.31	2.15	1.19	0.28	NS
PSY 18	The learner is not able to answer to the instructor	2.27	1.36	2.26	1.18	2.15	1.48	0.22	NS
PSY 19	Unwilling to get education	2.28	1.18	2.24	1.31	1.86	1.44	2.37	NS
PSY 20	Feeling that the age to study has passed	2.31	1.24	2.11	1.26	2.12	1.20	1.29	NS
PSY 21	Feeling shy to go to the centre	2.05	1.44	2.17	1.35	1.72	1.38	2.35	NS
PSY 22	Feeling that others would mock	2.12	1.41	2.27	1.27	2.28	1.43	0.65	NS
PSY 23	Easily getting tired	2.41	1.21	2.18	1.19	2.43	1.09	3.10	NS
PSY 24	Feeling why one should get educated when the age is so much	2.12	1.27	2.00	1.33	1.83	1.21	1.35	NS
PSY 25	Feeling that education is only for wealthy people	1.86	1.35	1.81	1.43	2.15	1.24	1.44	NS
PSY 26	Feeling shy during conversation with others	2.07	1.38	1.91	1.36	2.13	1.37	0.86	NS
PSY 27	Learners calling by nick-names	2.00	1.43	1.95	1.30	2.00	1.28	0.16	NS
PSY 28	The fellow learners do not listen to the thoughts and ideas	2.14	1.33	2.05	1.38	2.01	1.34	0.29	NS
PSY 29	Feeling that studying at the centre is a waste	2.15	1.39	2.01	1.21	2.43	1.40	2.83	NS
PSY 30	Feeling that learning at home instead of at the centre is better	1.98	1.39	1.91	1.26	2.12	1.38	0.52	NS

(Table Contd...)

1	2	3	4	5	6	7	8	9	10
FAM 31	Other family members refuse permission to attend during nights	2.11	1.37	2.19	1.37	2.43	1.31	1.98	NS
FAM 33	Other family members do not co-operate in matters of education	1.87	1.39	2.04	1.23	1.71	1.32	1.57	NS
FAM 34	The time of the centre is the supper time	2.12	1.29	2.10	1.32	2.13	1.35	0.12	NS
FAM 35	There is none else at home	2.27	1.34	2.14	1.41	2.40	1.31	0.90	NS
FAM 36	Unable to go to the centre because of heavy work	2.43	1.26	2.21	1.24	2.01	1.43	0.63	NS
FAM 37	The centre is not well maintained	1.82	1.20	1.82	1.40	1.95	1.34	0.27	NS
FAM 38	The instructor is not punctual to the centre	1.76	1.31	1.96	1.39	2.22	1.25	3.08	NS
FAM 39	The instructor is not well-versed with his teaching	1.99	1.32	1.94	1.50	1.87	1.43	0.17	NS
INS 40	There is no teaching experience to the instructor	2.02	1.36	1.86	1.25	1.75	1.43	1.13	NS
INS 41	The instructor is unable to explain clearly	1.84	1.31	2.06	1.26	2.16	1.37	2.02	NS
INS 42	The instructor does not treat all the learners equally	2.04	1.27	2.13	1.49	1.84	1.45	0.97	NS
INS 43	The instructor is negligent	2.03	1.41	1.91	1.43	2.15	1.29	0.72	NS
INS 44	The instructor does not accept criticism with open heart	1.92	1.34	2.04	1.35	1.84	1.16	0.58	NS
INS 45	The instruction is not relevant to the learners	2.02	1.29	2.17	1.32	1.86	1.39	1.29	NS
INS 46	The instructor lacks good voice and fluency	2.23	1.26	2.34	1.19	2.31	1.21	0.34	NS
INS 47	The instructor fails to enthuse the learners to participate	2.26	1.29	2.17	1.31	2.12	1.36	0.33	NS
INS 48	Instruction is limited only to literacy	2.30	1.33	2.13	1.31	1.83	1.39	3.05	NS

(Table Contd...)

1	2	3	4	5	6	7	8	9	10
INS 49	Providing too much information within a short time	2.01	1.28	2.05	2.07	1.50	1.32	0.07	NS
INS 50	The instructor does not reveal in learners progress	2.12	1.33	2.26	1.32	2.01	1.43	0.99	NS
INS 52	Teaching aids are not available at the right time	2.03	1.33	1.98	1.32	2.10	1.12	2.19	NS
INS 54	Related primary teaching books are not in order	2.07	1.36	2.04	1.42	1.74	1.12	1.59	NS
INS 55	The lessons are not according to the requirements and taste	2.10	1.28	2.15	1.28	2.13	1.29	0.06	NS
INS 56	The books are difficult to learn	2.39	1.40	2.20	1.20	1.93	1.29	3.12	NS
COM 59	Friends do not go to the centre	2.14	1.32	2.26	1.38	1.98	1.34	0.96	NS
COM 60	I am not permitted to go with my friends	2.27	1.31	2.25	1.39	1.84	1.26	2.69	NS
COM 61	Good friends are not available at the centre	2.02	1.32	2.16	1.28	1.86	1.37	1.23	NS
COM 62	The time of the centre is inconvenient	2.29	1.27	2.09	1.14	1.93	1.28	2.34	NS
COM 63	The centre is co-educated	2.19	1.35	2.06	1.35	1.77	1.31	2.36	NS
COM 64	No one else visits the centre except the instructor	1.90	1.28	2.18	1.39	2.28	1.23	2.50	NS
COM 65	The time of the programme is short	1.80	1.30	1.94	1.32	2.30	1.18	3.65	NS
PER 66	Becoming a slave to bad habits	2.15	1.47	1.81	1.39	2.21	1.46	2.83	NS
PER 67	Getting newly married	1.62	1.27	1.91	1.40	1.83	1.21	2.12	NS
PER 69	Quarrelling with other learners	1.60	1.36	1.90	1.28	2.06	1.25	3.75	NS
PER 70	Getting the marriage age	2.07	1.33	2.05	2.36	2.00	1.44	0.07	NS
PER 71	The other learners are much older	2.08	1.32	2.05	1.36	1.71	1.29	2.02	NS

(Table Contd...)

1	2	3	4	5	6	7	8	9	10
PER 72	The other learners are mocking because of my backwardness in learning	2.03	1.33	2.09	1.36	2.40	1.21	1.96	NS
PER 73	Getting discouraged after working hard to get educated and feeling that this attempt is useless	1.73	1.28	1.91	1.24	1.63	1.29	1.40	NS
PER 74	The other learners also are average in learning	1.86	1.32	2.12	1.26	2.07	1.29	1.82	NS
PER 75	The instructor is male	2.12	1.39	2.06	1.35	2.36	1.33	1.12	NS
PER 77	The relevant lessons are not taught at the centre	2.02	1.21	2.41	1.33	2.22	1.43	0.70	NS
PRO 78	Minimum amenities are not found at the centre (air/ventilation)	2.06	1.26	2.19	1.38	2.27	1.37	0.72	NS
PRO 79	The centre is started at inconvenient place/ environment with sounds and bad smell	2.12	1.28	2.02	1.29	2.03	1.27	0.27	NS

NS: Not-Significant

ECO: Economic problems

SOC: Social Problems area

PSY: Psychological problems

FAM: Familial Problems

INS: Instructor related Problems area

COM: Community related Problems area

PER: Personal Problems area

PRO: Programme related problems

2. There exists differences in the difficulty level felt among drop-outs belonging to different income groups on 10 problems the details of which are shown in Table 4.74.

a. **The difficulty experienced by "Rs. 20,000 and below income group" is higher than the 'Rs. 21-30 thousand income group' on 6 problems indicated below:**

3. Owners and landlords do not permit

51. The instructor uses difficult language, pictures and symbols.

53. The absence of audio-visual aids useful for instruction
58. There is no encouragement from the village elders.
76. Lack of knowledge about this programme.
80. The centre is at a distance.

b. The effect is more on "Rs. 21-30 thousand income group" than that of "Rs. 20,000 and below income group" with regard to only 3 problems i.e.,

32. Looking after the children.
57. The instructional methods specified by the government are not liked.
68. Due to ill-health.

c. The "Rs. 20,000 and below income group" experienced high difficulty in the case of 3 problems shown below compared to "Rs. 31 thousands and above income group".

53. The absence of audio-visual aids useful for instruction.
76. Lack of knowledge about this programme.
80. The centre is at a distance.

d. The "Rs. 21-30 thousand income group" felt more difficulty on to "Rs. 31 thousand and above income group" on the following 2 problems :

51. The instructor uses difficulty in language, pictures and symbols.
68. Due to ill-health.

f. The effect is more on "Rs. 31 thousand and above income group" than that of "Rs. 21-30 thousands income group" with regard to only one problem i.e.,

13. There are some fights in the village.

3. Seeing at the difficulty level of each problem experienced by different income groups, the following problem-wise conclusions are drawn:

Problem 3: Owners and Landlords do not permit

- This problem is high with "Rs. 20,000 and below income group" compared to "Rs. 21-30 thousands income group".
- There is no difference between "Rs. 21-30 thousands" and Rs. 31 thousands and above income group.
- There is no difference between "Rs. 21-30 thousands" and "Rs. 31 thousands and above income groups".

Problem 13: There are some fights in the village

- There is no difference between Rs. 20,000 and below income group and Rs. 21-30 thousands income group.
- This problem is more with "Rs. 31 thousand and above income group" compared to Rs. 20,000 and below income group.
- It is more with Rs. 31 thousands and above income group than that of Rs. 21-30 thousands income group.

Problem 32: Looking after the children

- This problem is more with Rs. 21-30 thousands income group compared to Rs.20,000 and below income group.
- There is no difference between Rs. 20,000 and below income group and Rs.31 thousands and above income group.
- There is no difference between Rs. 21-30 thousands income group and Rs. 31 thousands and above income group.

Problem 51: The instructor uses difficult language, pictures and symbols

- This problem is more with Rs. 20,000 and below income group compared to Rs.21-30 thousand income group.
- It has no difference between Rs. 20,000 and below and Rs. 31 thousands and above income groups.
- It is more with Rs. 21-30 thousand income group than that of Rs. 31 thousand and above income group.

Problem 53: The absence of audio-visual aids useful for instruction

- It is more with "Rs. 20,000 and below income group" compared to Rs. 21-30 thousands income group.
- This problem is more with Rs. 20,000 and below income group than that of Rs.31 thousand and above income group.
- There is no difference between Rs. 21-30 thousand and Rs. 31 thousand and above income group.

Problem 57: The instruction methods specified by the government are not liked

- This problem is more with Rs. 21-30 thousands income group compared to Rs.20,000 and below income group.
- It is more with Rs. 31 thousands and above income group than that of Rs. 20,000 and below income group.
- There is no difference between Rs. 21-30 thousands and Rs. 31 thousands and above income groups.

Problem 58: There is no encouragement from the village elders

- It is more with Rs. 20,000 and below income group compared to Rs. 21-30 thousands income group.
- This problem has no difference between Rs. 20,000 and below income group and Rs. 31 thousand and above income group.
- It has no difference between Rs. 21-30 thousand and Rs. 31 thousands and above income group.

Problem 68: Due to ill-health

- This problem is more with Rs. 21-30 thousand income group compared to Rs.20,000 and below income group.
- It has no difference between Rs. 20,000 and below income group and Rs. 31 thousand and above income group.
- It is more with Rs. 21-30 thousand income group compared to Rs. 31 thousand and above income group.

Problem 76: Lack of knowledge about this programme

- This problem is more with Rs. 20,000 and below income group compared to Rs.21-30 thousand income group.
- It is more with Rs. 20,000 and below income group compared to Rs. 31 thousand and above income group.
- There is no difference between Rs. 21-30 thousands and Rs. 31 thousand and above income groups.

Problem 80: The centre is at a distance

- This problem is high with Rs. 20,000 and below income group compared to Rs.21-30 thousand income group.
- It is greater with Rs. 20,000 and below income group compared to Rs. 31 thousand and above income group.
- There is no difference between Rs. 21-30 thousands and Rs. 31 thousands and above income group.

4. The hypothesis 5(vii) that "there is no difference in the effect of problems among drop-outs belonging to different income groups—Rs. 20,000 and below, Rs. 21-30 thousands and Rs. 31 thousands and above" is proved in the case of 70 problems found in Table 4.73 and not in the case of 10 problems found in the Table 4.74.

Table 4.74: Showing the problems on which differential effects exist among dropouts of different income groups

S.No. of problem in the rating scale	Problem	Group-1 Rs. 20,000 and below		Group-2 Rs. 21-30 thousands		Group-3 Rs. 31 and above		'F' Value	Significance	't' values		
		Mean	SD	Mean	SD	Mean	SD			Group 1-2	Group 2-3	Group 1-3
1	2	3	4	5	6	7	8	9	10	11	12	13
ECO 3	Owners and landlords do not permit	1.89	1.42	1.59	1.30	1.54	1.31	4.09	@@	2.72$^{@}$	0.26^{NS}	1.84^{NS}
SOC 13	There are some fights in the village	1.70	1.42	1.60	1.14	2.10	1.31	4.75	@@	1.39^{NS}	3.20$^{@}$	2.10$^{@@}$
FAM 32	Looking after the children	1.71	1.33	2.11	1.35	1.80	1.23	3.93	@	2.72$^{@}$	1.66^{NS}	0.50^{NS}
INS 51	The instructor uses difficult language, pictures and symbols	1.91	1.51	2.32	1.17	1.80	1.29	6.25	@@	3.15$^{@}$	2.63$^{@}$	0.58^{NS}
INS 53	The absence of audio-visual aids useful for instruction	2.26	1.16	1.76	1.24	1.75	1.23	8.27	@	3.75$^{@}$	0.11^{NS}	2.74$^{@}$
INS 57	The instructional methods specified by the government are not liked	1.76	1.18	2.10	1.27	2.42	1.49	7.51	@	2.56$^{@@}$	1.48^{NS}	3.26$^{@}$

(Table Contd...)

1	2	3	4	5	6	7	8	9	10	11	12	13
COM 58	There is no encouragement from the village elders	2.26	1.29	1.81	1.32	2.06	1.25	4.24	@@	3.01@	2.08NS	1.14NS
PER 68	Due to ill-health	1.95	0.14	2.40	1.33	2.01	1.28	4.79	@@	3.01@	0.36NS	0.33NS
PER 76	Lack of knowledge about this programme	2.35	1.28	1.94	1.38	1.87	1.19	5.82	@@	2.91@	0.36NS	2.74@
PRO 80	The centre is at a distance	2.42	1.20	2.04	1.25	1.80	1.41	12.90	@	4.01@	1.21NS	4.03@

@: Significant at 0.01 level
@@: Significant at 0.05 level
ECO: Economic problems
INS: Instructor related Problems area
SOC: Social Problems area
COM: Community related Problems
PRO: Programme related Problems
PER: Personal Problems

Effect of Problems on the Attendance of the Drop-outs

1. There exists 'no difference' in the difficulty level experienced among drop-outs of different attendance groups namely 1-2 months, 2-4 months and 4-6 months on 71 problems noted in Table 4.75.

Table 4.75: Showing the problems on which there is no difference in the effect of problems among drop-outs of different attendance groups

S.No. of problem in the rating scale	*Problem*	*1-2 months*		*2-4 months*		*4-6 months*		*F value*	*Significance*
		Mean	*SD*	*Mean*	*SD*	*Mean*	*SD*		
1	2	3	4	5	6	7	8	9	10
ECO 1	No immediate financial benefit by education	1.99	1.32	2.06	1.27	1.93	1.32	0.26	NS
ECO 2	Busy with farm work	1.95	1.42	2.22	1.32	1.95	1.33	1.60	NS
ECO 3	Owners and landlords do not permit for attending centres	1.87	1.35	1.55	1.43	1.69	1.32	1.13	NS
ECO 5	My family is economically backward	1.98	1.37	1.86	1.45	1.78	1.24	0.74	NS
ECO 6	There are no specific working hours in different professions	2.32	1.29	2.10	1.30	2.20	1.41	1.12	NS
SOC 7	The instructor does not belong to my place	1.87	1.39	1.97	1.33	2.12	1.36	1.00	NS
SOC 8	The instructor does not belong to my caste	2.02	1.44	2.02	1.41	2.42	1.29	3.37	NS
SOC 10	Personal position is at stake in the society	2.05	1.31	2.20	1.40	2.05	1.37	0.50	NS
SOC 11	Some learners have enmity in the centre	1.90	1.47	2.03	1.35	1.89	1.41	0.40	NS
SOC 12	The instructor and the learner are not friends	1.96	1.39	2.09	1.50	2.06	1.38	0.33	NS
SOC 15	There are some learners with bad behaviour in the centre	1.97	1.48	1.77	1.26	1.69	1.38	1.53	NS

(Table Contd...)

1	*2*	*3*	*4*	*5*	*6*	*7*	*8*	*9*	*10*
SOC 16	Attending functions and going to movies	2.20	1.37	1.96	1.32	2.18	1.50	1.27	NS
PSY 17	There is no understanding between the learner and the instructor	1.99	1.30	2.00	1.36	2.28	1.30	1.58	NS
PSY 18	The learner is not able to answer to the instructor	2.28	1.35	2.19	1.32	2.25	1.26	0.17	NS
PSY 19	Unwilling to get education	2.33	1.25	2.07	1.36	2.11	1.27	1.80	NS
PSY 20	Feeling that the age to study has passed	2.31	1.21	2.13	1.33	2.11	1.16	1.13	NS
PSY 21	Feeling shy to go to the centre	1.97	1.41	2.13	1.46	2.07	1.31	0.51	NS
PSY 22	Feeling that others would mock	2.11	1.49	2.25	1.25	2.31	1.23	0.85	NS
PSY 23	Easily getting tired	2.37	1.19	2.30	1.19	2.41	1.20	0.20	NS
PSY 24	Feeling why one should get educated when the age is so much	2.00	1.28	2.06	1.31	2.05	1.26	0.10	NS
PSY 25	Feeling that education is only for wealthy people	1.90	1.37	1.96	1.33	1.76	1.41	0.60	NS
PSY 26	Feeling shy during conversation with others	2.14	1.31	1.96	1.44	1.87	1.39	1.28	NS
PSY 28	The fellow learners do not listen to the thoughts and ideas	2.15	1.40	2.00	1.37	2.07	1.20	0.42	NS
PSY 29	Feeling that studying at the centre is a waste	2.14	1.38	2.27	1.23	2.00	1.38	1.33	NS
PSY 30	Feeling that learning at home instead of at the centre is better	1.97	1.28	1.93	1.33	2.05	1.48	0.20	NS
FAM 31	Other family members refuse permission to attend during nights	2.09	1.34	2.26	1.38	2.035	1.38	1.27	NS
FAM 32	Looking after the children	1.89	1.34	1.79	1.41	1.95	1.20	0.39	NS
FAM 33	Other family members do not co-operate in matters of education	1.90	1.31	1.92	1.37	1.92	1.33	0.00	NS
FAM 34	The time of the centre is the supper time	2.16	1.35	2.00	1.21	1.97	1.37	0.68	NS

(Table Contd...)

1	2	3	4	5	6	7	8	9	10
FAM 35	There is none else at home	2.28	1.36	2.11	1.34	2.36	1.41	0.94	NS
FAM 36	Unable to go to the centre because of heavy work	2.11	1.25	2.15	1.25	2.10	1.40	0.06	NS
FAM 37	The centre is not well maintained	1.74	1.23	1.81	1.31	2.11	1.40	2.51	NS
FAM 38	The instructor is not punctual to the centre	1.89	1.32	1.90	1.37	2.00	1.33	0.22	NS
FAM 39	The instructor is not well-versed with his teaching	2.10	1.37	1.80	1.42	1.86	1.44	2.02	NS
INS 40	There is no teaching experience to the instructor	1.78	1.26	2.14	1.30	1.88	1.49	2.68	NS
INS 41	The instructor is unable to explain clearly	1.90	1.35	2.03	1.33	2.04	1.16	0.52	NS
INS 42	The instructor does not treat all the learners equally	2.09	1.42	1.96	1.41	2.04	1.28	0.32	NS
INS 43	The instructor is negligent	2.08	1.41	1.87	1.39	2.04	1.38	0.86	NS
INS 44	The instructor does not accept criticism with open heart	1.94	1.31	1.91	1.36	2.03	1.26	0.23	NS
INS 45	The instruction is not relevant to the learners	2.09	1.35	2.09	1.33	1.90	1.24	0.66	NS
INS 48	Instructor is limited only to literacy	2.23	1.31	2.23	1.43	1.89	1.26	2.18	NS
INS 49	Providing too much information within a short time	2.08	1.42	2.19	1.20	1.71	1.46	3.59	NS
INS 50	The instructor does not reveal in learner's progress	2.12	1.33	2.27	1.33	2.06	1.39	0.73	NS
INS 51	The instructor uses difficult languages, pictures and symbols	1.96	1.13	2.13	1.31	2.09	1.26	0.82	NS
INS 52	Teaching aids are not available at the right time	2.26	1.31	1.95	1.24	2.21	1.29	2.28	NS

1	2	3	4	5	6	7	8	9	10
INS 53	The absence of audio-visual aids useful for instruction	1.98	1.24	2.07	1.29	1.95	1.24	0.28	NS
INS 54	Related primary teaching books are not in order	2.20	1.29	1.98	1.44	2.20	1.36	0.04	NS
INS 55	The lessons are not according to the requirements and taste	2.27	1.30	1.87	1.25	2.17	1.23	3.80	NS
INS 56	The books are difficult to learn	2.29	1.33	2.09	1.28	2.39	1.33	1.51	NS
INS 57	The instructional methods specified by the government are not liked	1.92	1.26	2.11	1.32	1.45	1.30	0.92	NS
COM 58	There is no encouragement from the village elders	2.14	1.31	2.08	1.36	1.93	1.21	0.79	NS
COM 59	Friends do not go to the centre	2.07	1.29	2.18	1.37	2.31	1.43	0.03	NS
COM 60	I am not permitted to go with my friends	2.28	1.35	2.04	1.29	2.23	1.38	1.19	NS
COM 61	Good friends are not available at the centre	2.21	1.23	1.81	1.44	2.04	1.26	3.36	NS
COM 62	The time of the centre is inconvenient	2.12	1.25	2.11	1.22	2.30	1.20	0.77	NS
COM 63	The centre is co-educated	2.21	1.39	2.07	1.28	1.87	1.31	3.07	NS
COM 64	No one else visits the centre except the instructor	1.97	1.34	2.19	1.32	2.03	1.29	1.09	NS
PER 66	Becoming a slave to bad habits	2.09	1.43	2.03	1.46	1.92	1.45	0.44	NS
PER 67	Getting newly married	1.81	1.36	1.65	1.29	1.82	1.33	0.65	NS
PER 68	Due to ill-health	2.06	1.35	2.32	1.32	1.97	1.46	2.00	
PER 69	Quarrelling with other learners	1.82	1.32	1.81	1.36	1.68	1.29	0.37	NS
PER 70	Getting the marriage age	2.01	1.27	2.18	1.46	1.94	1.39	0.98	NS
PER 71	The other learners are much older	2.12	1.33	1.89	1.29	1.93	1.39	1.33	NS
PER 72	The other learner are mocking because of my backwardness in learning	2.00	1.34	2.18	1.31	2.28	1.30	1.56	NS

(Table Contd...)

1	2	3	4	5	6	7	8	9	10
PER 73	Getting discouraged after working hard to get educated and feeling that this attempt is useless	1.65	1.25	2.00	1.30	1.73	1.23	2.79	NS
PER 75	The instructor is male	2.14	1.42	1.96	1.38	2.40	1.20	2.81	NS
PER 76	Lack of knowledge about this programme	2.07	1.24	2.14	1.35	2.21	1.27	0.40	NS
PER 77	The relevant lessons are not taught at the centre	2.07	1.29	2.04	1.33	2.25	1.25	0.74	NS
PRO 78	Minimum amenities are not found at the centre (air/ventilation)	2.18	1.30	2.29	1.34	1.87	1.32	2.69	NS
PRO 79	The centre is started at inconvenient place/ environment with sounds and bad smell	2.17	1.20	2.00	1.42	1.94	1.22	1.23	NS
PRO 80	The centre is at a distance	2.43	1.26	2.12	1.25	2.10	1.38	3.00	NS

NS: Not-Significant

ECO: Economic problems — *COM:* Community related Problems area

SOC: Social Problems area — *PER:* Personal Problems area

PSY: Psychological problems — *PRO:* Programme related problems

FAM: Familial Problems — *INS:* Instructor related Problems area

2. There exists differences among dropouts belonging to different attendance groups on 9 problems shown in Table 4.76.

a. The difficulty experienced by "1-2 months attendance group" is higher than the '2-4 months attendance group' on 3 problems indicated below :

9. The instructor utilised the learners for his personal work
27. Learners calling by nicknames.
47. The instructor fails to enthuse the learners to participate.

b. The effect is more on "2-4 months attendance group" than that of "1-2 months attendance group" with regard to only 2 problems i.e.,

13. There are some fights in the village
65. The time of the programme is short.

c. **The "1-2 months attendance group" felt high difficulty in the case of 2 problems shown below, compared to "4-6 months attendance group"**

4. There is no immediate use by getting education.
9. The instructor utilised the learners for his personal work.

d. **The "4-6 months attendance group" felt more difficulty on only one problem noted below compared to "1-2 months attendance group". The problem is**

74. The other learners also are average in learning.

e. **The "2-4 months attendance group" felt very high difficulty compared to "4-6 months attendance group" on the following only 1 problem. The problem is**

4. There is no immediate use by getting education.

f. **The effect is more on "4-6 months attendance group" than that of "2-4 months attendance group" with regard to 6 problems shown below:**

13. There are some fights in the village.
14. Many of the learners belong to upper caste.
27. Learners calling by nicknames.
46. The instructor lacks good voice and fluency.
65. The time of the programme is short.
74. The other learners also are average in learning.

3. Viewing at the difficulty level of each problem experienced by different attendance groups, the following problem-wise conclusions are drawn:

Problem 4: There is no immediate use by getting education

- There is no difference between 1-2 months and 2-4 months attendance group.
- It is more with 1-2 months attendance group compared to 4-6 months attendance group.
- The difficulty is high with 2-4 months attendance group than that of 4-6 months attendance group.

Problem 9: The instructor utilised the learners for his personal work

- The problem is more with 1-2 months attendance group compared to 2-4 months attendance group.
- It is more with 1-2 months attendance group than that of 4-6 months attendance group.
- There is no difference between 2-4 months attendance group and 4-6 months

Problem 13: There are some fights in the village

- This problem is more with 2-4 months attendance group compared to 1-2 months attendance group.
- There is no difference between 1-2 months and 4-6 months attendance groups.
- It is high with 4-6 months attendance group compared to 2-4 months attendance group.

Problem 14: Many of the learners belong to upper caste

- This problem has no difference between 1-2 months and 2-4 months attendance groups.
- There is no difference between 1-2 months and 4-6 months attendance groups.
- The difficulty is greater with 4-6 months attendance group than 2-4 months attendance group.

Problem 27: Learners calling by nicknames

- This problem is more with 1-2 months attendance group compared to 2-4 months attendance group.
- There is no difference between 1-2 months and 4-6 months attendance groups.
- The problem is more with 4-6 months attendance group compared to 2-4 months attendance group.

Problem 46: The instructor lacks good voice and fluency

- The problem has no difference between 1-2 months and 2-4 months attendance groups.

- There is no difference between 1-2 months and 4-6 months attendance groups.
- It is more with 4-6 months attendance group compared to 2-4 months attendance group.

Problem 47: The instructor fails to enthuse the learners to participate

- This problem is more with 1-2 months attendance group compared to 2-4 months attendance group.
- There is no difference between 1-2 months and 4-6 months attendance groups.
- There is no difference between 2-4 months and 4-6 months attendance groups.

Problem 65: The time of the programme is short

- This problem is more with 2-4 months attendance group compared to 1-2 months attendance group.
- There is no difference between 1-2 months and 4-6 months attendance groups.
- It is more with 4-6 months attendance group compared to 2-4 months attendance group.

Problem 74: The other learners also are average in learning

- This problem has no difference between 1-2 months and 2-4 months attendance groups.
- It is greater with 4-6 months attendance group compared to 1-2 months attendance group
- The difficulty of this problem is greater with 4-6 months attendance group than 2-4 months attendance group.

4. The hypothesis 5(viii) that "there is no difference in the effect of problems among drop-outs belonging to different attendance groups—1-2 months, 2-4 months, and 4-6 months" is proved in case 71 problems found in Table 4.75 and not in case of 9 problems found in Table 4.76.

Sum-up

The similarities and differences in the difficulty level or effects of the problems between/among different groups of drop-outs are presented. Implementations should be sensitive to the problems where significant differences are noticed and should put extra effort or care solve the problems of the group of dro-pouts concerned.

When significant differences are found between two groups, the effect will be more on one group than the other group. This must be kept in view and tackle such problems of the concerned group.

Table 4.76: Showing the problems on which differential effects exist among drop-outs of different attendance groups

S.No. of problem in the rating scale	Problem	Group-1 1-2 months		Group-2 2-4 months		Group-3 4-6 months		'F' Value	Significance	't' values		
		Mean	SD	Mean	SD	Mean	SD			Group 1-2	Group 2-3	Group 1-3
1	2	3	4	5	6	7	8	9	10	11	12	13
ECO 4	There is no immediate use by getting education	2.05	1.36	2.00	1.24	1.70	1.23	4.18	@@	1.08^{NS}	3.01$^{@}$	2.16^{NS}
SOC 9	The instructor utilises the learners for his personal work	2.09	1.40	1.67	1.33	1.55	1.35	5.88	@@	2.64$^{@}$	0.64^{NS}	3.02^{NS}
SOC 13	There are some fights in the village	1.60	1.26	2.300	1.36	1.46	1.32	5.28	@@	2.63$^{@}$	2.88$^{@}$	0.79^{NS}
SOC 14	Many of the learners belong to upper caste	1.92	1.46	2.20	1.35	1.64	1.39	4.07	@@	1.74^{NS}	2.91$^{@}$	1.51^{NS}
PSY 27	Learners calling by nicknames	2.05	1.35	1.68	1.37	2.34	1.28	6.47	@@	2.36$^{@@}$	3.58$^{@}$	1.70^{NS}
INS 46	The instructor lacks good voice and fluency	2.30	1.24	2.07	1.29	2.43	1.02	4.18	@@	1.62^{NS}	3.07$^{@}$	1.75^{NS}
INS 47	The instructor fails to enthuse the learners to participate	2.41	1.24	1.90	1.33	2.21	1.35	5.72	@@	3.39$^{@}$	1.66^{NS}	1.14^{NS}

(Table Contd...)

1	2	3	4	5	6	7	8	9	10	11	12	13
COM 65	The time of the programme is short	1.78	1.27	2.31	1.30	1.71	1.24	8.19	@	3.58@	3.40@	0.41NS
PER 74	The other learners also are average in learning	1.85	1.29	1.96	1.25	2.32	1.34	4.09	@@	0.72NS	2.03@@	2.78@

@: Significant at 0.01 level — @@: Significant at 0.05 level

ECO: Economic problems — *INS:* Instructor related Problems area

SOC: Social Problems area — *COM:* Community related Problems

PSY: Psychological Problems — *PER:* Personal Problems

5

Summary and Suggestions

It is increasingly recognized that traditional methods used in the adult education programmes for making illiterates literate are not yielding the results expected. Total literacy campaigns which are time- bound, age-specific, area-based and result-oriented are launched for rapid growth of literacy. Though large number of illiterates are enrolled in the campaign, many are dropping out from the programme without becoming literates. The scarce resources of money, men, material invested in the campaign are wasted. Drop-out is alarming. Indepth studies for unfolding the causes/problems of dropouts and thereby, help initiating appropriate actions to check/reduce drop-out rate are urgently needed and the present study is an attempt in this direction.

TITLE OF THE PROBLEM

An enquiry into the problems of drop-outs in Total Literacy Campaigns (TLC) of Kurnool district.

OBJECTIVES OF THE STUDY

The following are the objectives of the study.

1. To study the enrolment and drop-outs in TLC of Kurnool district.
2. To study the problems of drop-outs in TLC of Kurnool district as expressed by the dropouts:
   (i) to identify the problems which have same difficulty level/ same effect.

(ii) to identify the problems which have same difficulty level/ same effect.

(iii) to identify the very significant problems.

(iv) to identify the very significant problems of drop-outs in each problem area i.e., economic, social, psychological, familial, instructor related, community related, personal and programme related problems.

3. To study the differential effects (differences in the difficulty level) of each problem of drop-outs between the following groups of drop-outs.

   (i) Males and females (Sex)

   (ii) With previous schooling and no schooling (Education)

   (iii) Married and unmarried (Marital Status)

   (iv) With different age groups—20 years and below, between 21-35 years, and 36 years and above age groups (Age).

   (v) Belonging to different castes—Scheduled Caste (SC)/ Scheduled Tribe (ST), Backward Classes (BC), and Other Castes (OC) (Caste).

   (vi) Belonging to different occupations—Agriculture, labour, and others (Occupation).

   (vii) Different income groups-Rs. 20,000 and below, between Rs. 21-30 thousands, and 31 thousands and above per annum (Income).

   (viii) With different level of attendance at the centers —1-2 months, 2-4 months and 4-6 months (Attendance).

4. To study the differential effects of each problem area of drop-outs between the following groups of drop-outs:

   (i) Male and female.

   (ii) With previous schooling and no schooling.

   (iii) Married and unmarried.

   (iv) Age 20 years and below, between 21-35 years and 36 years and above years.

(v) Belonging to different castes—Scheduled Caste (SC)/ Scheduled Tribe (ST), Backward Classes (BC), and Other Castes (OC) (Caste).

(vi) Agriculture, labour and others.

(vii) Income Rs. 20,000 and below, between Rs. 21-30 thousands and Rs. 31 thousands and above per annum.

(viii) Learners who have attended the centers upto 6 months and dropped out.

5. To study the relative effect of the problem areas on total drop-outs.

6. To suggest remedial measures for solving the problems of drop-outs.

HYPOTHESES OF THE STUDY

Hypothesis 1

The drop-out rate in TLC of Kurnool district is higher than 50.

Hypothesis 2

The problem of drop-outs are various and varied.

Hypothesis 3

The problems of drop-outs have varying levels of difficulty/ effect.

Hypothesis 4

There are some groups of problems which have same difficulty levels/effect.

Hypothesis 5

There is no difference in the effect/difficulty levels of each problem between the following groups of drop-outs.

(i) Male and Female (Sex)

(ii) With previous schooling and no schooling (Education)

(iii) Married and unmarried (Marital Status)

(iv) With different age groups—20 years and below, between 21-35 years, and 36 years and above age groups (Age).

(v) Belonging to different castes— Scheduled Caste, Scheduled Tribe (SC/ST), Backward Castes (BC) and Other Castes (OC) (Caste)

(vi) Belonging to different occupations— agriculture, labour and others (Occupation).

(vii) Different annual income groups—Rs. 20,000 and below, between Rs. 21-30 thousands and Rs. 31 thousands and above (Annual Income).

(viii) With different levels of attendance at the centres—1-2 months, 2-4 months, and 4-6 months (Attendance).

SELECTION AND DEVELOPMENT OF THE TOOL

Three point rating scale was selected for identifying the problems of drop-outs.

The problems (items) of the rating scale were prepared after surveying the literature available, meeting the experts and drop-outs. 15 experts helped in the selection of problems and problems areas. The rating scale consisting of 96 problems was tried out on a sample of 370 drop-outs selected from Velugodu, Atmakur, Banaganapalli Mandals of Kurnool district. After reading out the problems, the drop-outs were requested to give one of the three alternatives for each problem. The three responses given by the drop-outs were scored by giving a value of 1, 2, 3 to the responses 'Not at all', 'To some extent' and 'Much' respectively. Using the top 27% and the lowest 27% of the sample as 'high' and 'low' groups, item analysis was done. The items with 't' values less than 1.75 were rejected. The final form of the rating scale consists of 80 items, divided into 8 problems areas—economic problems, social problems, psychological problems, familial problems, instructor related problems, community related problems, personal problems and programme related problems. The rating scale has validity (face .9327). The rating scale has high reliability, the test-retest correlation co-efficient being 87.

LOCALE OF THE STUDY

The locale of the study is Kurnool district.

SAMPLE SELECTION

A total sample of 400 drop-outs from 100 centres, at the rate of 4 from each centre were randomly selected from Kurnool, Nandyal and Adoni Revenue Divisions of Kurnool district by using stratified random sampling technique, stratification being revenue division and mandal. The 6 mandals selected include—Paepalli, Kodumur (Kurnool Division), Dornipadu, Nandyal (Nandyal Division), Chippagiri and Gonegandla (Adoni Division). The sample covered different groups of drop-outs based on sex, education, marital status, age, caste, occupation, income and attendance at the centres.

DATA COLLECTION

With the permission of the nodal officers at the mandal level, the Researcher took in help of centre organiser for identifying and contacting the drop-out from the centres. After establishing the rapport with the drop-outs, the items of the rating scale were read out to them. They were requested to indicate the extent of difficulty faced by choosing one of the three alternatives and alternatives were noted by the researcher. The three alternatives—'Not at all', 'To some extent' and 'Much' were scored by giving a value of 1, 2 and 3 respectively. The information relating to learners enrolled and dropped out was collected from the Deputy Director of Adult Education, Kurnool district.

STATISTICAL TECHNIQUES USED IN THE STUDY

I. The drop-out rate was calculated by using the following method.

$$\text{Drop-out Rate } \frac{\text{No. of Learners left the centre}}{\text{No. of Adults enrolled in the centres}} = \times 100$$

II. The difficulty level/effect of the problem was found by calculating mean difficulty of the problems.

III. On the basis of the mean difficulty of the problems, the problems were classified as very significant problems, significant problems and less significant problems, if the difficulty values range from 2.14 to 2.43, 1.84 to 2.13 and 1.53 to 1.83 respectively.

IV. The differential effects of different problems and problem areas on different groups of drop-outs were found by calculating the mean and S.D. of the groups and by using 't' test for checking the significant difference between means of the two groups to be compared are more than two. When 'F' test was significant indicating the difference among the groups, the exact groups which differ from each other were found by employing 't' test.

MAJOR FINDINGS

Enrolment and Drop-out Rate

The number of learners enrolled in TLC of Kurnool district is 5,84,027 and the number of drop-outs who left the centres without completing even Primer I and before 6 months of starting the centre is 1,93,292. The drop-out rate is 33.1

Problems of Drop-outs

The problems of 22 groups of drop-outs are presented, indicating the very significant, significant and less significant problems of each group and the distribution of these problems, problem area-wise.

1. Total drop-outs

   (i) Out of 80 problems, the difficulty levels of 17 problems appear to be different from each other and such problem are found in Table 4.01.

   (ii) With regard to the remaining 63 problems, they fall under 20 groups of problems which have same difficulty levels, so far as the group is concerned, but each group differs from the other. The list of such problems is seen in Table 4.02.

   (iii) The very significant, significant and less significant problems are found in Tables 4.03, 4.04 and 4.05 respectively.

   (iv) The very significant, significant and less significant problems in the areas of (1) economic problems, (2) social problems, (3) psychological problems, (4) familial

problems, (5) instructor related problems, (6) community related problems, (7) personal problems, and (8) programme related problems are found in Tables 4.06 to 4.13.

There are 21 very significant problems, 54 significant problems and 5 less significant problems

The 21 very significant problems area-wise are given below :

Economic Problem—1

1. There are no specific working hours in different professions.

Social Problems—1

1. There are no very significant problems in the social problems area.

Psychological Problems—6

1. Easily getting tired.
2. The learners is not able to answer to the instructor.
3. Unwilling to get educated.
4. Feeling that others would mock.
5. Feeling that studying at the centre is a waste.
6. Feeling that the age to study has passed.

Familial Problems—2

1. There is none else at home.
2. Other family members refuse permission to attend during nights.

Instructor related problems—6

1. The instructor lacks good voice and fluency.
2. The books are difficult to learner
3. The instructor fails to enthuse the learner to participate.
4. Instructor is limited only to literacy.
5. The instructor does not personally reveal any development.
6. Teaching aids are not available at the right time.

Community related Problems—3

1. I am not permitted to go with my friends.
2. Friends do not go to the centre.
3. The time of the centre is inconvenient.

Personal Problems—1

1. The instructor is male.

Programme related Problems—2

1. The centre is at a distance.
2. Minimum amenities are not found at the centre (air/ventilation)

The very significant, significant and less significant problems of the following groups of drop-outs are found.

The problem of Male Dropouts

There are 28 very significant problems, 47 significant problems and 5 less significant problems—wide Table 4.15. Area-wise distribution of the problems is found in Table 4.16. The very significant problems are given below:

Economic Problems—1

1. There are no specific working hours in different professions.

Social Problems—3

1. Personal position is at stake in the society.
2. The instructor does not belong to my caste.
3. Attending functions and going to movies.

Psychological Problems—6

1. Easily getting tired.
2. Unwilling to get educated.
3. The learners are not able to answer to the instructor.
4. Feeling that others would mock.
5. Feeling that the age to study has passed.
6. The fellow learners do not listen to the thoughts and ideas.

Familial Problems—1

1. There are none else at home.

Instructor related problems—8

1. The instructor fails to enthuse the learner to participate.
2. The instructor does not personally reveal any development.
3. The books are difficult to learner.
4. Teaching aids are not available at the right time.
5. The instructor lacks good voice and fluency.
6. Providing too much information within a short time.
7. Instruction is limited only to literacy.
8. Primer and follow-up books are not in order.

Community related Problems—2

1. Providing too much information within a short time.
2. I am not permitted to go with my friends.

Personal Problems—5

1. Due to ill-health.
2. The other learners also are average in learning.
3. The other learners are mocking because of my backwardness in learning.
4. The relevant lessons are not taught at the centre.
5. Lack of knowledge about this programme.

Programme related Problems—2

1. Minimum amenities are not found at the centre (air/ ventilation)
2. The centre is started at inconvenient place/having much sounds and bad smell.

Problems of Female Drop-outs

There are 20 very significant problems, 41 significant problems and 5 less significant problems—wide Table 4.16. area-wise distributions of problems is found in the Table 4.17. The very significant problems are given below:

Economic Problems—1

1. There are no specific working hours in different professions.

Social Problems—0

There is no very significant problems in this area.

Psychological Problems-6

1. Easily getting tired.
2. The learners are not able to answer to the instructor.
3. Feeling why one should get educated when the age is so much.
4. Feeling that the age to study has passed.
5. Feeling that studying at the centre is a waste.
6. Feeling that others would mock.

Familial Problems—4

1. Other family members refuse permission to attend during nights.
2. Unable to go to the centre because of heavy work.
3. There are none else at home.
4. The time of the centre is the supper time.

Instructor related problems—2

1. The instructor lacks good voice and fluency.
2. The books are difficult to learn.

Community related Problems—5

1. Co-educational centre.
2. The time of the centre is inconvenient.
3. I am not permitted to go with my friends.
4. There is no encouragement from the village elders.
5. Friends do not go to the centre.

Personal Problems—1

1. The instructor is male.

Programme related Problems—1

1. The centre is at a distance.

The problems of "Previous Schooling Dropouts"

There are 30 very significant problems, 45 significant problems and 5 less significant problems-wide Table 4.19. Area-wise distribution of the problems is found in the Table 4.20.

Economic Problems—1

1. There are no specific working hours in different professions.

Social Problems—3

1. Attending functions and going to movies.
2. Personal position is at stake in the society.
3. The instructor does not belong to my caste.

Psychological Problems—8

1. Easily getting tired.
2. Feeling that the age to study has passed.
3. The learner is not able to answer to the instructor.
4. Feeling that studying at the centre is a waste.
5. Feeling that others would mock.
6. Due to ill-health.
7. There is no understanding between the learner and the instructor.
8. Unwilling to get educated.

Familial Problems—3

1. Unable to go to the centre because of heavy work.
2. There are none else at home.
3. Other family members refuse permission to attend during nights.

Instructor related problems—8

1. The books are difficult to learn.
2. The instructor lacks good voice and fluency.
3. Teaching aids are not available at the right time.
4. The instructor fails to enthuse the learners to participate.
5. The lessons are not according to the requirements or tastes.
6. The instructional methods used by the instructor are not liked.
7. The instructor does not treat all the learners equally.
8. Teaching aids are not available at the right time.

Community related Problems—2

1. The time of the centre is inconvenient.
2. I am not permitted to go with my friends.

Personal Problems—3

1. The other learners are mocking because of my backwardness in learning.
2. The relevant lessons are not taught at the centre.
3. The time of the centre is the supper time.

Programme related Problems—2

1. The centre is at a distance.
2. Minimum amenities are not found at the centre (air/ ventilation)

The problems of "No Schooling Drop-outs"

There are 18 very significant problems, 52 significant problems and 10 less significant problems—wide Table 4.21. Area-wise distribution of the problems is found in the Table 4.22.

Economic Problems—2

1. Busy with farm work.
2. There are no specific working hours in different professions.

Social Problems—2

1. Many learners belong to the upper caste.

2. The instructor and the learner are not friendly

Psychological Problems—4

1. Easily getting tired.
2. Unwilling to get educated.
3. The learner is not able to answer to the instructor.
4. Feeling that others would mock.

Familial Problems—1

1. Other family members refuse permission to attend during nights.

Instructor related problems—4

1. The instructor lacks good voice and fluency.
2. Instruction is limited only to literacy.
3. The instructor does not reveal in learner's progress.
4. The instructor fails to enthuse the learners to participate.

Community related Problems—2

1. Friends do not go to the centre.
2. I am not permitted to go with my friends.

Personal Problems—2

1. The instructor is male.
2. Lack of knowledge about this programme.

Programme related Problems—1

1. The centre is at a distance.

The problems of "Married Drop-outs"

There are 22 very significant problems, 52 significant problems and 6 less significant problems—wide Table 4.23. Area-wise distribution of the problems is found in the Table 4.24. The very significant problems given below:

Economic Problems—2

1. There are no specific working hours in different professions.
2. Busy with farm work.

Social Problems—1

1. Personal position is at stake in the society.

Psychological Problems—8

1. Easily getting tired.
2. Feeling that others would mock.
3. The learner is not able to answer to the instructor.
4. Unwilling to get educated.
5. Feeling that the age to study has passed.
6. Feeling that studying at the centre is a waste.
7. Feeling shy to go to the centre.
8. The fellow learners do not listen to the thoughts and ideas.

Familial Problems—2

1. Other family members refuse permission to attend during nights.
2. There are none else at home.

Instructor related problems—6

1. The books are difficult to learn.
2. The instructor lacks good voice and fluency.
3. Instruction is limited only to literacy.
4. The instructor does not reveal in learner's progress.
5. The lessons are not according to the requirements and tastes.
6. The instructional methods used by the instructor are not liked.

Community related Problems—2

1. The instructor does not reveal in learner's progress.
2. Instruction is limited only to literacy.

Personal Problems—0

There are no very significant problems in the personal problems area.

Programme related Problems-1

1. The centre is at a distance.

The problems of "Unmarried Drop-outs"

There are 25 very significant problems, 41 significant problems and 14 less significant problems—wide Table 4.25. Area-wise distribution of the problems is found in the Table 4.26.

Economic Problems—1

1. There are no specific working hours in different professions.

Social Problems—2

1. Attending functions and going to movies.
2. The instructor does not belong to my caste.

Psychological Problems—5

1. Easily getting tired.
2. Feeling shy during conversation with other.
3. Feeling that the age to study has passed.
4. The learner is not able to answer to the instructor.
5. Feeling that the age to study has passed.

Familial Problems-1

1. There are none else at home.

Instructor related problems—6

1. The instructor fails to enthuse the learners to participate.
2. The instructor lacks good voice and fluency.
3. Teaching aids are not available at the right time.
4. The books are difficult to learn.
5. The instructor does not accept criticism with open heart.
6. The instructor does not reveal in learner's progress.

Community related Problems—4

1. I am not permitted to go with my friends.
2. Co-educational centre.
3. Good friends are not available at the centre.
4. Friends do not go to the centre.

Personal Problems—4

1. Getting the marriage age.
2. Lack of knowledge about this programme.
3. The other learners are mocking because of my backwardness in the centre.
4. The instructor is male.

Programme related Problems—2

1. The centre is at a distance.
2. Minimum amenities are not found at the centre (air/ ventilation).

The problems of "20 years and below age group drop-outs"

There are 26 very significant problems, 39 significant problems and 15 less significant problems-wide Table 4.27. Area-wise distribution of the problems is found in the Table 4.28.

Economic Problems—1

1. There are no specific working hours in different professions.

Social Problems—2

1. The instructor does not belong to my caste.
2. Attending functions and going to movies.

Psychological Problems—5

1. Easily getting tired.
2. The learner is not able to answer to the instructor.
3. Unwilling to get educated.
4. Feeling that the age to study has passed.
5. There is no understanding between the learner and the instructor.

Familial Problems—1

1. There are none else at home.

Instructor related problems—6

1. The instructor fails to enthuse the learners to participate.

2. The instructor lacks good voice and fluency.
3. Teaching aids are not available at the right time.
4. The books are difficult to learn.
5. The absence of audio-visual aids useful for instruction
6. The instructor does not treat all the learners equally.

Community related Problems—5

1. I am not permitted to go with my friends.
2. Good friends are not available at the centre.
3. Co-educational centre.
4. Friends do not go to the centre.
5. The time of the centre is inconvenient.

Personal Problems—4

1. Lack of knowledge about this programme.
2. The other learners are mocking because of my backwardness in learning.
3. Getting the marriage age.
4. The instructor is male.

Programme related Problems—2

1. The centre is at a distance.
2. Minimum amenities are not found at the centre (air/ventilation).

The problems of "21-35 age group drop-outs"

There are 21 very significant problems, 46 significant problems and 13 less significant problems—wide Table 4.29. Area-wise distribution of the problems is found in the Table 4.30.

Economic Problems—0

There is no very significant problems in the economic problems area.

Social Problems—1

1. Some co-learners have enmity in the centre.

Psychological Problems—5

1. Easily getting tired.
2. Feeling that others would mock.
3. Feeling shy to go to the centre.
4. Feeling that studying at the centre is a waste.
5. Unwilling to get educated.

Familial Problems—2

1. Other family members refuse permission to attend during nights.
2. There are none else at home.

Instructor related Problems—5

1. The books are difficult to learn.
2. The instructor lacks good voice and fluency.
3. The lessons are not according to the requirements and tastes.
4. The instructor does not reveal in learner's progress.
5. The instructor does not accept criticism with open heart.

Community related Problems—3

1. The time of the programme is short.
2. Friends do not go to the centre.
3. There is no encouragement from the village elders.

Personal Problems—3

1. Becoming a slave to bad habits.
2. Quarrelling with other learners.
3. The relevant lessons are not taught at the centre.

Programme related Problems—2

1. Minimum amenities are not found at the centre (air/ventilation).
2. The centre is at a distance.

The problems of "36 years above age drop-outs"

There are 39 very significant problems, 38 significant problems and 3 less significant problems—wide Table 4.31. Area-wise distribution of the problems is found in the Table 4.32.

Economic Problems—3

1. Busy with farm work.
2. There are no specific working hours in different professions.
3. There is no immediate use by getting educated.

Social Problems—5

1. Attending functions and going to movies.
2. Personal position is at stake in the society.
3. Many learners belong to the upper caste.
4. The instructor and the learners are not friendly.
5. The instructor does not belong to my caste.

Psychological Problems—10

1. The learner is not able to answer to the instructor.
2. Instructor is limited only to literacy.
3. Easily getting tired.
4. Feeling that the age to study has passed.
5. There is no understanding between the learners and the instructor.
6. The instructor utilise the learners for his personal work.
7. Feeling that others would mock.
8. Feeling that studying at the centre is a waste.
9. Feeling that learning at home instead of at the centre, is better.
10. Instructor uses difficult language, pictures and symbols.

Familial Problems—5

1. The time of the centre is the supper time.
2. Unable to go to the centre because of heavy work.

3. Other family members refuse permission to attend during nights.
4. There are none else at home.
5. Looking after the children.

Instructor related problems-7

1. Instructor is limited only to literacy.
2. The absence of audio-visual aids useful for instruction.
3. The instructor does not treat all the learners equally.
4. Teaching aids are not available at the right time.
5. The instructor fails to enthuse the learners to participate.
6. The instructor fails to enthuse the learners to participate.
7. The books are difficult to learn.

Community related Problems—3

1. No one else visits the centre except the instructor.
2. Co-educational centre.
3. The time of the centre is inconvenient.

Personal Problems—4

1. Quarrelling with other learners.
2. The other learners are much older.
3. Lack of knowledge about this programme.
4. The other learners also are average in learning.

Programme related Problems—2

1. The centre is at a distance.
2. The centre is started at inconvenient place/having much sounds and bad smell.

The problems of "SC/ST caste group drop-outs"

There are 23 very significant problems, 42 significant problems and 15 less significant problems—wide Table 4.33. Area-wise distribution of the problems is found in the Table 4.34.

Economic Problems—1

1. There are no specific working hours in different professions.

Social Problems—2

1. Personal position is at stake in the society.
2. The instructor does not belong to my caste.

Psychological Problems—5

1. Easily getting tired.
2. Feeling that the age to study has passed.
3. Feeling that others would mock.
4. There is no understanding between the learners and the instructor.
5. Feeling that studying at the centre is a waste.

Familial Problems—2

1. Other family members refuse permission to attend during nights.
4. There are none else at home.

Instructor related Problems—5

1. The instructor does not treat all the learners equally.
2. Instructor is limited only to literacy.
3. The instructor uses difficult language, pictures and symbols.
4. The books are difficult to learn.
5. The instructor fails to enthuse the learners to participate.

Community related Problems—3

1. I am not permitted to go with my friends.
2. Co-educational centre.
3. The time of the centre is inconvenient.

Personal Problems—4

1. The other learners are mocking because of my backwardness in learning.

2. The instructor is male.
3. The relevant lessons are not taught at the centre.
4. Getting the marriage age.

Programme related Problems—1

1. The centre is at a distance.

The problems of "BC caste group drop-outs"

There are 30 very significant problems, 43 significant problems and 7 less significant problems—wide Table 4.35. Area-wise distribution of the problems is found in the Table 4.36.

Economic Problems—1

1. There are no specific working hours in different professions.

Social Problems—5

1. The instructor does not belong to my caste.
2. There are some learners with bad behaviour in the centre.
3. The instructor and the learner are not friendly.
4. Some co-learners have enmity in the centre.
5. Personal position is at stake in the society.

Psychological Problems—5

1. The learner is not able to answer to the instructor.
2. The fellow learners do not listen to the thoughts and ideas.
3. Unwilling to get educated.
4. Feeling shy during conversation with other.
5. Easily getting tired.

Familial Problems—3

1. Looking after the children.
2. The time of the centre is the supper time.
3. Other family members refuse permission to attend during nights.

Instructor related problems—5

1. The books are difficult to learn.
2. The instructor is not well versed with his teaching.
3. The instructor lacks good voice and fluency.
4. Teaching aids are not available at the right time.
5. The instruction is not relevant to the learners.

Community related Problems—5

1. I am not permitted to go with my friends.
2. Good friends are not available at the centre.
3. There is no encouragement from the village elders.
4. The time of the centre is inconvenient.
5. Good friends are not available at the centre.

Personal Problems—5

1. Due to ill-health.
2. The other learners are much older.
3. Becoming a slave to bad habits.
4. Lack of knowledge about this programme.
5. The instructor is male.

Programme related Problems—1

1. Minimum amenities are not found at the centre (air/ ventilation).

The problems of "Other caste group drop-outs"

There are 27 very significant problems, 41 significant problems and 12 less significant problems—wide Table 4.37. Area-wise distribution of the problems is found in the Table 4.38.

Economic Problems—1

1. There are no specific working hours in different professions.

Social Problems—2

1. Attending functions and going to movies.

2. Some co-learners have enmity in the centre.

Psychological Problems—8

1. Feeling that others would mock.
2. Feeling that studying at the centre is a waste.
3. Feeling that learning at home instead of at the centre, is better.
4. Easily getting tired.
5. Feeling that the age to study has passed.
6. There is no understanding between the learner and the instructor.
7. Feeling that the age to study has passed.
8. Unwilling to get educated.

Familial Problems—3

1. There are none else at home.
2. Unable to go to the centre because of heavy work.
3. Other family members refuse permission to attend during nights.

Instructor related Problems—7

1. The instructor fails to enthuse the learners to participate.
2. The instructor lacks good voice and fluency.
3. The instructor does not reveal in learner's progress.
4. Instruction is limited only to literacy.
5. The lessons are not according to the requirements or tastes.
6. The instructional methods used by the instructor are not liked.
7. Primer and follow-up books are not in order.

Community related Problems—1

1. No one else visits the centre except the instructor.

Personal Problems—2

1. The other learners also are average in learning.
2. Lack of knowledge about this programme.

Programme related Problems—3

1. Minimum amenities are not found at the centre (air/ ventilation).
2. The centre is at a distance.
3. The centre is started at inconvenient place/having much sounds and bad smell.

The problems of "Agriculture group drop-outs"

There are 19 very significant problems, 48 significant problems and 13 less significant problems—wide Table 4.39. Area-wise distribution of the problems is found in the Table 4.40.

Economic Problems—1

1. There are no specific working hours in different professions.

Social Problems—1

1. Attending functions and going to movies.

Psychological Problems—5

1. Easily getting tired.
2. The learner is not able to answer to the instructor.
3. Unwilling to get educated.
4. Feeling that studying at the centre is a waste.
5. The fellow learners do not listen to the thoughts and ideas.

Familial Problems—3

1. There are none else at home.
2. Unable to go to the centre because of heavy work.
3. Other family members refuse permission to attend during nights.

Instructor related Problems—3

1. The instructor lacks good voice and fluency.
2. The instructor fails to enthuse the learners to participate.
3. The instructor does not reveal in learner's progress.

Community related Problems—2

1. Good friends are not available at the centre.
3. I am not permitted to go with my friends.

Personal Problems—2

1. Due to ill-health.
2. Lack of knowledge about this programme.

Programme related Problems—2

1. The centre is at a distance.
2. Minimum amenities are not found at the centre (air/ventilation).

The problems of "Labour group drop-outs"

There are 20 very significant problems, 44 significant problems and 4 less significant problems—wide Table 4.41. Area-wise distribution of the problems is found in the Table 4.42.

Economic Problems—2

1. There are no specific working hours in different professions.
2. No immediate financial benefit by education.

Social Problems—0

There is no very significant problem in the social problems area.

Psychological Problems—5

1. Feeling that learning at home instead of at the centre is better.
2. Feeling that the age to study has passed.
3. Unwilling to get educated.
4. Feeling that others would mock.
5. Easily getting tired.

Familial Problems—3

1. There are none else at home.
2. The time of the centre is the supper time.

3. Other family members refuse permission to attend during nights.

Instructor related problems—4

1. The books are difficult to learn.
2. Teaching aids are not available at the right time.
3. Instruction is limited only to literacy.
4. The instructor lacks good voice and fluency.

Community related Problems—2

1. I am not permitted to go with my friends.
2. The time of the centre is inconvenient.

Personal Problems—3

1. The instructor is male.
2. Getting the marriage age.
3. The relevant lessons are not taught at the centre.

Programme related Problems—1

1. The centre is at a distance.

The problems of "Other group drop-outs"

There are 49 very significant problems, 27 significant problems and 4 less significant problems—wide Table 4.43. Area-wise distribution of the problems is found in the Table 4.44.

Economic Problems—1

1. There are no specific working hours in different professions.

Social Problems—7

1. The instructor and the learner are not friendly.
2. The instructor does not belong to my caste.
3. The time of the centre is inconvenient.
4. Attending functions and going to movies.
5. The instructor does not belong to my place.
6. Some co-learners have enmity in the centre.
7. Many learners belong to the upper caste.

Psychological Problems—10

1. Easily getting tired.
2. Feeling that others would mock.
3. Feeling that education is only for wealthy people.
4. The learner is not able to answer to the instructor.
5. Feeling shy during conversation with other.
6. Feeling that learning at home instead of at the centre is better.
7. Feeling that studying at the centre is a waste.
8. Learners calling by nicknames.
9. Feeling that the age to study has passed.
10. There is no understanding between the learner and the instructor.

Familial Problems—3

1. Other family members refuse permission to attend during nights.
2. The time of the centre is the supper time.
3. There are none else at home.

Instructor related problems—14

1. The absence of audio-visual aids useful for instruction.
2. The instructor is not relevant to the learners.
3. Instructor is limited only to literacy instruction.
4. The instructor is negligent.
5. The books are difficult to learn.
6. The lessons are not according to the requirements or tastes.
7. The instructor fails to enthuse the learners to participate.
8. Teaching aids are not available at the right time.
9. The instructor is not well versed with his teaching.
10. The instructor does not treat all the learners equally.
11. The instructor uses difficult language, pictures and symbols.

12. The instructor lacks good voice and fluency.
13. The instructor does not reveal in learner's progress.
14. The instructor is not punctual to the centre.

Community related Problems—5

1. Friends do not go to the centre.
2. The time of the centre is inconvenient.
3. No one else visits the centre except the instructor.
4. Co-educational centre.
5. There is no encouragement from the village elders.

Personal Problems—7

1. Becoming a slave to bad habits.
2. The other learners also are average in learning.
3. The relevant lessons are not taught at the centre.
4. The other learners are mocking because of my backwardness in learning.
5. Quarrelling with other learners.
6. Due to ill-health.
7. The other learners are much older.

Programme related Problems—2

1. Minimum amenities are not found at the centre (air/ventilation).
2. The centre is started at inconvenient place/having much sounds and bad smell.

The problems of "Rs. 20,000 and below income group drop-outs"

There are 25 very significant problems, 45 significant problems and 10 less significant problems-wide Table 4.45. Area-wise distribution of the problems are found in the Table 4.46.

Economic Problems—1

1. There are no specific working hours in different professions.

Social Problems—2

1. The instructor and the learner are not friendly.
2. The instructor does not belong to my caste.

Psychological Problems—6

1. Easily getting tired.
2. Feeling that the age to study has passed.
3. Unwilling to get educated.
4. The learner is not able to answer to the instructor.
5. Feeling that studying at the centre is a waste.
6. The fellow learners do not listen to the thoughts and ideas.

Familial Problems—2

1. Unable to go to the centre because of heavy work.
2. There are none else at home.

Instructor related problems—6

1. The books are difficult to learn.
2. Instruction is limited only to literacy.
3. Teaching aids are not available at the right time.
4. The absence of audio-visual aids useful for instruction.
5. The instructor fails to enthuse the learners to participate.
6. The instructor lacks good voice and fluency.

Community related Problems—5

1. The time of the centre is inconvenient.
2. I am not permitted to go with my friends.
3. There is no encouragement from the village elders.
4. Co-educational centre.
5. Friends do not go to the centre.

Personal Problems—2

1. Lack of knowledge about this programme.
2. Becoming a slave to bad habits.

Programme related Problems—1

1. The centre is at a distance.

The problems of "Rs. 21-30 thousands income group drop-outs"

There are 24 very significant problems, 49 significant problems and 7 less significant problems—wide Table 4.47. Area-wise distribution of the problems is found in the Table 4.48.

Economic Problems—1

1. There are no specific working hours in different professions.

Social Problems—1

1. Attending functions and going to movies.

Psychological Problems—5

1. Feeling that others would mock.
2. The learner is not able to answer to the instructor.
3. Unwilling to get educated.
4. Easily getting tired.
5. Feeling shy to go to the centre.

Familial Problems—3

1. Unable to go to the centre.
2. Other family members refuse permission to attend during nights.
3. There are none else at home.

Instructor related problems—7

1. The instructor lacks good voice and fluency.
2. The instructor uses difficult language, pictures and symbols.
3. The instructor does not reveal in learner's progress.
4. The books are difficult to learn.
5. The instruction is not relevant to the learners.
6. The instructor fails to enthuse the learners to participate.
7. The lessons are not according to the requirements and tastes.

Community related Problems—4

1. Friends do not go to the centre.
2. I am not permitted to go with my friends.
3. No one else visits the centre except the instructor.
4. Good friends are not available at the centre.

Personal Problems—2

1. Due to ill-health.
2. The relevant lessons are not taught at the centre.

Programme related Problems—1

1. Minimum amenities are not found at the centre (air/ventilation).

The problems of "Rs. 31 thousands and above income group drop-outs"

There are 23 very significant problems, 37 significant problems and 20 less significant problems—wide Table 4.49. Area-wise distribution of the problems is found in the Table 4.50.

Economic Problems—1

1. No immediate financial benefit by education.

Social Problems—2

1. Attending functions and going to movies.
2. The instructor does not belong to my caste.

Psychological Problems—6

1. Easily getting tired.
2. Feeling that studying at the centre is a waste.
3. Feeling that others would mock.
4. There is no understanding between the learner and the instructor.
5. The learner is not able to answer to the instructor.
6. Feeling that education is only for wealthy people.

Familial Problems—2

1. Other family members refuse permission to attend during nights.
2. There are none else at home.

Instructor related problems—5

1. The instructional methods used by the instructor are not liked.
2. Unable to go to the centre because of heavy work.
3. The instructor is not punctual to the centre.
4. The instructor is unable to explain clearly.
5. The instructor is negligent.

Community related Problems—2

1. The time of the programme is short.
2. No one else visits the centre except the instructor.

Personal Problems—4

1. The other learners are mocking because of my backwardness in learning.
2. The instructor is male.
3. The relevant lessons are not taught at the centre.
4. Becoming a slave to bad habits.

Programme related Problems—1

1. Minimum amenities are not found at the centre (air/ventilation).

The problems of drop-outs with "1-2 months attendance in the centre"

There are 26 very significant problems, 47 significant problems and 7 less significant problems—wide Table 4.51. Area-wise distribution of the problems is found in the Table 4.52.

Economic Problems—1

1. There are no specific working hours in different professions.

Social Problems—1

1. Attending functions and going to movies.

Psychological Problems—7

1. Easily getting tired.
2. Unwilling to get educated.
3. Feeling that the age to study has passed.
4. The learner is not able to answer to the instructor.
5. The fellow learners do not listen to the thoughts and ideas.
6. Feeling that studying at the centre is a waste.
7. Feeling shy during conversation with other.

Familial Problems—2

1. There are none else at home.
2. The time of the centre is the supper time.

Instructor related problems—7

1. The instructor fails to enthuse the learners to participate.
2. The instructor lacks good voice and fluency.
3. The books are difficult to learn.
4. The lessons are not according to the requirement or tastes.
5. Teaching aids are not available at the right time.
6. Instruction is limited only to literacy.
7. Primer and follow-up books are not in order.

Community related Problems—4

1. I am not permitted to go with my friends.
2. Co-educational centre.
3. Good friends are not available at the centre.
4. There is no encouragement from the village elders.

Personal Problems—1

1. The instructor is male.

Programme related Problems—3

1. The centre is at a distance.
2. Minimum amenities are not found at the centre (air/ ventilation).

3. The centre is started at inconvenient place/having much sounds and bad smell.

The problems of drop-outs with "2-4 months attendance in the centre"

There are 22 very significant problems, 48 significant problems and 10 less significant problems—wide Table 4.53. Area-wise distribution of the problems is found in Table 4.54.

Economic Problems—1

1. Busy with farm work.

Social Problems—2

1. Many learners belong to the upper caste.
2. Personal position is at stake in the society.

Psychological Problems—4

1. Easily getting tired.
2. Feeling that studying at the centre is a waste.
3. Feeling that others would mock.
4. The learner is not able to answer to the instructor.

Familial Problems—3

1. Other family members refuse permission to attend during nights.
2. The time of the centre is the supper time.
3. Unable to go to the centre because of heavy work.

Instructor related Problems—4

1. The instructor does not reveal in learner's progress.
2. Instruction is limited only to literacy.
3. Teaching aids are not available at the right time.
4. There is no teaching experience to the instructor.

Community related Problems—3

1. The time of programme is short.
2. No one else visits the centre except the instructor.
3. Friends do not go to the centre.

Personal Problems—4

1. Due to ill-health.
2. The other learners are mocking because of my backwardness in learning.
3. Getting the marriage age.
4. Lack of knowledge about this programme.

Programme related Problems—1

1. Minimum amenities are not found at the centre (air/ ventilation).

The problems of drop-outs with "4-6 months attendance in the centre"

There are 24 very significant problems, 43 significant problems and 13 less significant problems-wide Table 4.55. Area-wise distribution of the problems is found in Table 4.56.

Economic Problems—1

1. There are no specific working hours in different professions.

Social Problems—2

1. The instructor does not belong to my caste.
2. Attending functions and going to movies.

Psychological Problems—5

1. Easily getting tired.
2. Learners calling by nicknames.
3. Feeling that others would mock.
4. There is no understanding between the learner and the instructor.
3. The learner is not able to answer to the instructor.

Familial Problems—2

1. There are none else at home.
2. Other family members refuse permission to attend during nights.

Instructor related problems—6

1. The instructor lacks good voice and fluency.
2. The books are difficult to learn.
3. Teaching aids are not available at the right time.
4. The instructor fails to enthuse the learners to participate.
5. Primer and follow-up books are not in order.
6. The lessons are not according to the requirements or tastes.

Community related Problems—3

1. Friends do not go to the centre.
2. The time of the centre is inconvenient.
3. I am not permitted to go with my friends.

Personal Problems—5

1. The instructor is male.
2. The other learners also are average in learning.
3. The other learners are mocking because of my backwardness in learning.
4. The relevant lessons are not taught at the centre.
5. Lack of knowledge about this programme.

Programme related Problems—0

There is no very significant problems in the programme related problems area.

3. Among 22 groups of drop-outs, including total drop-outs, the other occupation group (other than agriculture and labour) has highest number of very significant problems, followed by above 36 years age group, 'previous schooling' group and BC caste group. The 'no schooling' group has lowest number of very significant problems, followed by agriculture occupation group, labour occupation group and females. The range of very significant problems felt by different groups of drop-outs vary from 49 (61.25%) to 18 (22.50%). The number of very significant problems of total drop-outs is 21 and it amounts to 26.25% of total problems vide Table 4.57 as seen from Table 4.58.

4. Among very significant problems, the problem which was felt as very significant problem by all the 22 groups of drop-outs is S.No. 23 (easily getting tired) followed by the problems numbers are:

   6. There are no specific working hours in different professions.
   18. The learner is not able to answer to the instructor.
   35. There are none else at home.
   46. The instructor lacks good voice and fluency.

The problem 23 is also the No. 1 very significant problem of total drop-outs. The 24 problems which are felt as very significant problems by 50% of drop-outs groups are:

23. Easily getting tired.

6. There are no specific working hours in different professions.

35. There are none else at home.

46. The instructor lacks good voice and fluency.

56. The books are difficult to learn.

22. Feeling that others would mock.

19. Unwilling to get educated.

31. Other family members do not co-operative in matters of education.

60. I am not permitted to go to the centre.

20. Feeling that the age to study has passed.

29. Feeling that studying at the centre is a waste.

47. The instructor fails to enthuse the learners to participate.

78. Minimum amenities are not found at the centre (air/ventilation).

80. The centre is at a distance.

16. Attending functions and going to movies.

59. Friends do not go to the centre.

8. The instructor does not belong to my caste.
48. Instruction is limited only to literacy.
52. Teaching aids are not available at the right time.
62. The time of the centre is inconvenient.
76. Lack of knowledge about this programme.
50. The instructor does not reveal in learners progress; and
75. The instructor is male.

All the 21 problems found to be very significant problems for total drop-outs group are also found to be very significant problems by 50% of the drop-out groups.

All the 80 problems were found to be very significant problems to one group or the other except the 6 problems shown below:

3. Owners and landlords do not permit for attending centres.
5. My family is economically backward.
9. The instructor utilises the learners for his personal work.
13. There are some fights in the village.
67. Getting newly married; and
73. Getting discouraged after working hard for sometime to get educated and feeling that this attempt is useless, which are not at all very significant problems for any group.

Differential effects of each problem of drop-outs on their sex, education, marital status, age, caste, occupation, income and attendance in centres.

The differences in the effect of each problem on different groups of dropouts are summarised below :

I. Sex

1. The effect or the difficulty of the problems experienced by the male and female drop-outs is the same on 60 problems shown in Table 4.59.
2. In the case of the 17 problems, the effect or difficulty experienced by male drop-outs is higher, compared to female

dropouts and these problems are found in Table 4.60. The 17 problems are:

10. Personal position is at stake in the society.
11. Some learners have enmity in the centre.
13. There are some fights in the village.
37. The centre is not well maintained.
38. The instructor is not punctual to the centre.
41. The instructor is unable to explain clearly.
44. The instructor does not accept criticism with open heart.
47. The instructor fails to enthuse the learners to participate.
49. Providing too much information with in a short time.
50. The instructor does not personally reveal any development.
52. Teaching aids does not available at the right time.
54. Related primary teaching books are not in order.
68. Due to ill health.
73. Getting discouraged after working hard to get educated and feeling that this attempt is useless.
74. The other learners also are average in learning.
78. Minimum amenities are not found at the centre (air/ventilation); and
79. The centre is started at inconvenient place/environment with sounds and bad smell.

The effect or difficult felt by female drop-outs is higher than the male drop-outs with regard to the three problems shown in Table 4.61. The 3 problems are:

24. Feeling why one should get educated when the age is so much.
63. The centre is co-educated; and
80. The centre is at a distance.

II. Education

1. The drop-outs with "Previous schooling" and "No schooling" experienced "No difference" in the difficulty or effect in the case of 73 problems shown in Table 4.62.

2. The "Previous schooling" drop-outs felt more difficulty than the "No schooling" drop-outs on 7 problems indicated in Table 4.63. The 7 problems are:

   28. The fellow learners do not listen to the thoughts and ideas.
   36. Unable to go to the centre in the supper time.
   38. The instructor is not punctual to the centre.
   42. The instructor does not treat all the learners equally.
   51. The instructor uses difficult language, pictures and symbols.
   57. The instructional methods specified by the government are not liked; and
   65. The time of the programme is short.

3. There are no problems where the "No schooling" felt more difficulty (effect is more) than the "Previous schooling" drop-outs.

III. Marital Status

1. There exists "No difference" between married drop-outs and unmarried drop-outs on the difficulty /effect felt in respect of 65 problems shown in Table 4.64.

2. The effect experienced by married drop-outs is higher than that of the unmarried drop-outs on 7 problems noted in Table 4.65. The 7 problems are:

   2. Busy with farm work.
   25. Feeling that education is only for wealthy people.
   32. Looking after the children.
   38. The instructor is not punctual to the centre.
   57. The instructional methods specified by the government are not liked.

64. No one else visits the centre except the instructor; and

74. The other learners also average in learning.

3. The effect felt by the unmarried drop-outs is greater than that of the married drop-outs on 8 problems found in Table 4.66. The 8 problems are:

16. Attending functions and going to movies.

26. Feeling shy during conversation with others.

44. The instructor does not accept criticism with open heart.

47. The instructor fails to enthuse the learners to participate.

60. I am not permitted to go with my friends.

61. Good friends are not available at the centre.

63. The centre is co-educated; and

70. Getting the marriage age.

IV. Age

1. There exist "No difference" in the effect experienced among drop-outs of different age groups namely 20 years and below, 21-35 years and 36 years and above on 65 problems noted in Table 4.67.

2. There exists difference in the effect of problems among drop-outs belonging to different age groups on 15 problems, the details which are shown in Table 4.68. The 15 problems are :

16. Attending functions and going to movies.

17. There is no understanding between the learner and the instructor.

18. The learner is not able to answer to the instructor.

28. The fellow learners do not listen to the thoughts and ideas.

32. Looking after the children.

48. Instruction is limited only to literacy.

53. The absence of audio-visual aids useful for instruction.

57. The instructional methods specified by the government are not liked.

60. I am not permitted to go with my friends.
61. Good friends are not available at the centre.
63. The centre is co-educated
67. Getting newly married.
70. Getting the marriage age.
74. The other learners also are average in learning; and
76. Lack of knowledge about this programme.

(a) The effect experienced by "20 years and below age group" is higher than the "21-35 years age group" on 8 problems, the details of which are shown in Table 4.68.

16. Attending functions and going to movies.
17. There is no understanding between the learner and the instructor.
53. The absence of audio-visual aids useful for instruction.
60. I am not permitted to go with my friends.
61. Good friends are not available at the centre.
63. Getting newly married.
70. Getting the marriage age; and
76. Lack of knowledge about this programme.

(b) The effect is more on "21-35 years age group" than that of "20 years and below age group" with regard to only one problem i.e., 57, namely,

57. The instructional methods specified by the government are not liked.

(c) The "36 years and above age group" experienced more effect compared to the age group "21-35" in the case of 3 problems, found in Table 4.68. The problems are:

60. I am not permitted to go with my friends.
61. Good friends are not available at the centre; and
63. Getting newly married.

(d) The "36 years and above age group" felt more effect, compared to "20 years and below age group" on 8 problems with S.No. 16, 18, 28, 32, 48, 57, 67 and 74 found in Table 4.68. The 8 problems are:

16. Attending functions and going to movies.
18. The learner is not able to answer to the instructor.
28. The fellow learners do not listen to the thoughts and ideas.
32. Looking after the children.
48. Instruction is limited only to literacy.
57. The instructional methods specified by the government are not liked.
67. Getting newly married; and
74. The other learners also average in learning.

(e) The "36 years and above age group" felt more effect compared to "21-35 age group" on 7 problems found in Table 4.68. The 7 problems are :

17. There is no understanding between the learner and the instructor.
18. The learner is not able to answer to the instructor.
28. The fellow learners do not listen to the thoughts and ideas.
48. Instruction is limited only to literacy.
53. The absence of audio-visual aids useful for instruction; and
76. Lack of knowledge about this programme.

V. Caste

1. There exist "No difference" in the difficulty/effect experienced among drop-outs of different caste groups namely SC/ST, B.C. and on 67 problems noted in Table 4.69.
2. There exists difference among drop-outs belonging to different caste groups on 13 problems, the details of which are shown in Table 4.70. The 13 problems are:

8. The instructor does not belong to my caste.
11. Some learners have enmity in the centre.
15. There are some learners with bad behaviour in the centre.
17. There is no understanding between the learner and the instructor.
28. The fellow learners do not listen to the thoughts and ideas.
30. Feeling that learning at home instead of at the centre is better.
32. Looking after the children.
35. There is none else at home.
39. The instructor is not well versed with his teaching.
68. Due to ill-health.
69. Quarrelling with other learners.
71. The other learners are much older; and
78. Minimum amenities are not found at the centre (air/ventilation).

(a) The difficulty experienced by "B.C. caste group" is higher than the "SC/ST caste group" on 8 problems found in Table 4.70. The 8 problems are:

11. Some learners have enmity in the centre.
15. There are some learners with bad behaviour in the centre.
28. The fellow learners do not listen to the thoughts and ideas.
32. Looking after the children.
39. The instructor is not well versed with his teaching.
68. Due to ill-health.
71. The other learners are much older; and
78. Minimum amenities are not found at the centre (air/ventilation).

(b) The effect is more on "SC/ST caste group" than that of "BC caste group" with regard to only 2 problems found in Table 4.70. The 2 problems are:

17. There is no understanding between the learner and the instructor; and

69. Quarrelling with other learners.

(c) The "OC caste group" experienced more difficulty, compared to "SC/ST caste group" on 3 problems found in Table 4.70. The 3 problems are :

11. Some learners have enmity in the centre.

30. Feeling that learning at home instead of at the centre is better.

35. There is none else at home.

(d) The "BC caste group" felt more difficulty, compared to "OC caste group" on 7 problems found in Table 4.70. The 7 problems are:

8. The instructor does not belong to my caste.

15. There are some learners with bad behaviour in the centre.

28. The fellow learners do not listen to the thoughts and ideas.

32. Looking after the children.

39. The instructor is not well versed with his teaching.

68. Due to ill health; and

78. Minimum amenities are not found at the centre (air/ventilation).

(e) The "OC caste group" felt more difficulty compared to "BC caste group" on the following 5 problems found in Table 4.70. The 5 problems are:

17. There is no understanding between the learner and the instructor.

30. Feeling that learning at home instead of at the centre is better.

35. There is none else at home.
69. Quarrelling with other learners; and
78. Minimum amenities are not found at the centre (air/ventilation).

VI. Occupation

1. There exists "No difference" in the difficulty level/effect experienced among drop-outs of different occupation groups namely agriculture, labour and others on 68 problems noted in Table 4.71.
2. There exists difference among drop-outs belonging to different occupation groups on 12 problems, the details of which are shown in Table 4.72. The 12 problems are:

   9. The instructor utilises the learners for his personal work.
   11. Some learners have enmity in the centre.
   12. The instructor and the learner are not friends.
   25. Feeling that education is only for wealthy people.
   33. Other family members do not co-operate in matters of education.
   38. The instructor is not functional to the centre.
   45. The instructor is not relevant to the learners.
   59. Providing too much information with a short time.
   66. Becoming a slave to bad habits.
   69. Quarrelling with other learners.
   74. The other learners are average in learning; and
   80. The centre is at a distance.

(a) The difficulty experienced by "agriculture group" is higher than the "labour group" on 3 problems found in Table 4.72. The 3 problems are:

   9. The instructor utilises the learners for his personal work.
   11. Some learners have enmity in the centre; and
   38. The instructor is not functional to the centre.

(b) The effect is more on "Labour group" than that of "Agriculture group" with regard to only 2 problems i.e., 33 and 45 found in the Table 4.72. The 2 problems are:

33. Other family members do not co-operate in matters of education; and

45. The instruction is not relevant to the learners.

(c) The "Other group" experienced more difficulty, compared to "Agriculture group" on 6 problems found in Table 4.72. The 6 problems are:

12. The instructor and the learner are not friends.

25. Feeling that education is only for wealthy people.

59. Providing too much information with a short time.

66. Becoming a slave to bad habits.

69. Quarrelling with other learners; and

74. The other learners are average in learning.

(d) The "Other group" felt more difficulty, compared to "Labour groups" on 10 problems found in Table 4.72. The 10 problems are:

9. The instructor utilises the learners for his personal work.

11. Some learners have enmity in the centre.

12. The instructor and the learner are not friends.

25. Feeling that education is only for wealthy people.

38. The instructor is functional to the centre.

45. The instruction is not functional to the centre.

59. Providing too much information with a short time.

66. Becoming a slave to bad habits.

69. Quarrelling with other learners; and

74. The other learners are average in learning.

VII. Income

1. There exists "No difference" in the difficulty level experienced among drop-outs of different income groups namely Rs. 20,000

and below Rs. 21-30 thousands and 31 thousands and above per annum on 70 problems noted in Table 4.73.

2. There exists difference in the difficulty level felt among drop-outs belonging to different income groups on 10 problems, the details of which are shown in Table 4.74. The 10 problems are:

   3. Owners and landlords do not permit.
   13. There are some fights in the village.
   32. Looking after the children.
   51. The instructor uses difficult language, pictures and symbols.
   53. The absence of audio-visual aids useful for instruction.
   57. The instructional methods specified by the government are not liked.
   58. There is no encouragement from the village elders.
   68. Due to ill-health.
   76. Lack of knowledge about this programme; and
   80. The centre is at a distance.

(a) The difficulty experienced by "Rs. 20,000 and below income group" is higher than the "Rs. 21-30 thousands income group" on problems found in Table 4.74. The 6 problems are:

   3. Owners and landlords do not permit.
   51. The instructor uses difficult language, pictures and symbols.
   53. The absence of audio-visual aids useful for instruction.
   58. There is no encouragement from the village elders.
   76. Lack of knowledge about this programme; and
   80. The centre is at a distance.

(b) The effect is more on "Rs. 21-30 thousands income group than that of "Rs.20,000 and below income group" with regard to only 3 problems namely found in Table 4.74. The 3 problems are:

32. Looking after the children.

57. The instructional methods specified by the government are not liked; and

68. Due to ill-health.

(c) The "Rs. 20,000 and below income group" experienced high difficulty, compared to "Rs. 31 thousands and above income group" on 3 problems found in Table 4.74. The 3 problems are:

53. The absence of audio-visual aids useful for instruction.

76. Lack of knowledge about this programme; and

80. The centre is at a distance.

(d) The "Rs. 31,000 and above income group" felt more difficulty compared to "Rs.20,000 and below income group" on 2 problems found in Table 4.74. The 2 problems are :

13. There are some fights in the village; and

57. The instructional methods specified by the government are not liked.

(e) The "Rs. 21-30 thousand income group" felt more difficulty compared to "Rs. 31 thousand and above income group" on the 2 problems 51 and 68 found in Table 4.74. The 2 problems are:

51. The instructor uses difficult language, pictures and symbols;

68. Due to ill-health.

(f) The effect is more on "Rs. 31 thousand and above income group" than that of "Rs. 21-30 thousands income group" with regard to only one problem i.e., 13 found in Table 4.74. The problem is:

13. There are some fights in the village.

VIII. Attendance

1. There exists "No difference" in the difficulty level experienced among drop-outs of different attendance groups namely 1-2 months, 2-4 months and 4-6 months on 71 problems noted in Table 4.75.

2. There exists difference among drop-outs belonging to different attendance groups in 9 problems shown in Table 4.76. The 9 problems are:

   4. There is no immediate use by getting education.
   9. The instructor utilised the learners for his personal work.
   13. There are some fights in the village.
   14. Many of the learners belong to upper caste.
   27. Learners calling by nicknames.
   46. The instructor lacks good voice and fluency.
   47. The instructor fails to enthuse the learners to participate.
   65. The time of the programme is short; and
   74. The other learners also are average in learning.

(a) The difficulty experienced by "1-2 months attendance group" is higher than the "2-4 months attendance group on 3 problems found in Table 4.76. The 3 problems are :

   9. The instructor utilised the learners for his personal work.
   27. Learners calling by nicknames; and
   47. The instructor fails to enthuse the learners to participate.

(b) The effect is more on "2-4 months attendance group" than that of "1-2 months attendance group" with regard to only 2 problems 13 and 65 found in Table 4.76. The 2 problems are:

   13. There are some fights in the village; and
   65. The time of the programme is short.

(c) The "1-2 months attendance group" felt high difficulty compared to "4-6 months attendance group" on 2 problems S.No. 4 and 9 found in Table 4.76. The 2 problems are:

   4. There is no immediate use by getting education; and
   9. The instructor utilised the learners for his personal work.

(d) The "4-6 months attendance group" felt more difficulty compared to "1-2 months attendance group" on only one problem i.e., 74 found in Table 4.76. The problem is:

   74. There is no immediate use by getting education.

(e) The "2-4 months attendance group" felt very high difficulty compared to "4-6 months attendance group" on the only one problem i.e., 4 found in Table 4.76. The problem is:

4 There is no immediate use by getting education.

(f) The effect is more on "4-6 months attendance group" that of "2-4 months attendance group" with regard to 6 problems found in Table 4.76. The 6 problems are:

13. There are some fights in the village.
14. Many of the learners belong to upper caste.
27. Learners calling by nicknames.
46. The instructor lacks good voice and fluency.
65. The time of the programme is short; and
74. The other learners also are average in learning.

SUGGESTIONS FOR SOLVING THE PROBLEMS OF DROP-OUTS

Several suggestions for solving the problems of drop-outs are made. The suggestions have to be implemented by (1) learners, (2) family members of learners, (3) instructor volunteer, (4) programme/planners and implementers, (5) experts in care of preparation of teaching-learning and post-literacy materials and (6) community members as detailed below:

1. The Learners

- The learners should be friendly with other learners.
- They should not involve in village fights/rivalries, at least during the total literacy campaign period.
- They should participate in the recreational activities in the centre.
- They should not feel that they are too old to learn age for studies is over.
- They should not feel shy to attend the centre.
- They should not mind to sit with upper caste co-learners.
- They should ignore if other co-learners mock at/ridicule them.

- On the other hand, they should mock at those who ridicule them.
- They should understand that education is not meant only for wealthy persons and it is needed most for poor people to understand the conditions under which they live and to take measures to improve their living conditions.
- They should not feel shy during conversation with other learners.
- The learners should not mind if the co-learners call them by nicknames.
- They should not feel shy to call the co-learners by nicknames if it's comes to.
- They should ignore, if the co-learners do not agree with their opinion.
- They should attend the centres regularly.
- They may supplement the learning by additional study at home.
- If the instructor is not regular, they have to request him / her to be regular.
- They should not mind to learn from instructors who are younger than the learners.
- They should be friendly with the instructor.
- They should not take it to heart, if they are not able to answer the questions put by the instructor.
- They should demand from the instructor for information about income generating activity.
- They should take up income generating activities by forming small self-help groups.
- If the timing of the centre is not convenient, they should inform the instructor.
- If the location of the centre is not suitable, they should inform the instructor and help to secure suitable accommodation.

- If the working hours of the centre is clashing with the working hours of the jobs they are doing, they should request the management to change the working hours or provide leisure time within the working hours for attending the centres.

The instructor and higher officials incharge of implementation of the centres should visit the centres frequently and persuade the learners to do the activities mentioned above.

2. The Family Members

The family members should permit the learners to attend the centres during night time and that the learners may go in groups after the class, if they expect any trouble from others during night time. The classes should not be held during very late hours of the night.

- Make the learners free from taking care of the children and house and from domestic work, farm work.
- Co-operate with the learners and encourage them to attend centres.
- See that the learners are not involved in local village fights.
- Motivate the learners to join TLC and continue till the end.
- Advise the learners not to mind the ridicule by co-learners and ignore it.
- Explain the need of education to the learners in the present local context.
- Watch whether the learners are attending the classes regularly on time and also watch their progress.
- Persuade the learners to complete the course, by extending the marriage date, if it comes to.

3. The Instructor

The instructor has to keep in mind that learners enter the centres after hard work. They are tired. They expect a pleasant evening. Recreational activities have to be provided at the centre to make them happy and they should feel that learning is a pleasurable activity. The instruction should never be boring, the learners should go home with a sense of satisfaction.

- Should be punctual to the centre.
- Has to acquaint with latest teaching methods.
- Has to update and upgrade his/her knowledge.
- Has to explain clearly to the learners.
- Should treat all the learners equally.
- Should not be negligent to his/her duties.
- Should accept criticism with open heart.
- Should teach subjects that are relevant to the teachers.
- Should have pleasing voice and fluency.
- Should encourage the learners to participate in learning activity.
- Should not limit teaching to literacy only. Functionality and social awareness components have to be added. Subject experts may be invited to the centres.
- Should not provide too much information in short time.
- Should inform the learners their progress in learning.
- Should use vocabulary within the comprehension of the learners.
- Should secure the aids on time.
- Should use latest teaching-learning techniques.
- Should contact the learners personally when they are absent or get information about them through co-learners and persuade them to join, after knowing the problems.
- Should be friendly with the learners.
- Should avoid the questions which the learners may not be able to answer.
- Should not use learners for doing his/her personal work.
- Should have proper understanding of the learners.

- Should avoid long class hours.
- Should inform the learners in advance if he/she is going on leave and make alternate arrangements to run the centre.
- May allow the learners to attend the centres with their children, if need be.
- Should choose time convenient to the learners for attending centres—avoid supper time.
- Should choose suitable place for locating the centre.
- Should keep the centre clean and green.

4. Programme Planners and Implementations

- Should supply teaching-learning material on time.
- Should see that suitable, adequate and relevant aids are supplied on time.
- Should select right primers.
- Should see that the content of the primers and post-literacy materials reflect the needs, interests and problems of the learners.
- Should arrange training programme for the instructors to do their specific functions effectively.
- Involve the learners even from planning stage of the programme.
- Learners should feel that it is their programme. It must be developed with the learners and not simple for learners.
- Should supervise the programme frequently and provide guidance.
- Should know the problems of learners and instructors and solve them as quickly as possible.
- Should select the instructors with pleasing voice, good conversation skills, from the same place and caste.
- As far as possible, co-education centres should be avoided.

- Should check whether the instructor is attending the centre regularly or not.
- Should select members with some previous experience to work as instructors.
- Should appoint women as instructors to women centres.
- Should provide medical facility for the learners who are ill.
- Should publicise the programme adequately so that the learners may have knowledge and join the centres.
- Should choose convenient time for running the centre.
- Should select place which is centrally located, accessible to all, with proper ventilation and lighting for locating the centre. The centre should not be at a distance.
- The owners and landlords may be convinced to permit the workers to attend the centre.
- The duration of the programme should not be short.
- Should be sensitive to the problem of special groups, women, SC/ST etc., and taken appropriate action.
- In the training programme for different functionaries, the problems of drop-outs and solutions should be emphasised.

5. Material Preparation Experts

The material preparation experts should do the following:

- The language used in the primers should not be difficult and the vocabulary should be graded.
- The primers should include practice exercise to help slow learners to progress at their own speed and phase.
- The primers should have small units so that learners may go home every day with the feeling of some achievement.
- The context and format of the books should be enjoyable.
- Large print letters, illustrations should find a place in primers.

- Content of the primers, post-literacy and continuing education materials should reflect the needs, interests and problems of the learners.

6. Community Members

- Should encourage the learners to join the centres.
- Should never demotivate the learners.
- Should allow the workers in their organisations to attend the centres.
- Should change the working hours of different occupations so that workers may have free time to attend the centres.
- Should provide leisure time within the working hours for workers to attend the centres.
- Should see whether the learners are attending the centres.
- Should watch whether the instructor is regularly coming to the centres.
- Should help in choosing suitable location for the centre.

2. In the case of problems and problem areas where significant differences are found between/among different groups of drop-outs, the programme planners and implementers should be sensitive to these differences and take special/additional care to solve the problems of the groups concerned. When significant differences are found between two groups, the effect will be more on one group than the other. This must be kept in view and tackle such problems and problem areas of the concerned group.

SUGGESTIONS FOR FURTHER RESEARCH

— Relationship between drop-out rate and the variable like sex, age, caste, occupation, marital status and income.

— Who influenced the decision to drop-out from the campaign may be explored.

— Cost-benefit analysis of TLC, with special reference to drop-out.

— Analysis of drop-out rate at different intervals of the programme, monthly, quarterly and half-yearly.

— Analysis of reasons for attending TLC centres.

Bibliography

BOOKS

Bajpai, R. (1960). *Methods of Social Survey and Research* (Fifteenth Edition), Kitab Ghar, Kanpur-3.

Edwards, A.L. (1957). *Techniques of Attitude Scale Construction*. Appleton Century Craft, INC, New York, p. 153.

Edwards, A.L. (1969). *Techniques of Attitude Scale Construction*. Vakils Preffer and Simmons Private Ltd., Bombay.

Edwards, A.L. and Kilpatric, Quoted (1984). *Social Analysis and the Measurement of Social Attitude*, Ibid.

Fernald, C. James (1919). *Desk Standard Dictionary,* Frink and Managnalles Co., New York and London, 1919, p. 620.

Garret, H.E. (1958). *Statistics in Psychology and Education,* New York, Longmans Green and Co.

Garret, Henry, E. (1981). *Statistics in Psychology and Education*, 5th Edition, New York.

Guilford, J.P. (1954). *Psychometric Methods,* New York, McGraw Hill Book Company.

Hamadachi, A. (1973). *Alphabetization Factionnelle (Loas) Project de la plain de Vientiane*, Abstract in the Problem of Dropouts, Tehran: International Institute for Adult Literacy Methods.

Howell (1965). *Adult Education in India*. Indian Adult Education Association, 17-B, Indraprastha Estate, New Delhi, 1986, p. 15.

Indian Adult Education Association (1980). *A Hand Book for Adult Education Instructors*, New Delhi, 1986, p. 15.

Indian Adult Education Association, (1980). *A Hand Book for Adult Education Instructors*, New Delhi, Indian Adult Education Association.

International Encyclopedia of Education (1980), Vol. 1, p. 135.

International Institute for Adult Literacy Methods (1980). The Problem of Dropouts, Tehran.

Jayagopal, R. (1985). *Adult Learning: A Psycho-social Analysis in the Indian Context*, Madras, University of Madras.

Jhansi (1981). *Participants, Non-participants and Dropouts in Jesudasan* V., Roy, P. and Koshy, T.A. *Non-formal Education for Rural Women*, New Delhi, Allied Publishers.

Lindquist, E.F. (1966). *Educational Measurement*, Washington D.C., American Council on Education, p. 672.

Lowe, J. (1975). *The Education for Adults: A World Perspective* in Jayagopal, R., (1985). *Adult Learning: A Psycho-social Analysis in Indian Contest*, Madras: University of Madras.

Madras Institute for Development Studies (1983). *Adult Education Programme in Tamil Nadu: An Appraisal of the Programme Implementation by the Universities and Colleges*, Madras, MIDS.

Mail, M.G. (1984). *Adult Education in India*, New Delhi: Deep & Deep Publications.

Oxford English Dictionary, Oxford University Press, Amen House, London, p. 4.

Phillip, H. Coombs and Mazdoor Ahmed (1975). *Non-formal Education*, A Hand Book.

Standard Desk Dictionary (1977). *Standard Desk Dictionary of the English Language*, Institutional Edition, Funk & Wagnalls, New York.

The First International Conference (1949). Adult Education in Denmark.

The New Oxford Encyclopedic Dictionary (1981). Oxford University Press.

Webster's Dictionary (1967). *Webster's Dictionary of the English Language*, UNABRIDGED, Encyclopedic Edition, J.G. Ferguson Publishing Company, Chicago.

Yadav, S.K. (1986). *National Policy on Education: A Hand Book on Non-formal Educational: New Policy Perspective*, First Edition, Shree Publishing House, S.V. Printers, New Delhi, 1987, p. 3.

JOURNALS

Ahmad, M. (1972). Functional Literacy Experimental Project in Zambia. Reasons for Dropouts, *Indian Journal of Adult Education*, Vol. 33, No. 8.

Avery (1997). *Student Absenteeism: An American Indian/Native American Community Perspective*. The University of Arizona, 1997, p. 145,

International Dissertation Abstracts, Vol. 58, No. 4, October, 1997.

Bhandari, J.S. and Mehta, R.C. (1974). *"Personal Characteristics of Persisters and Dropouts in Functional Literacy Classes"*, Prasar, Vol. 3.

Boss, M.W. (1985). Locus of Control and Course Completion in Adult Basic Education. *Adult Literacy and Base Education*, Vol. 9, No. 1.

Cutz (1997). *Reasons for the Non-participation of Adults in Rural Literacy Programme in Western Guatemala*. Ball State University, 1997, p. 222.

Dissertation Abstracts International, Vol. 58, No. 3, September, 1997.

Dreza Jean (1996). *Indian Economic Development*, Delhi, Oxford University Press, 1996. *Indian Journal of Adult Education*, Vol. 58, No. 1, p. 39, January-March, 1997.

Fanning (1996). *A Study of the Perceptions and Understanding of Professional Educators concerning the effects of the Back-to-the Basics Reforms Movement on the Dropouts Rate of selected suburban high schools since 1982*. Booster College, 1996, p. 160. *Dissertation Abstracts International*, Vol. 58, No. 3, September, 1997.

Frederick Stephen (1960). *"Stratification in Representative Sampling"* Journal of Marketing, 1960, pp. 124-125.

Ganguli et al. (1984). A Study on Adults Learners in different Blocks of Bihar State *Developed Profiles of Adult Learners.*

Hussain Ch. G. (1980). A Study in the Socio-economic Factors associate with the acceptance of Adult Literacy Programme in Gujaranwala Tehsil. Gujaranwala District, *Abstract in the Problems of Dropouts.* Tehran: International Institute for Adult Literacy Methods, 1980.

International Encyclopedia of Education (1980), Vol. 1, p. 135.

Irish, G. (1978). Persistence and Dropouts in Adult Education, their relation to differential reinforcement of Attendance, Ph.D. Thesis, Columbia University, *Indian Journal of Adult Education,* Vol. 54, No. 3, July-Sept., 1993.

Manjeet Ahluwalia (1997). A Study of Dropouts in the Literacy Campaign, *Indian Journal of Adult Education,* Vol. 58, No. 1, January-March, 1997, pp. 39-47.

Naik and Nurullah (1951). *Vernacular Literature, National Seminar on Adult Education,* Vol. 43, No. 4.

Natarajan, R. (1982). *Adult Education and Dropouts. Indian Journal of Adult Education,* Vol. 43, No. 4.

Pangotra, N. and Sween (1989). Non-formal Adult Education, Identification of Motivational Strategies and Linkages of Learning Needs, *Journal of Indian Education,* Vol. 15, No. 2.

Pestonjee, D.M. et al. (1981). *National Adult Education Programme in Rajasthan,* Second Appraisal, Ahmedabad, National Institute of Management.

Rajyalakshmi (1986). *Motivational Problems in Functional Literacy Programme in Mahaboobnagar District of Andhra Pradesh, on the basis of the Study conducted on Women.*

Ramakrishna, K. (1980). *National Adult Education Programme: An Appraisal of the Role of Voluntary Agencies in Tamil Nadu,* Madras, Madras Institute of Developmental Studies.

Rao, K. (1983). *A Comparative Study of the Relative Effectiveness of Methods of Teaching Literacy to Adults,* Research in Adult Education, New Delhi, Indian Adult Education Association.

Ray, G.L. and Nandi, S.K. (1981). Dropouts from Adult Education Centres in West Bengal, *Indian Journal of Adult Education*, Vol. 42, No. 7, pp. 7-8.

Reddy, D.J. (1986). Selection of Adult Education Instructors: A Study, *Indian Journal of Adult Education*, Vol. 47, No. 11.

Robertson (1998). A Comparative Analysis of Student and Instructor Perceptions of the Effectiveness of International Practices. Wilmington College (Delware), 1998, p. 83. *Dissertation Abstracts International*, Vol. 58, No. 9, March, 1998.

Smith, B. (1987). Investigating Dropout from the Open Foundation Course, *Australian Journal of Adult Education*, Vol. 27, No. 1.

Tepper (1997). Literacy Development: Teacher/Student Interaction in a whole Language Classroom. The University of North Dakota, 1997. *Dissertation Abstracts International*, Vol. 58, No. 9, March 1998, p. 122.

Towards a Literate World: *National Literacy Mission*. Directorate of Adult Education, Government of India, New Delhi (1973).

Tylor, M.C. and Boss, M.W. (1985). Locus of Control and Course Completion in Adult Education. *Adult Literacy and Basic Education*, Vol. 9, No. 1.

Varma, R. et al. (1981). *Adult Education for Development: A Study of the National Adult Education Programme in Bihar*, Patna, A.N. Sinha Institute of Social Studies.

REPORTS

Acharji, N. (1983). *Adult Education in Bihar*, Jamshedpur, Xavier Labour Relations Institute.

Adult Basic Education Pakisthan (1973). Interim Report of the Lifelong Literacy Project. Abstract in the Problem of Dropouts. Tehrom International Institute for Adult Literacy Methods (1980).

Aikara, J. (1984). *Adult Education Programme in Maharashtra: An Appraisal*, Bombay, Tata Institute of Social Science.

Centre for Advanced Study in Education (1981). *Evaluation of the National Adult Education Programme in Seven Districts of Gujarat—An Interim Report*, Baroda, M.S. University of Baroda.

Day, B.R. and Natarajan, R. (1981). *Evaluation of Adult Education Programme in Nine Districts of Bihar*, Jamshedpur, Xavier Labour Relations Institute.

Directorate of Adult Education (1973). *Farmers Training and Functional Literacy: A Pilot Evaluation Study of Functional Literacy Project in Lucknow District*, New Delhi, Directorate of Adult Education, Government of India.

Experimental World Literacy Programme (1973). Work oriented Adult Literacy in Iran. A Experiment (Final Technical Report), *Abstract in the Problems of Dropouts*, Tehran International Institute for Adult Literacy Methods, 1980.

Fourth Five Year Plan (1966-70). Government of India, Planning Commission, New Delhi.

Fourteenth National Seminar on Adult Education (1966). *Indian Journal of Adult Education: A Report*, New Delhi, 1966.

Ganguli (1983). *Adult Education in Bihar, Fifth Appraisal* (Dumka District), Patna, A.N.S. Institute of Social Studies.

Harihar, R. and Rao, T.V. (1982). *Adult Education in Rajasthan, Third Appraisal*, Ahmedabad, Indian Institute of Management.

Hebsur et al. (1981). *National Adult Education Programme in Maharashtra, Evaluation*, Bombay, Tata Institute of Social Science.

Indian Education Commission (1985). Submitted Report, Made Rules, Provide Night Schools for Adults, Government of India.

Krishna Murthy et al. (1991). *Evaluation of Total Literacy Campaign in Chittoor District: A Report*, University of Hyderabad.

Laharia, S.N. and Dixit, D. (1981). *National Adult Education Programme in Rajasthan, Second Appraisal*, Ahmedabad, Indian Institute of Management.

Live Right and Haygood (1966). The External Papers. *Report of the First International Conference on the Comparative Study of Adult Education Extension*. Centre for the Study of Liberal Education for Adults, Boston University, Boston, Massachusetts, 1996, p. 9.

Mathew, T. (1983). *Adult Education Programme in Gujarat, Fourth Evaluation*, Ahmedabad, Sardar Patel Institute of Economic and Social Research.

Ministry of Human Resource Development, (1988). *National Literacy Mission*, New Delhi, Ministry of Human Resource Development (Department of Education), Government of India.

Journal of Adult Education Programme in Visakhapatnam District (1988), Himalaya Publishing House, New Delhi.

Okara, J. (1975). *The Psychological Approach and its effect on the Problem of Dropouts in Literacy Classes: An Experimental Investigation Carried out in Kibera Division*, Birobi in the problem of dropouts, Tehran, International Institute for Adult Literacy Methods.

Omena, S. (1989). *An Enquiry into the Reasons for Dropping-out from the Adult Education Centres*, Field Work Report, Trivendrum, University of Kerala, Kerala.

Parik, G.O. (1985). *Adult Education Programme in Gujarat. A Study of Community Involvement*, Ahmedabad, Sardar Patel Institute of Economic and Social Research.

Pathak (1983). *Adult Education in Bihar (Fifth Appraisal)*, A.N.S. Institute of Social Studies, Patna.

Pillai, K.S. (1974). Dropouts from Functional Literacy Classes, *Literacy News*, Calcutta, Abstracts in the Problem of Dropouts, Tehran, International Institute for Adult Literacy Methods.

Pillai, K.S. (1987). *Impact of Adult Education Programme in Kerala (1983-84): An Evaluation Study*, DAE Project Report, CAEE, University of Kerala.

Sachidananda et al. (1989). *Voluntary Efforts in Adult Education in Bihar*, Patna, A.N. Sinha Institute of Social Studies.

Sarma, A. et al. (1979). *Adult Education in Gujarat: An Appraisal Revisited*, Ahmedabad, Sardar Patel Institute of Social Research.

Sarma et al. (1981). *Adult Education Programme in Gujarat*, Revisited, Ahmedabad, Sardar Patel Institute of Economic and Social Research.

Seaman, D.F. (1971). Preventing Dropouts in Adult Basic Education. *Abstract in the Problem of Dropouts*, Tehran, International Institute for Adult Literacy Methods, 1980.

Shah, K.R. (1983). *Adult Education Programme of Gujarat, Third Evaluation*, Ahmedabad, Sardar Patel Institute of Economic and Social Research.

State Planning Board (1980). *A Study of Dropout in Primary Education*, Trivendrum, State Planning Board, Government of Kerala.

UNESCO (1984). *The Dropout Problem in Primary Education: Some Case Studies*, Bangkok, UNESCO Regional Office for Education in Asia and Pacific.

Visaria and Mathew (1983). *Adult Education Programme in Gujarat, Fourth Evaluation*, Ahmedabad, Sardar Patel Institute of Economic and Social Research.

DISSERTATION

Bhandari, J.S. (1974). Factors effecting Persistency and Dropouts of Adult Literacy Classes in Udaipur. Ph.D. Thesis, Udaipur University, Udaipur.

Garrisow, D.R. (1983). Prediction of Adult Learners Dropouts using a Psychological System Model (Doctoral Dissertation). University of British Colombia, 1983.

Khajapeer, M. (1978). A Study of the Academic Performance of the Farmers Functional Literacy Programme Participants in relation to some Socio-psychological Factors, Ph.D. Thesis, S.V. University, Tirupati.

Rao (1980). A Comparative Study of Relative Effectiveness of Four Methods of Teaching Literacy of Adults, Ph.D. Thesis, Osmania University, Hyderabad.

Reddy, P.A. (1989). A Study of certain Socio-psychological Factors relating to the Adult Education Instructors Effectiveness, Ph.D. Thesis, S.V. University, Tirupati.

Reddy, G.L. (1981). A Study of certain Personality Characteristics of Active Participants and Dropouts enrolled in Adult Education Centres of Srikalahasthi Project, Chittoor District, M.A. Dissertation, S.V. University, Tirupati.

Index

Q

R

S

T

U

V

Z